Reforging Shakespeare

Reforging Shakespeare

The Story of a Theatrical Scandal

Jeffrey Kahan

Lehigh
University
Press

Bethlehem: Lehigh University Press
London: Associated University Presses

Associated University Presses
440 Forsgate Drive
Cranbury, NJ 08512

Associated University Presses
16 Barter Street
London WC1A 2AH, England

Associated University Presses
P.O. Box 338, Port Credit
Mississauga, Ontario
Canada L5G 4L8

The paper used in this publication meets the requirements
of the American National Standard for Permanence of Paper
for Printed Library Materials Z39.48-1984.

Library of Congress Cataloging-in-Publication Data

Kahan, Jeffrey, 1964–
    Reforging Shakespeare : the story of a theatrical scandal /
Jeffrey Kahan.
        p.   cm.
    Includes bibliographical references (p.   ) and index.
    ISBN 0-934223-55-6 (alk. paper)
    Shakespeare, William, 1564–1616—Forgeries—Ireland.
    2. Literary forgeries and mystifications—History—18th century.
    3. Ireland, W. H. (William Henry), 1777–1835—Stage history.
    4. Ireland, W. H. (William Henry), 1777–1835. Vortigern.
    5. Ireland, W. H. (William Henry), 1777–1835. 6. Theater—England—
History—18th century. 7. Vortigern, fl. 450—In literature.
    I. Title.
    PR2950.K35   1998
    822.3'3—dc21
                                                                    98-9200
                                                                    CIP

In dedication to Robert and Stuart Kahan for their support, Doctors Brock and Matheson for their advice, and to the only begetter of this ensuing book Mr. W.H. (William-Henry)—all happiness and that eternity promised by our ever-lasting poet, wisheth the well-wishing adventurer in setting forth.

J. K.

Contents

Preface   9
Abbreviations   13

1. Background: *Vortigern* and the Criminal Quill   17
2. The Shakspeare Papers: The Master Plan   41
3. Why *Vortigern?*   71
4. More Forgeries: The Authentication of *Vortigern*
   Continues   82
5. Talbot and Wallis: Two Cases of Blackmail?   96
6. Lies and More Lies: The Truth About the Ireland
   Family   108
7. Negotiations and the Rewriting of *Vortigern*   124
8. In Defense of the Realm: The Critics Strike Back   145
9. Prologue to Tragedy   166
10. Opening Night: The Play's the Thing. . . .   178
11. Aftermath: Confession and Disgrace   188
12. The Legacy of *Vortigern*   213
13. Postscript   223

Notes   225
Works Cited   254
Index   267

Preface

Iᴛ is fitting that I begin this book about a forger with a brief discussion of its originality. Any critic of Shakespeare will tell you that a new study of William-Henry Ireland's Shakespeare forgeries has been needed for years. Recent trends in Shakespeare scholarship have made such a study an imperative.

In the last few years a mass of critical studies has reexamined Shakespeare's function in the Enlightenment (including Maria De-Grazia's study, *Shakespeare Verbatim* (1991), which was wholly devoted to Edmond Malone, the Shakespeare critic who exposed William-Henry Ireland and his forgeries). Moreover, much of our literary culture is presently preoccupied with forgery and pastiche, which may well make the Irelands available for rediscovery not only as master criminals, but also as pioneering postmodernists. Previously treated as a mere historical curiosity, the time may be ripe to reexamine the forgeries not just as a wonderful story but as a decisive case history in the development of our current respect for antiquity, appreciation of autheticity, and understanding of bardolatry.

There are several accounts of the forgeries and how they were received: the newspapers commented upon them almost daily; critics such as James Boaden and scholars such as Edmond Malone published studies attempting to expose the forger. After William-Henry was exposed, his father, Samuel Ireland, published an account. William-Henry himself wrote two full confessions. The hitherto accepted confessions by the forger were in themselves his ultimate forgeries. For he successfully recast himself as a well-meaning, misunderstood genius, interested only in pleasing his innocent and obsessive father. According to the forger, he was forced by circumstances beyond his control into "finding" more and more documents and finally a lost play.

In fact, William-Henry's true history is far more interesting and less altruistic. Here was no young man trying to please his unwitting father but a calculating criminal who came very close to successfully perpetrating a fraud that might well have rewritten our knowledge of Shakespeare. Along the way, he planned to secure

9

for himself the royalties to almost every major Shakespeare play, a fraud that would have made him one of the wealthiest men in the realm.

There have been several modern studies of the forgeries. The twentieth century has seen the publication of very small studies by Haraszti, Bodde, and Jaggard, as well as two major, book-length studies: Mair's *The Fourth Forger* (1938) and Grebanier's *The Shakespeare Forgery* (1965). All of them unquestioningly accepted the forger's confessions. The most famous account of the forgeries is, of course, Schoenbaum's, in his highly enjoyable *Shakespeare's Lives* (1970). Schoenbaum's account does not differ substantially from Mair's or Grebanier's in that it accepts the forger's confessions as sincere.

Schoenbaum's purpose, however, was not to reexamine the forger's confessions but simply to record what he evidently thought was a well-investigated and verified chapter of Shakespeare history. Unfortunately, Mair and Grebanier's studies suffer from a variety of minor inaccuracies, gross blunders, and oversights. For instance, Mair seems unaware that the title of his book is in reference to Samuel Ireland, not William-Henry. He makes no attempt to link the forgeries to other eighteenth-century forgers, or trends in eighteenth-century theater or eighteenth-century biographies and editions of Shakespeare. He gives a very good account of the negotiations between the Irelands and Drury Lane and a reconstruction of the performance, but fails to quote from the performance text. Furthermore, he seems unaware that many of the original manuscripts of the play are still extant. Most exasperating of all, he fails to document any of his quotations or properly date the release of each forgery. Nor does he properly differentiate between the letters he quotes from: some are originals, some are copies.

Grebanier briefly covers the careers of the other great eighteenth-century literary forgers, Macpherson and Chatterton, but only in the context of Herbert Croft's novel *Love and Madness* (1880). He fails to realize that William-Henry was part of a literary tradition learning, evolving, and testing its methods against contemporary standards of literary authentication. Though he must be credited with many of the details herein referred to, particularly the unscrupulous business activities of Samuel Ireland and a titillating theory concerning the housekeeper, Mrs. Freeman, still, Grebanier has fallen short. Like Mair, Grebanier fails to document his information. Like Mair, Grebanier does not distinguish between original letters and copies of letters, or the possible ramifications of such documentation, considering that the subject in question is a forger. And like Mair, he is equally sketchy on the release dates of the forgeries. Had either writer simply checked all the dates against the forger's confessions, many of their opinions might have been very different. Furthermore, Grebanier ignores Mair's strong arguments as to the "loyalty" of Montague Talbot. He briefly notes that William-Henry tried to buy the Shakespeare birthplace, but fails to recognize the significance of this attempt. His theory that Alice Crudge was involved in the forgeries lacks any credible evidence whatsoever, although Grebanier was correct in suspecting "outside" help. Grebanier also states that the manuscripts for *Vortigern* were destroyed in a fire in 1879. In actuality, no less than seven "original" manuscripts of *Vortigern* are extant.

While the majority of this book consists of my reconstruction of what I believe were the true motives of the Irelands, their supporters, and their enemies, the introduction and conclusion attempt to place *Vortigern* and the accompanying forgeries, collectively known as the "Shakspeare Papers" (our spelling of Shakespeare is a relatively recent one), in their historical context. *Vortigern* is more than just a play that strutted and fretted its three hours upon the stage to be heard no more. It is a tale based on trends in eighteenth-century theater, forgery, Shakespeare studies, and contemporary literary theory. *Vortigern* was a failure, in part, not because it was bad, but because it was so much of the eighteenth century that it could hardly be of any other.

I should point out that the study of Shakespeare's cultural significance in the eighteenth century has, to a large extent, been well-documented. Aside from DeGrazia's wonderful study, critics such as Gary Taylor and Michael Dobson have written about that century's cultural appropriation of Shakespeare for naive and cynical purposes. Further theoretical studies and historical surveys, such as Antony Grafton's *Forgers and Critics* (1990) and Paul Hamilton's erudite *Historicism* (1996), have successfully mapped out the often blurry limits of forgery and history. While drawing upon these sources, I have also broken new ground. This is the first study of the Shakspeare Papers to relate the creation of *Vortigern* to trends in eighteenth-century drama. The generalizations I have made concerning Shakespeare and eighteenth-century theater are the results of statistical analyses that show a constant pattern for every decade of that century. All printed prologues and epilogues mentioning Shakespeare during the period have been examined in an attempt to ascertain some eighteenth-century tragedians' views on the Bard's dominance. Also unique to this study is the information on the content and nature of the major eighteenth-century Shakespeare imitations.

William-Henry Ireland's ideas were directly informed by the success of previous eighteenth-century forgers. Contemporary scholars and satirists alike compared the Shakspeare Papers to the forgeries of Lauder, Macpherson, Chatterton, and others. I have, therefore, dedicated part of my introduction linking the Shakspeare Papers to the historical development of literary forgery and the eighteenth century's increased use of documentation as a method of authentication. This information, I believe, can tell us valuable things about what William-Henry was trying to achieve, how he tried to achieve it, who was out to stop him and why.

Further, this is the first study of the forgeries to document all the quoted letters by the Ireland family back to their primary sources. (However, like the former writers, I have silently emended the use of shorthand and superscript in letters.) This is also the first study to list the actual release order of the forgeries and to question Albany Wallis's role in the fraud, to explore the source material for *Vortigern* and to reassess the entire Ireland family's collaboration in the play, and to quote from the performance text.

The tone of much of this book will surprise some. I have tried to make this a scholarly work, documenting all my sources, but I have also tried to make this an entertaining read. I encourage the reader to follow me on a complex trail of literary detection. Together, we will question suspects, examine letters, diaries, affidavits, and published confessions from some of the most famous literary, political, and theatrical figures of the day. We will uncover fraud, conspiracy, blackmail, and sexual scandal. As a famous fictional detective, quoting Shakespeare, was fond of saying, "The game's afoot!"

List of Abbreviations and Symbols

A.D.   Anno Domini, or "in the year of our lord"

BL   British Library

ca.   circa, or "about"

cf.   cliff note found on page

ex   for example

MS   manuscript

Pl.   plate of illustration

p.m.   post meridian

PR   public relations

Rev.   Reverend

sic   thus used

v/r   verso or recto: The Ireland Papers in the British Library consist of letters and newspaper cuttings either glued onto sheets or straight into the binding. Many of the letters are several pages glued onto one sheet. Most have writing on both sides. Locating passages in these letters using the more traditional "page" and "opposite page" system proved impractical. The letters "v" and "r" refer to which side of the sheet I have quoted. The verso side refers to quoted passages that fall on the left-hand side of the open book, recto refers to pages that fall on the right-hand side. (ex: BL MS 30346, 19v–20r.)

<>   lacuna

[]   editorial insertion

Reforging Shakespeare

1

Background: *Vortigern* and the Criminal Quill

On 2 April 1796, a packed house sat in judgment as the curtain rose on the most controversial play of the entire eighteenth century. The playbill advertised "A Play Called *Vortigern*." No author was cited but it was far from an anonymous work. Some believed it was a lost play by Shakespeare, others that it was a masterful fraud calculated to part the public from its collective purse.

Certainly by conventional stylistic tests, *Vortigern* is, to say the least, Shakespearean. The play opens with King Constantius dividing the power of his kingdom with Vortigern, as Lear did with his sons-in-law. Left alone to reflect on his newfound fortune, Vortigern decides to murder the king, as in *Macbeth*. Meanwhile, Vortigern's wife, Edmunda, laments that her husband no longer loves her, though there seems to be no logical reason for the sudden change, as with Hermione in *A Winter's Tale*. Her daughter Flavia tries to cheer her up. Pascentius, Flavia's brother, then enters with news that Vortigern is now coruler of the realm. This news throws Edmunda into deeper despair, as she believes that Vortigern no longer loves her because he's now in love with power. Meanwhile, the Fool enters and does his best Touchstone impression.

Vortigern has yet to commit the murder and is plagued by Macbeth-like doubts and Hamlet-like soliloquies on the oddities of human nature. Realizing (again like Macbeth) that the murder of the king means the loss of his soul, he presses on anyway. Like Lady Macbeth, he calls on the forces of night and Hecate to serve him.

Two murderers enter and he instructs them when to kill the king. However, when it comes to the deed, the two murderers suffer doubts, as with Clarence's murderers in *Richard III*. One kills the other and the remaining murderer kills the king, although the murder scene itself was cut for the stage and the king's death is only reported. As in *Macbeth,* Vortigern deftly casts suspicion on an

17

innocent party, in this case the Scots. The barons elect him protector until the next-in-line, Aurelius, can be reached in Rome. Vortigern piously leads the procession of mourners out, as in *Richard III*.

However, when alone, Vortigern decides again on murder as the quickest way to the crown. As with *Macbeth* and *Richard III*, Vortigern launches a plot to kill the princes. However, Vortigern has more than power on his mind as he soon after reveals his incestuous love for his own daughter, as in *Pericles*. However, this scene is watered down in the stage version to read like one of Shakespeare's festive comedies. Flavia is to be married to a man she doesn't love. Her real love is the banished Prince Aurelius. She disguises herself as a man and, accompanied by her brother and the fool, sets off for the forest—shades of Ganymede.

Meanwhile, Aurelius and his brothers are informed that their father was murdered by Vortigern and that he also has plans to kill them. They decide to raise an army in Scotland. Similar scenes are found in *King Lear* and *Macbeth*. Aurelius is especially upset that Vortigern has killed his father. He is in love with Vortigern's daughter, Flavia.

Vortigern blames the defection of his children on Edmunda who, like Lady Macbeth, is having trouble sleeping and is slowly going mad. She decides to induce sleep as in *Romeo and Juliet*. In the forest, Flavia and Pascentius are entertained by the Fool, who sings a song. The three then meet a postman, as Edgar does in *King Lear*, who tells them that Vortigern is openly accused of killing Constantius and that the princes have landed with an army. Flavia and her brother decide, *As You Like It*-like, to rent a cottage in the woods.

Vortigern decides to hire Saxon mercenaries to help out the English against the Scots. The barons, led by the Buckingham-like Baron 1, approve and proclaim Vortigern as king. Aurelius has also claimed his right as lawful king, but shows a more Henry V-like piousness. The Saxons arrive and pledge their allegiance to Vortigern.

In the woods, Flavia misses her family, and sings a melancholic, Feste-like song. The Fool cheerfully adds his nonsense. But they are soon disturbed by troops from Aurelius's camp, much like scenes in both *King Lear* and *Cymbeline*. Edmunda has since gone mad, talking to birds, though unlike Lear, she does not feed them cheese. She then sings a song, though in the stage version the song was given to an attendant to sing.

Aurelius congratulates Flavia on her clever and incredibly original idea of cross-dressing. They embrace before Aurelius leaves for the battle. But the virtuous lose, as in *King Lear*. Horsus is killed by Catagrinus, though in Holinshed he is killed. Despite the loss of Horsus, it is still a great victory for Vortigern's side. At the victory celebration, Vortigern meets Hengist's daughter, Rowena. He immediately falls in love with her and unceremoniously dumps Edmunda, proclaiming Rowena his new queen. Vortigern's sons are outraged and soon after defect to Aurelius's camp, as the princes do in *King John*.

A second battle is fought and Vortigern loses. As in *Julius Caesar*, Vortigern can't find anyone to help him kill himself. He decides to fight on. Meanwhile, Pascentius and Flavia are reunited with their mother. A *Lear*-like recognition scene then unfolds.

In a series of *Macbeth* parallels, Vortigern prepares against a final assault. He is then informed that Rowena has taken poison. Upset by news of Rowena's death, Vortigern stoically reflects on free will and destiny. Vortigern fights on, killing many, but he is eventually taken prisoner. Aurelius is about to kill him but is stopped by Flavia who pleads for her father's life. The harsh justice of *Macbeth* and *Richard III* give way to the sentimental. Instead, Vortigern is forced to resign, as in *Richard II*. Aurelius is then legally proclaimed king. The Fool closes the play with a long speech directed to the audience, as in *As You Like It*.

This "lost" Shakespeare was only one among many documents and curiosities "discovered" by William-Henry Ireland. Among the items on display were legal deeds and promissory notes, a profession of religious faith, a love letter from Shakespeare to Anne Hathaway (complete with a lock of the poet's hair), correspondences between Shakespeare and Leicester, Shakespeare and Southampton, Shakespeare and Queen Elizabeth, Shakespeare and his printer, signed and annotated books from Shakespeare's library, as well as the original manuscript of *King Lear* and a fragment of *Hamlet,* both with significant variants. Among the "Believers," as they called themselves, were Shakespeare critics, biblical and Greek scholars, novelists, journalists, the poet laureate, the Prince of Wales (the future George IV) and the Duke of Clarence (the future William IV). Boswell was so impressed with the pieces that he fell to his knees and kissed the "sacred relics."

How, we wonder, could people have been taken in by this obviously derivative play and moldy papers? Yes, in hindsight, it all sounds very silly. We are perhaps too quick to agree with Peter Martin's recent assessment that the Ireland forgeries were "audacious, impudent, and blundering."[1] To our eyes they may seem so. But given the aesthetics of the era, the tests for documentational verisimilitude and the growing interest in Shakespeare, these for-geries (known collectively as the "Shakspeare Papers") were ex-pertly designed to fool both laymen and literati. As forgery expert Hans Tietze pointed out, the forger combines two charms:

> He presents a work that by its aspect seems to belong to a highly valued period or master and which, on the other hand, is in tune with the taste of its own period. It is this combination that makes it so attractive and irresistible.[2]

Surprisingly, these forgeries were not the works of an established playwright or of a Shakespeare scholar but the first poetic bur-blings of a nineteen-year-old boy. And yet, despite his youth and lack of formal education, William-Henry Ireland succeeded in fooling some of the best minds of his age. Even more astonish-ingly, the presentation of these relics was only the first phase of a master plan. Had *Vortigern* succeeded, new poems, manuscripts, masques, and an entire cycle of history plays were to be "newly discovered" and staged. These discoveries were to be made at a property that had recently come up for sale: that property was Shakespeare's birthplace.

William-Henry Ireland was a literary forger. By literary forger, I mean someone who creates a work in an acknowledged style and then lies about its legitimate authorship. A literary forger is not a parrot or a copyist. He creates anew but within preexisting stylistic parameters. By such a definition, a literary forger has much in common with a legitimate artist who merely creates what is popu-lar and marketable. What makes the forger different from the imita-tor is that he understands that imitation of a popular style is in itself not enough to ensure its success. Any marketing consultant will tell you that a no-name brand does not sell as well as an established brand name, though often the quality of the two items is on par.

The impulse to forge may be far more complex than the impulse to imitate. But they share one common trait: both the imitator and the forger respond to contemporary tastes. After all, to succeed, their works must be noticed, must be relevant. Ireland forged a Shakespearean tragedy. This chapter will attempt to gauge what the majority of eighteenth-century critics and theatergoers thought of Shakespeare's work. I am especially interested in their percep-tions concerning the genre of tragedy and how their views might have influenced contemporary playwrights. I am interested as to whether audiences were receptive to new tragedies, and if so, how a Shakespearean tragedy would fare. When dealing with such broad questions, there is the danger of making inaccurate generalizations. In an attempt to avert this danger, I have computed the numbers of Shakespeare tragedies acted in each decade of the eighteenth century, studied all the popular Shakespeare imitations and read hundreds of eighteenth-century plays, prologues, and epilogues. The results have convinced me that as a new tragedian, William-Henry Ireland would have had little success had he marketed *Vortigern* as a new play, or as a Shakespeare imitation. In purely practical terms, forging Shakespeare was probably the only way to ensure a positive response for a new tragedy written in the mid 1790s. Moreover, as I will explain, Ireland was not the first to choose forgery as a way of circumventing the often hostile reception of new literary works.

WHY FORGE? SHAKESPEARE AND THE STAGE

Why did Ireland forge a lost Shakespeare play? Was he simply criminally minded? Possibly, but there were aesthetic concerns at work as well. In practical terms, "discovering" a lost Shakespeare may have been the only way to ensure a new tragedy was well received or at least fairly judged. To oversimplify the critical taste of the late eighteenth century: if it wasn't old, it wasn't good. This was a retrospective age; an age obsessed with the past. Gibbon's *Decline and Fall of the Roman Empire* was found on a table in every residence. Pope's translation of *The Iliad* was considered a poetic pinnacle in terms of subject and taste. In literature, Walpole's novels, with their old castles, knights, and ghosts created and responded to a Romantic attraction to the decayed and forgotten. The repertoire of the two main London theaters, Drury Lane and Covent Garden, depended upon Shakespeare, a poet who had died nearly two hundred years before. The few new plays regularly staged were constructed upon old, Neoclassical principles.[3]

Modern critics such as Gary Taylor agree that if the era's theater lacked one strong element, it was a first-rate, new tragedian capable of rivaling Shakespeare.[4] Not one tragedy from this period survives in our repertoire. And though this point may say as much about our theater as it does about theirs, the fact remains that in the eighteenth century new tragedies, with very few exceptions, were not the favorite of artists or audiences. It was not that eighteenth-century dramatists never wrote tragedies: it was more a case of the dramatists not being able to reach the contemporary critics' high standards, which might be reductively defined as Shake-speare's tragic themes mingled with the rules of Neoclassicism.

NEOCLASSICAL SHAKESPEARE

Neoclassical rules were intended to create an atmosphere of verisimilitude. The action on the stage was to resemble reality. These rules were known as "The Three Unities." They consisted of (1) the Unity of Action—governing the structure of action uni-formly directed towards one intended effect. Tragedy was not to be mixed with comedy. Unnecessary scenes were to be omitted; (2) the Unity of Place—requiring the action to be limited to a single location; and (3) the Unity of Time—that the play cover a timespan of no more than twenty-four hours.

But it seems to me that too much is made of Neoclassicism's popularity on the contemporary stage. All the reprints of Addison's *Cato* (1713) and undergraduate classes in the genre aside, the fact is that Neoclassicism was never a serious rival to Shakespeare. Only an average of 7.3 Neoclassical plays per season were staged at Drury Lane between 1747–76; at Covent Garden only 7 perfor-mances per season were staged.[5]

Nonetheless, Neoclassical theory did have an enormous effect upon Shakespeare, who had long been considered an unschooled genius. In a brilliant critique of the period, Michael Dobson has surveyed how Shakespeare, while considered imperfect, could be improved with Neoclassical cutting, adapting, and altering.[6] Muti-lating Shakespeare was not an eighteenth-century curiosity. The trend had started during the author's own life but by the eighteenth century such mutilations had come to dominate Shakespeare theat-rical representations. Indeed, by the eighteenth century such changes were not regarded as curiosities but necessities. Indeed, many of Shakespeare's plays were rewritten drastically. Every nu-ance of the Bard's writings came under scrutiny: his language, his humor, his morality. His puns were deemed to be in bad taste. They were removed. The funny bits in sad plays and the sad bits in funny plays were erased. His characters were inconsistent. Adap-tors simplified Shakespeare's heroic men into plain heroes and his distressed women into recognizable damsels in distress. Similarly, the themes of many of Shakespeare's plays were often found to be noninstructive. The most commonly cited criticism was that Cordelia's death served no moral purpose. *King Lear* was changed.

In fact, in the commonly played Tate adaption, Cordelia wouldn't die at all!

Some plays needed music and dance to be palatable. Gildon added a masque to *Measure for Measure;* Granville added one to *Merchant of Venice;* Purcell's music was added to *Timon of Athens;* a symphony was added to *The Merry Wives of Windsor.*[7] Some plays, even in adapted form, were almost forgotten. During the entire eighteenth century *Titus Andronicus* was performed professionally in London only sixteen times, and *Troilus and Cressida* was performed only twelve times, *Antony and Cleopatra* appeared only ten times, *Coriolanus* appeared nine times and *Pericles* only twice. *Love's Labour's Lost* was not performed at all.[8] On the other hand, in this new, tidied-up form, Shakespeare reached new heights of popularity. As Aaron Hill, an adaptor of Shakespeare, said, "tragedy, unfarc'd, invites full houses."[9]

Literary critic Harold Bloom believes that every writer must confront and wrestle his literary father. Any strong literary work must misinterpret a precursor. The prize is canonical inclusion. With the exception of Addison and possibly Rowe, no eighteenth-century tragedian has entered the canon.[10] Theory and fact, in this case, are not unrelated. Unfarced Shakespeare dominated the stage.

Unfarced, Shakespeare was by far the most respected and often played tragedian of the century. One of every six plays staged in London was a Shakespeare.[11] Of the sixty-five nights devoted to tragedy on the London stage in the season of 1703–04, twenty of them were devoted to Shakespeare's tragedies.[12] In the following year, Drury Lane presented twenty-eight nights of tragedy, thirteen were Shakespeare's tragedies. In 1708–9, Shakespeare again dominated tragic theater: thirteen of thirty-eight nights were Shakespeare's, while on two other nights Dryden's rewritings of *Antony and Cleopatra* (retitled *All For Love*) and *Troilus and Cressida* were presented. In all, plays by Shakespeare or plays Shakespearean were performed for fifteen of thirty-eight nights. If we again count Dryden's adaptations in the figures, in the season of 1718–19, Shakespearean plays were presented twenty-four times, plus two nights of Rowe's 1714 Shakespeare imitation, *Jane Shore.* Ten years later the numbers for the four main theaters (Drury Lane, Covent Garden, The Haymarket, and Lincoln's Inn) are much the same: twenty-nine nights of Shakespeare plays, three nights of Dryden's *All for Love,* one night of Theobald's Shakespearean adaption *The Double Falsehood.* In all, thirty-three nights were devoted to Shakeapeare or Shakespearean tragedy. For the season of 1738–39,

Drury Lane records fifty-eight evenings devoted to tragedy, twenty-one Shakespeare's, with an additional performance of *Jane Shore*. Covent Garden staged sixty evenings of tragedy, nineteen Shakespeare's, two evenings of *Jane Shore*, and three evenings of Dryden's *All for Love*. Ten years later, the numbers are more impressive: eighty-six tragedy performances at Drury Lane, forty-four Shakespeare's. At Covent Garden, fifty-seven evenings of tragedy, merely six of which were Shakespeare's, but ten performances were staged of Thomson's adaptation of *Coriolanus*, and seven evenings were devoted to *Jane Shore*.[13] Overall figures for succeeding decades tell a similar story. Between the years 1747 and 1776 Shakespeare was the most popular dramatist. On average, his tragic plays were performed seventeen times a season. Of the top five tragedies of this era, four were Shakespeare's.

Five Most Popular Tragedies at Drury Lane, 1747–76

Play	Number of Performances
Romeo and Juliet	141
Hamlet	114
King Lear	82
The Mourning Bride	78
Macbeth	76[14]

During the same period, Shakespeare's *Much Ado About Nothing* and *Cymbeline* were the second- and fifth-most-played comedies, while *Richard III* and *Henry VIII* were the second- and fifth-most-performed miscellaneous category plays. At Covent Garden, we see much the same numbers: three of the five most popular tragedies are Shakespeare's and one is Shakespearean.

Five Most Popular Plays at Covent Garden 1747–76

Play	Number of Performances
Romeo and Juliet	188
Jane Shore	93
Hamlet	81
The Rival Queens	74
Othello	61[15]

In addition, *Macbeth* was the sixth-most-popular tragedy, *Merry Wives of Windsor* was the fourth-most-popular comedy, *Richard III* was the third-most-popular miscellaneous play.[16]

In the last years of the century (1776–1800) the only tragedies to place in the top ten were Shakespeare's. *Hamlet* was the fifth-most-popular play of this era, *Macbeth* the seventh; *Romeo and Juliet* was the tenth-most-popular play. But if we consider tragedy as a genre, these three works rank as the top three plays of the period.[17] And the overall numbers for his four most popular tragedies for the entire century are mind-boggling:

Play	Number of London Performances
Hamlet	601
Macbeth	558
Romeo and Juliet	495
Othello	441

Calculating eighteenth-century performances of his tragedies, even while excluding his comedies and histories, Shakespeare was staged a staggering 3,208 times. Including the popular *Richard III*, a play which in many ways resembles Shakespeare's tragedies, the performances total an astonishing 3,731.[18] In this new, altered form, Shakespeare represented all that was best and beautiful. No one could match him or replace him.[19] In fact, according to a distinguished eighteenth-century theater critic, the contemporary playwright was lucky if his new play was performed three times. But what was three times to 3,731?

REJECTING SHAKESPEARE

Comparisons of new plays to Shakespeare's were inevitable. No one likes to lose, so few wrote new plays and those who did did so nervously, afraid to offend the jealous dramatic god. Instead, a large number of eighteenth-century tragedians allowed Shakespeare to overshadow their own work. They gave tribute—the sacrifice was their identity. Those who did not met much opposition.

As early as 1721, some eighteenth-century dramatists were trying to break down traditional theater. On 21 December 1721 Aaron

Hill announced his intention to manage and direct The Haymarket. The scenes were to be

> contriv'd after a Fashion entirely new, the Habits . . . all new; the principal Characters of the Men, and all the Woman Characters, . . . [were to] be play'd by Persons who never appear'd upon the Stage before . . . [the] chief End and Design of this Theatre is the . . . Benefit and Encouragement of Authors, whose Works very often, tho' good, . . . [were] despis'd and set aside.[20]

In the end Hill got his theater but shied away from his promise. Indeed, he became one of the era's chief adaptors of Shakespeare. What choice did he have? To stage a new play was to risk financial ruin. Barton Booth, a theatrical entrepreneur during Garrick's period, said that "he and his partners lost money by new plays; and that, if he were not obliged to it, he would seldom give his consent to perform one of them."[21] The audiences for the entire century, by and large, agreed.

Theobald noted in his prologue to George Jeffrey's *Edwin* (1724) that the audiences did not much care for and were unfairly critical of new plays:

> Oft have you mourn'd, in this degenerate Age,
> How low is sunk the noble Tragic Rage.[22]

Unsuccessful playwrights always complain.

But the contemporary dramatist was at a definite disadvantage. Even a successful tragedian like Nicholas Rowe complained:

> Most kinds of Poetry, but especially Tragedies, come into the world now, like Children born under ill stars: a general indifference, or rather disinclination, attends like a bad influence upon them; and after having bustled through ill usage, and a short life, they sleep, and are forgotten.[23]

Poor Rowe, even his criticism paraphrased Shakespeare.

Frustration and resentment on the part of contemporary authors was common. In his prologue to his *The West Indian* (1771), Richard Cumberland gave a conventional tip of the hat to the natural genius:

> And in this humble sketch, we hope you'll find
> Some emanations of a noble mind;
> Some little touches, which, tho' void of art,

> May find perhaps their way into the heart.[24]

But Cumberland, like many of the dramatists of his age, was weary of the endless comparisons with his primitive, but powerful and godlike, predecessors:

> You say we write not like our fathers- true,
> Nor were our fathers half so strict as you,
> Damn'd not each error of the poet's pen,
> But, judging man, remember'd they were men.[25]

So the dramatist was in a double bind: if he followed any new artistic movement he was not like Shakespeare, and if he followed Shakespeare he was only an imitator—someone who based his aesthetics upon the works of a primitive, copying all that was lowly without the compensation of achieving godlike status. No wonder writers disliked critics. In the prologue to Charles Johnson's *The Country Lasses or The Custom of the Manor* (1715), the author condemns critics who

> . . . gravely tell you what you knew before,
> How Ben and Shakspere wrote in days of yore:
> Then damn the critics first, that envious train,
> Who, right or wrong, resolve to damn again.[26]

Even the critics agreed. Dr. Johnson, for example, called it an age "crush'd by rules, and weaken'd as refined."[27]

Some tried to break out of the restraints imposed by classicists and bardolaters. The playwright Richard Cumberland wanted to shed the classical baggage, the tradition, the inhibition, the Shakespeare. In the prologue to *The Brothers* (1769), he wrote:

> Some, in our English classics deeply read,
> Ransack the tombs of the illustrious dead;
> Hackney the muse of Shakspere o'er and o'er,
> From shoulder to the flank, all drench'd in gore.[28]

His contemporary, Samuel Foote, agreed and set out to do something different:

> We scorn, like our brethren, our fortunes to owe
> To Shakspere, and Southern, to Otway and Rowe.
> Though our judgement may err, yet justice is shewn,
> For we promise to mangle no works but our own.[29]

Needless to say, Samuel Foote was never a popular author.

But even this attempt to break away from Shakespeare was an acknowledgment of his power. While watching a new play, you heard echoes of his; if you saw something completely different to Shakespeare you were specifically aware of that difference. And while watching the play you were bound to see playbills for coming Shakespeare productions. There was no escape. Shakespeare was the phantom of the playhouse.

HISSING NEW PLAYS

R. B. Sheridan, the successful comic dramatist and later manager of Theatre Royal Drury Lane, envisioned the perfect first-night audience:

> For my own part, I see no reason why the Author of a Play should not regard a First Night's Audience, as a candid and judicious friend attending, in behalf of the Public, at his last Rehearsal.[30]

In reality, it wasn't like that at all. According to Scouten, "spectators frequently engaged in conversation while the play was going on, they brought their dogs with them on occasion, and there would be sporadic outbursts of noise."[31] But if all contemporary plays were met merely with indifference, most opening-night dramatists would have been very happy. New plays were often met with catcalls, hisses, even peltings of fruit.

It would be wrong, of course, to say that this phenomenon was unique to the eighteenth century. Ben Jonson's *The New Inn* "LIVED NOT . . . TO HAVE IT SPOKEN."[32] But certainly it can be said that the eighteenth century marked an intensified phase in open, organized hostility towards new plays and their authors. Said one spectator who had been at the premiere of Colley Cibber's *The Refusal* (14 February 1721):

> *Mr. Cibber's* Enemies . . . began to hiss it [the play] before they had heard it, and I remember very well, began their Uproar, on the first Night, as soon as he appeared to speak the Prologue.[33]

According to Richard West, his play *Hecuba* (2 February 1726) did not succeed because "It was not heard. A Rout of Vandals in the Galleries, intimidated the young Actresses, disturb'd the Audience, and prevented all Attention."[34] At the premiere of *The*

Village Opera (6 February 1729), "People got together, and fell a Hissing before the Performers utter'd a Word."[35] In 1738, Miller's *Art and Nature* was "damn'd at the Theatre Royal [Drury Lane] . . . not one Word of it being heard, from the Disturbance that was in the House the only Night it was acted."[36] One year later, William Shirley complained that his play, *The Parricide*, was ruined by

> twenty or thirty Persons . . . [who commonly] enter[ed] into an Association against a Person or his Productions, without having the least knowledge of either, but that it was a New Play, and had been Licens'd.[37]

On 22 February 1748, Lord Hubbard organized a party to ruin the premiere of *The Foundling*. The reason he gave was that it was too long.[38] How he knew it was too long is a matter of speculation, since he damned the play before it even ran.

The anonymous author of the 1751 *Guide to the Stage* disapproves of the "ambitious youths, who thus love to signalize themselves." The old plays are to be respected. However, this same critic adds that he "shall leave a new play to their mercy."[39] Mrs. Q, a character in the epilogue to Garrick and Colman's *The Clandestine Marriage* (1766), indicates that such an occupation was not strictly part of the male domain. For it seems her niece "Has made a party . . . to damn the piece." The only plays she and her friends like are Shakespeare's:

> *Sir Pat.* King Lare is touching!- And how fine to see
> Ould Hamlet's ghost!-"To be, or not to be."-
> What are your op'ras to Othello's roar?
> Oh, he's an angel of a Blackamoor!
> *Lord Min.* What, when he chokes his wife?-
> *Col. T.*   And calls her whore?
> *Sir Pat.* King Richard calls his horse- and then Macbeth,
> Whene'er he murders- takes away the breath.
> My blood runs cold at ev'ry syllable,
> To see the dagger-that's invisible. *(All laugh.*
> *Sir Pat.* Laugh if you please, a pretty play-
> *Lord Min.*   Is pretty.
> *Sir Pat.* And when there's wit in't-
> *Col.T.*   To be sure 'tis witty.
> *Sir Pat.* I love the playhouse now-so light and gay
> With all those candles they have ta'en away! *(All laugh.*
> For all your game, what makes it so much brighter?
> *Col. T.* Put out the light, and then-
> *Lord Min.*   'Tis so much lighter.

> *Sir Pat.* Pray do you mane, sirs, more than you express?
> *Col. T.* Just as it happens-
> *Lord Min.*   Either more, or less.
> *Mrs. Q.* An't you ashamed, sir?   *(To* SIR PAT.
> *Sir Pat.* Me!- I seldom blush.-
> For little Shakespeare, faith! I'd take a push.[40]

In this passage, Shakespeare's tragedies are seen as the ideal plays for the technically sophisticated, modern theater.

Some new authors decided to fight fire with fire. For the premiere of Addison's *Cato,* Richard Steele secured an "Audience . . . [so] it should be impossible for the Vulgar to put its Success or due Applause to any Hazard."[41] Rowe hired part of an audience for the premiere of his play *Lady Jane Grey* (1715).[42] In *The Humours of the Court* (1732), Fielding noted sarcastically that a dramatist must hire

> a little Army of Friends in the Pit, with good oaken Towels, and long Swords, to make them look terrible, and let them clap you lustily, and no-body will dare hiss, for fear of being knocked down.[43]

Football supporters would have felt at home in an eighteenth-century theater.

It was inevitable that two opposing factions attended the same performance. On the night of 6 June 1727 the audience of Giovanni Bononcini's opera, *Astyanax,* "carried on by Hissing on one Side, and Clapping on the other; but proceeded at length to catcalls, and other great Indecencies."[44]

While it might be too strong to say that contemporary plays had no place on the stage, it is clear that a new playwright, especially a tragedian, was faced with an enormous amount of prejudice toward his craft. Indeed, Arthur Scouten states that new tragedy "very nearly became extinct."[45]

IMITATING SHAKESPEARE

One of the most common tactics to circumvent this open disdain for new tragedies seems to have been the imitation of Shakespeare. The Bard was a huge drawing card and many new playwrights simply strengthened their reputations by linking their names to his.[46] In return, these playwrights paid a heavy price. By confining themselves to a reiteration of Shakespearean characters and situations, they simply reinforced the prevalent notion that all the good tragedies had already been written.[47]

In 1714 Nicholas Rowe, poet laureate, and the first eighteenth-century Shakespeare editor, wrote *The Tragedy of Jane Shore. Written in Imitation of Shakespear's Style.* Rowe wrote his play in the "good old taste."[48] There is no doubt it was Rowe's most popular play. Indeed, it was one of the most popular plays of that century. It, like all of Rowe's plays, was little more than an "eighteenth-century frontispiece . . . to the plays of Shakespeare."[49]

However, the play is not entirely Shakespearean. Rowe modified Shakespeare's style with Neoclassical decorum. Further, Rowe's play is a domestic tragedy, a form Shakespeare seldom dabbled in; a bedroom biography dealing with the evils of infidelity:

> Let those, who view this sad example, know
> What fate attends the broken marriage-vow;
> And teach their children in succeeding times,
> No common vengeance waits upon these crimes;
> When such severe repentance could not save
> From want, from shame, and an untimely grave.[50]

Other writers followed Rowe's example of following Shakespeare's modified example. William Havard's *Charles the First* (1737) is subtitled *in the imitation of Shakespeare.* King Charles is to be tried for his crimes against the state. He ponders, Richard II-like, on his loss of power and impending death. Cromwell confronts Charles but the king sneers at him. He is only accountable to God.

> *King.* Where is your right from Heaven?
> *Crom.* Power!
> The right of nature and the free-born man.
> *King.* Leave me.
> *Crom.* You speak as if you were still king.
> *King.* If not, what am I then?
> *Crom.* Charles Stuart, nothing more.[51]

The play ends supporting the concept of monarchy.

In William Shirley's *Edward the Black Prince* (1750) the author reveals that he is "fired by England's ancient fame, / (And humbly aiming at great Shakspere's flame!)."[52] In Shakespeare's *Henry the Fifth,* the French king recalls that Henry is a descendant of Edward the Black Prince, who humiliated the French in battle.[53] This is the storystem to which Shakespeare referred but never wrote. France invades the English territories on mainland Europe. King Edward consults his dukes and decides to fight the French at Poitiers. He then promotes his childhood friend, Arnold, to the post at Milford. It turns out that Arnold is in love with a French prisoner, Mariana. Torn between woman and country, Arnold eventually chooses country and dies bravely in England's glorious victory.

M'Namara Morgan was so impressed with Henry Jones's *The Earl of Essex* (1751), that he asked the author if "great Shakspere's transmigrated shade / Inform'd thy mass, or lent thee friendly aid[?]"[54] The story concerns the supposed love affair of Elizabeth and Essex. Though well-constructed in its use of characters, tone, setting, and timespan, the play is marred occasionally by singsong verse such as:

> This sudden shock, my lord, this weighty stroke,
> Must press him headlong down to deep destruction:
> Indignant fate marks out this dreaded man,
> And fortune now has left him.[55]

A Frenchman, M. De la Harpe, wrote *The Earl of Warwick,* translated into English by Dr. Franklin in 1766.[56] Like the previous imitations, *The Earl of Warwick* is a combination of selected Shakespeare characters and themes placed within a Neoclassical framework. King Edward is in love with Elizabeth, who is in love with Warwick, who has gone to France to propose to Lewis's daughter Bona on behalf of Edward. But Edward does not love Bona, though he is equally sure Elizabeth does not love him. By the play's close, Warwick will sacrifice himself for the love of his girl and his king.

Also in 1766, William Kenrick wrote a play entitled *Falstaff's Wedding, a Comedy in the Imitation of Shakspere.* It was considered by one theater critic to be among the best of the Shakespeare imitations.[57] Falstaff is to go into a monastery. Shallow wants his thousand pounds. Ursula has inherited £400 a year. Falstaff decides to marry her. Pistol is also in love with Ursula but settles for her maid. Shallow, unable to collect his cash, challenges Sir John to a duel. Falstaff refuses on the pretext that Shallow is too thin to present a target. Peto takes sick so Dr. Caius, of *The Merry Wives of Windsor,* comes in to nurse him. Shallow falls in love with Mistress Quickly and Slender falls for Doll Tearsheet. Falstaff convinces them that the women are whores and tricks the women into marrying Pistol and Nym.

Listing and describing all other Shakespeare imitations for the period would be a book in itself. However, some productions do deserve mention: Edward Young's *The Revenge* (1721) is an imitation of *Othello,* except that in this version the Moor has Iago's personality. John Home's *Douglas* (1757), stars the hostage that started all the trouble in Shakespeare's *Henry IV* cycle.

Samuel Johnson wrote that Shakespeare "Exhausted worlds, and then imagin'd new."[58] These plays operated within Shakespeare's known imaginative worlds. The contemporary playwright did not imitate so much as record the further adventures of well-known favorites such as Falstaff, or chronicle, as Shakespeare might have, the history of Edward the Black Prince. Though often termed as mere imitations, the generic is a simplification. These plays did not imitate Shakespeare but rather the later Neoclassical adaptors of his plays. Much like a forger, the imitator imagined a play Shakespeare might have written and then adapted it to contemporary aesthetics.

If so, then why didn't William-Henry simply release *Vortigern* as an imitation of Shakespeare? The reception of the "imitation Shakespeares" provides us with an answer. However aesthetically acceptable and useful a pattern these appropriations of Shakespearean characters and themes might prove to Neoclassical sensibilities, commercially most were failures. Even a good Shakespeare imitation could not ensure a play's success. Shirley's *Edward the Black Prince* "was receiv'd with great applause, [and] only a little groaning at some of the love scenes." After a mere nine performances, it disappeared for over twenty-five years.[59]

New tragedies were jeered, imitations tolerated, a lost Shakespeare might well succeed. Indeed, Henry Fielding, in his preface to his spoof *Tragedy of Tragedies or Tom Thumb* (1730), came very close to anticipating *Vortigern:*

> I shall waive at present what hath caused such feuds in the learned world, whether this piece was originally written by Shakespeare, though certainly that, were it true, must add a considerable share to its merit; especially with such who are so generous to buy and to commend what they never read, from an implicit faith in the author only: a faith which our age abounds in as much as it can be call deficient in any other.[60]

Fielding satirically expressed the problematic reception of new tragedies in the 1730s. Little had changed by the 1790s. William-Henry simply made good on Fielding's earlier satiric offer. If the public wanted Shakespeare, he would give it to them.[61]

MANUSCRIPT HUNTERS

But finding a "lost" play created several logistical problems. Where was it found? Were the paper, ink, and word usage legitimate? What kind of authentication process would the piece have to undergo?

In terms of finding a lost Shakespeare, the Bard's unique theatrical position actually improved the chances of its favorable reception. As Dobson's study has indicated, Shakespeare was usually performed in adapted form. Recognizing exactly what constituted Shakespeare was no easy matter for the average theater audience. As for papers and inks, the general public had far less knowledge about manuscripts than a Shakespeare editor. But even for the layperson, "Ancient literature was afforded a greater historical value than were modern reconstructions of the past."[62] Indeed, Lawrence Lipking has gone so far as to say that a "less sympathetic reader might maintain that poetry of the mid-[eighteenth] century is a footnote to antiquarianism."[63] These aesthetic factors contributed to a period which is retrospectively referred to as "the classical period of English literary forgeries. . . ."[64] James Boaden, a critic and key figure in the exposure of William-Henry Ireland, wrote that "the present is not an age in which this wretched ignorance can find credit."[65] But there was great ignorance, even among the seemingly learned. William-Henry was not the first forger of his age. Indeed, recent role models were easy enough to come by.

In 1703 George Psalmanzer passed himself off as an oriental, cannibal prince of faraway Formosa (modern-day Taiwan). He wrote a history of Formosa and made a fortune. He gave up the charade by 1728. But he kept the cash. He died in 1763, at age 83, a close friend of Dr. Johnson.[66] Johnson compared him favorably to the saints.[67]

In 1719, the public was engrossed by the lurid account of one Robinson Crusoe. Of course today we know this account to be by Daniel Defoe. With the benefit of hindsight, we are all too ready to agree with Anthony Burgess's analysis of Defoe when he wrote, "Defoe keeps a straight face, but everyone knows its a novel." But according to Ian Watt, at the time of its first publication "Robinson Crusoe itself was widely regarded as authentic."[68] And as late as 1743, Henry Fielding referred to Defoe as an "historian."[69]

Even those who realized that Crusoe's "true account" was nothing more than a novel by Defoe, also admitted that Defoe's power laid in his great ability to fool his audience. In 1718, *Reed's Journal* judged Defoe more a criminal than artist, stating, that "little Art he is truly Master of, [is] of forging a Story, and imposing it on the World for Truth."[70]

In 1747, Charles Julius Bertrum gave Dr. William Stukeley a manuscript history of Roman Britain by one Richard of Westminster, a priest of the fifteenth century. Bertrum published the manuscript in 1757. It sold well and was taken as fact. Gibbon included references to it in his *Decline and Fall of the Roman Empire*. It was only in 1866, more than one hundred years after its first publication, that Bertrum was exposed as a forger. In 1765, Thomas Percy published his *Reliques of Ancient English Poetry*. He claimed the poems came from a genuine manuscript he had discovered.[71]

In 1784, Edward Jones published his *Musical and Poetical Relicks of the Welsh Bards: Preserved by Tradition and Authentic Manuscripts From Remote Antiquity; Never Before Published*. Neither Jones nor Percy displayed their "authentic" manuscripts. Both editors were later exposed as forgers.[72] During much of the 1760s, James Macpherson "recorded" the oral poems by an unknown Scottish poet, Ossian. He published them in handsome, leather-bound editions; each had a preface, an introduction, and even critical apparatus. The poems fooled much of Europe and while Boswell and Johnson attacked them as fakes, a full study proving them so would be published only in 1805.[73] In 1768, Thomas Chatterton "discovered" a trunk full of manuscripts, among them poems by an unknown medieval poet, Rowley. In 1769, independent of the financially more successful Macpherson, Chatterton "found" some of Ossian's poems! All Chatterton's apparently genuine documents displayed a curious and unique spelling system. Today we refer to the spelling as "Chattertonian." But in the 1760s very little was known about the history of the English language and many believed the poems to be genuine. Further, although he often produced manuscripts, and even sold them, no one during his lifetime studied the authenticity of these papers.[74] The authorship and authenticity of many of these pieces were a source of debate as late as 1792.[75]

Perhaps it is too much to argue that the eighteenth century displays a Leavisite tradition of forgery. Nevertheless, William-Henry masterfully combined the techniques of his predecessors. Like all his predecessors, William-Henry acted as discoverer; like Macpherson, he released the forgeries to the public in a scholarly edition, enhancing their academic credibility and financial value. But the most obvious sign of influence in the Shakspeare Papers is that of Thomas Chatterton.

In the firmament of forgers, Chatterton was William-Henry's guiding light. Like Chatterton's Rowley poems, William-Henry's Shakspeare Papers represent an urge to imagine the history of Britain in a pervasive style. The papers are a range of interconnected allusions to a past age, from its small towns to its London stages. Linked by similar orthography and paleography, the documents of William-Henry Ireland, like those of Thomas Chatterton, create a circular verisimilitude of literature and history validating each other.

Indeed, in some ways William-Henry's forgeries are even greater than Chatterton's works. Edmond Malone, a Shakespeare scholar who had helped expose Chatterton, praised Chatterton's ability to write thirty-six hundred lines in about eighteen months on a variety of subjects, but speculated that "it would have been still more astonishing, if he had transcribed in that time the same number of lines, written on parchment, in a very ancient hand. . . ."[76] William-Henry wrote well over ten thousand lines of documents, letters, poems, and lost plays by Shakespeare, his contemporaries, and his sources. And all would be transcribed into his version of Chatterton's "ancient hand." William-Henry was nothing if not industrious.

In terms of his own shadowy craft, William-Henry was the Shakespeare of forgery. Indeed, like the Bard, who often based his plays on moldy tales, William-Henry Ireland understood that this thirst for the recovery of knowledge was linked to a sentimental regard for a past golden age. The forgers gave the eighteenth century their Camelots. And *Vortigern* was the sword in the stone that heralded new works by Shakespeare, the dramaturgical once and future king.

SPECIFIC INSTANCES OF FORGING SHAKESPEARE

William-Henry's forgeries were not the first attempt to pass off "lost" papers related to Shakespeare. Lewis Theobald, a lawyer and Shakespeare scholar, announced the discovery of a "new" Shakespeare play, *The Double Falsehood,* in 1728. He was careful to note that the find was an unusual one and that he possessed three manuscripts—the original, written for a "Natural Daughter," and "Two other Copies"—but Theobald never allowed anyone to see them.[77]

Theobald made judgment more difficult by further adding that he had rewritten the play for the stage.[78] Theobald never admitted to forging the play, but failed to include it in his edition of Shakespeare in 1733. Nor did he ever show the manuscripts to anyone. They have since disappeared. Opinion has varied on the legitimacy of Theobald's statements. Richard Farmer thought bits of the play were actually by Shirley; Malone identified it as Massinger's. Isaac Reed thought the play a forgery by Theobald.[79] Late twentieth-century scholarship has been more kind. John Freehafer has suggested that Theobald owned at least one Shakespeare-Fletcher manuscript.[80] Wells and Taylor follow Freehafer in the belief that *The Double Falsehood* was based on the lost Shakespeare play *Cardinio*.[81] Recent historical linguistic tests also agree with Freehafer.[82] Nonetheless, Theobald's dedication makes it clear that many of his contemporaries deemed the play a forgery. If "You shall think fit to pronounce this Piece genuine," he proposes to his reader, "it will silence the Censures of those *Unbelievers,* who think it impossible a Manuscript of *Shakespeare* could so long have lain dormant."[83] *The Grub Street Journal* was not convinced:

> See Theobald leaves the lawyer's gainful train
> To wrack with poetry his tortured brain;
> Fired or not fired, to write resolves with rage,
> And constant pours o'er Shakespeare's sacred page;
> -Then staring cries, I something will be thought,
> I'll write- then- boldly swear 'twas Shakespeare wrote.
> Strange! he in poetry no forgery fears,
> That knows so well in law he'd loose his ears.[84]

In 1748, the Shakespeare actor, Charles Macklin, said he owned a Caroline pamphlet that mentioned Shakespeare in conjunction with Ford and Jonson. Macklin later said he lost the pamphlet at sea in 1760. In 1790, Malone accused Macklin of making up the story in order to create interest for his staging of a Ford play.[85] Another eighteenth-century Shakespeare editor, George Steevens, was at the center of another authorial controversy. In 1763, Steevens published a letter from Peele to Marlowe that made mention of Shakespeare:

Friend Marlo,- I must desyre that my syster hyr watche and the cookerie book you promysed may be sent bye the man. I never longed for thy company more than last night. We were all very merry at the Globe, when Ned Alleyn did not scruple to affyrme plesauntely to thy friende Will that he had stolen his speeche about the qualityes of an actor's excellencye in "Hamlet," hys tragedye, from conversations manyfold which had passed between them, and opinyons given Alleyn touchinge the subjecte. Shakespeare did not take this talke in good sorte, but Jonson put an end to the strife with wittylye remarkinge: "This affaire needeth no contentione; you stole it from Ned no doubte; have you not seen him act, tymes out of number?" Believe me, most syncerilie yours, G. Peele.[86]

This letter was published in *Theatrical Review* and was for many years a source of confusion to scholars.[87] It has since been dismissed as a hoax by Steevens.

His other great forgery is just as comical. In 1790, he fooled the Society of Antiquaries with some engraved Anglo-Saxon letters on a chunk of marble that he tried to pass off as a genuine, ancient artifact. The scrawl read, "Here King Hardcnut drank a wine-horn dry, stared about him, and died."[88]

This hoax was only four years prior to William-Henry's first Shakespeare forgery. And there was yet another successful Shakespeare forger operating at the very same time. His name was John Jordan. Jordan lived in Stratford-upon-Avon. Although he never forged Shakespeare's hand, he did tell some tall tales about the Bard. Many of these tales concerned Shakespeare's drinking prowess and were recorded on paper and sold. Jordan's story of Shakespeare passing out under a crabapple tree outside of Bidford is typical. It begins:

> Our Poet was extremely fond of drinking hearty draughts of English Ale and glory'd in being thought a person of superior eminence in that profession if I may be alowed [*sic*] the phrase.[89]

Jordan sold these stories and papers to tourists, collectors, and scholars. One poem, which he claimed he had found in a chest of drawers, was sold to Edmond Malone, who included it in his 1790 edition of Shakespeare.[90] But Jordan's greatest achievement was the "discovery" of John Shakespeare's Profession of Faith.[91] Although a facsimile exists, the original document has since disappeared.

AUTHENTICATION DEBATE

Why were so many intelligent, educated scholars so easily fooled? Partially it was a mark of the forger's artistic skill and craftsmanship, but equally, it was symptomatic of a literary elite that suffered too readily from a suspension of disbelief when it came to forgery. For while the eighteenth century was an age in which the regard for the aesthetic merits of past ages and their personages had reached maturity, it was, paradoxically, an age in which bibliography and paleography were in their infancy.[92] The techniques for dating deeds, papers, inks, and seals were relatively primitive, as was the study of Elizabethan secretary-hand. These were new sciences, impatient to make connections with the past. There were those who were eager to find and there were those equally eager to supply. Among the suppliers were found the forgers, with their dusty boxes, moldering manuscripts, and long-lost treasures of fool's gold. Covered in the dust of antiquity, their often excellent, sometimes drab works gained an instant audience more interested in venerating than judging the rediscovered. Further, the situation was muddled by many scholars' lack of consensus concerning their methodology of authentification.

According to Maria DeGrazia, Edmond Malone's 1790 edition of Shakespeare was the culmination of a remarkable eighteenth-century scholarly movement toward the use of history and documents as a litmus test for authenticity.[93] But while it is true that periodization, chronology, and historical correspondence were the keys to Edmond Malone's critical theory of legitimization, I disagree with DeGrazia's theory that Malone's emphases were "a compelling and novel response to the absence of a fixed and independent standard by which to prepare and present Shakespearean materials."[94] Rather, Malone was consciously opposing an older, existing standard with which he disagreed. Edmund Burke noted that Malone merely revived "the spirit of that sort of criticism by which false pretense and imposture are detected."[95] This older system, which Burke judged inferior for cases of literary detection, weighed authenticity on aesthetic principles.

This aesthetic standard accepted material as "Shakespearean" on the basis of whether it was suffused with his genius. Rowe, Pope, and Warburton, among others, were scholars who looked for the spirit of the man, not the paper it was writ upon, as evidence of authorship. Such a system was by its nature abusive, an excuse to include or exclude anything the editor liked or disliked. If a story was told congenially and said what the public wanted to hear, there was a good chance the story would be accepted without question. Once it had insinuated itself into a larger accepted narrative, the lie became interlinked with historical reality.[96] As Lord Kames pointed out in 1761:

> when events are related in a lively manner, and every circumstance appears as passing before us, we suffer not patiently the truth of the facts to be questioned.[97]

In 1782, Thomas Warton defined the two prevailing scholarly approaches then in practice, and the party he had favored when commenting on Chatterton's papers:

> It is not from the complexion of ink or of parchment, from the information of cotemporaries [sic], the tales of relations, the recollections of apprentices, and the prejudices of friends, nor even from the doomsday-book, pedigrees in the herald's office, armorial bearings, parliamentary rolls, inquisitions, indentures, episcopal registers, epitaphs, tomb-stones, and brass-plates, that this controversy is to be finally and effectually adjusted. Our arguments should be drawn from principles of taste, from analogical experiment, from a familiarity with antient poetry, and from gradations of composition.[98]

Documentational authenticity was a secondary issue. The litmus of authenticity lay in a document's aesthetics, not its historical accuracy.

Malone's system was an attempt to replace this kind of thinking; to transform the texts and their related documents into one object lodged in the past, rather than tracts riddled with current cultural concerns.[99] William-Henry's forgeries were designed to fool scholars who studied ink, paper, and seals from the Elizabethan era, and those who studied images and echoes from Shakespeare's plays. Many experts were fooled and much of the public, approaching these forgeries with no theoretical framework at all, were similarly taken in. But historical trends, artist merit, documentational verisimilitude, and methodological uncertainty had not fooled Edmond Malone. Unable to study the original documents, Malone attacked the Irelands with a combination of pure intellect and malice. On the line was the integrity of the Shakespeare canon. It was a watershed moment in history, with the future of Shakespeare scholarship hanging in the balance.

2

The Shakspeare Papers: The Master Plan

DESPITE his youth, William-Henry was a master criminal, a boy who plotted to deceive the world. It is a testament to his genius that for over two hundred years the forger's true motives remained concealed. In 1796, 1805, and again in 1832, William-Henry published confessions of his crimes. His version of the events has been accepted unquestioningly by scholars as great as Edmond Malone and as recent as Samuel Schoenbaum.

The accepted story runs as follows: In 1793, Samuel Ireland, a collectibles dealer and travel writer, is obsessed with anything having to do with William Shakespeare. He travels to Stratford-upon-Avon in order to search for documents pertaining to Shakespeare. Accompanying him is Samuel's apparently dim-witted son, William-Henry. Father and son knock on doors asking if any old papers are about. They fail, buy a few worthless trinkets and depart. The father is crushed by his lack of success.

Soon after their return from Stratford, William-Henry informs his father that he has met a gentleman, whom he refers to as "Mr. H." Mr. H. has some old papers in a trunk and has offered them to William-Henry. Some apparently bear Shakespeare's signature. William-Henry returns to the house with one of these documents and gives it to his father who then has it inspected. It is validated as a legitimate Shakespeare signature, a find of tremendous significance and monetary value. Samuel orders the boy back to his friend's trunk to see what else he can find. The boy goes, very reluctantly. He just wants to please his father. He returns with a Profession of Faith, Shakespeare's signed adherence to Protestantism. It, too, is examined and validated. The scholarly world takes notice. The son is sent back to search the trunk. He unearths a letter from Shakespeare to Anne Hathaway. Accompanying the letter is a love poem and a lock of Shakespeare's hair. Amazingly, hair, letter, and poem are validated. On his next search, yet more documents are found. Again, each is accepted as a lost Shake-

The dull-eyed dreamer, William-Henry Ireland, age nineteen. Photo obtained from the Shakespeare Birthplace Trust.

speare document. Days later, William-Henry "discovers" a hand-written version of *King Lear* and a fragment of *Hamlet*. The trunk seems bottomless. The father begins plans to exhibit the papers. He sets Shakespeare's hairs in rings and sells them. He publishes the papers. Money rolls in. An industry begins. The father demands more papers. The son, afraid to confess to his crimes, suddenly finds himself at the center of a major public fraud, his writing heralded as the work of a genius. It dawns on the boy that perhaps, yes, he is a genius, capable of writing as well as Shakespeare. More papers appear: letters from Elizabeth and Southampton, land deeds, receipts, books from Shakespeare's library, a portrait of the dramatist before his house, a reversible portrait with Shakespeare on one side and Shylock on the other, and a deed of gift bequesting a large measure of Shakespeare's royalties to the Ireland family. Incredulity has no bounds and all the documents are validated by a group calling themselves "Believers." On 3 January 1795, William-Henry Ireland announces that he has discovered an unknown Shakespeare play called *Vortigern.*

Samuel is ecstatic, and the press announces the discovery. Debate rages in the newspapers and gentlemen's clubs. Experts and celebrities flock to the papers. Boswell falls to his knees and kisses the "sacred relics." Father and son are invited to meet the Prince of Wales. Theatres Royal, Drury Lane, and Covent Garden begin a bidding war for the lost play. The finest Shakespeare actor of the day, John Philip Kemble, is cast in the title role, and the duke of Clarence becomes a patron of the play. The poet laureate writes the prologue.

IS THE FORGER ALSO A LIAR?

The version I have just presented is a conflation, a composite of his various confessions pieced together.[1] Still, in one important feature they are all identical: to the end of his life William-Henry denied his forgeries were part of an organized plan or cohesive pattern. He wrote, "I did not act upon any premeditated plan of deception, but was as it were unwittingly led into error. . . ."[2] He maintained that the forgeries were done to please his father, that there was no monetary impetus behind them, no rhyme, nor reason, nor overall scheme in his mind. According to the author of the Shakspeare Papers, he was too young to fully understand his crimes.

The question is, do we believe him? Had he forged the papers to please his father; was this simply a youthful prank that got out of hand? Certainly many of the people who had been fooled by the papers did believe his story. John Byng, an early, ardent supporter, believed that William-Henry had simply found himself out of his depth: "to cover one Deceit [he] has told a thousand Lies. But they have begat each other, and were not intended at starting."[3]

Was Byng correct, or had he been duped yet again? A forger is a professional falsifier, and William-Henry was a very good forger. As the *Morning Chronicle* noted, "W.H. Ireland has come forward and announced himself author of the papers attributed by him to Shakspeare; which, if *true,* proves him to be a *liar.*"[4]

In this chapter I will, for the first time, test the assertions of William-Henry's story by examining the variations in his confessions, and comparing them where possible with contemporaneous reportage, letters, and diaries. The results of this investigation have convinced me that William-Henry was not an innocent babe but a deliberate and calculating fraud. However, the facts are so patched with his fictions that we must sometimes pull at the stitchings of the truth to reveal the seams of his lies. There is evidence to suggest that the boy-forger spent many years contemplating the art of forgery, and even passed off some early frauds before attempting his masterwork, the Shakspeare Papers. And like the Shakspeare Papers, these early forgeries centered on literary obsession and his relationship with his father.

WILLIAM-HENRY IRELAND'S HEROS: CHAUCER AND CHATTERTON

William-Henry Ireland was born 2 August 1775. At the time of the first Shakspeare Papers forgery, William-Henry was a nineteen-year-old clerk in a law firm and a part-time book collector.[5] Little is known of his upbringing except that he went to college in France. His contact with his father seems to have been centered on Shakespeare. The boy-forger had what he called "daily opportunities of hearing Mr. Samuel Ireland extol the genius of Shakspeare, as he would very frequently in the evening read one of his [Shakespeare's] plays aloud, dwelling with enthusiasm on such passages as most peculiarly struck his fancy."[6]

However, William-Henry did not share his father's enthusiasm for the Bard. Rather, his interests lay with two other writers—Chaucer and Chatterton. His love of Chaucer was, like his father's love of Shakespeare, obsessional. He wished not only to collect and read Chaucer but to enter into his fictions. He often

> sighed to be the inmate of some gloomy castle; or that having lost my way upon a dreary heath, I might, like Sir Bertram, have been conducted to some enchanted mansion. Sometimes I have wished that by the distant chime of a bell I had found the hospitable porch of some old monastery, where, with the holy brotherhood, having shared at the board their homely fare, I might afterwards have enjoyed upon the pallet a sound repose, and, with the abbots, blessing the ensuing morn, have hied me in pursuit of fresh adventures.[7]

As with the later Shakespeare forgeries, William-Henry began in part to actualize his medieval fantasies. He collected old armor. He might have become a real-life Don Quixote. Certainly, if he were not quixotic he appears to have been borderline psychotic. He described his bedroom as "a regular armoury" and himself as the knight-errant, who "sat upright in [his] bed, and pictured scenes from my lord Orford's Castle of Otranto, &c."[8] The missing parts of his armor were filled in with pasteboard substitutes, based on his readings of Grose's *Ancient Armoury.* Even early on William-Henry realized that verisimilitude could be reached by a mixture of research and imaginative resourcefulness.

But no matter how real the effort, the result was still fantasy; make-believe; play; fiction. It did not take long for William-Henry to realize that if he could not interact in the creative world of a writer, he could supplant the creator and make that world his own. Such an attempt is found in William-Henry's acrostic to Chaucer. The piece has two titles. The first title is:

ACROSTIC ON GEOFFREY CHAUCER,

> In the Style of John Lydgate, a writer of that period,
> and a disciple and friend of the Father of English poetry.

The second title reads:

> *Lynes by thilke lerned clerke Dan Jan Lydgate, a monke of Burye, wrotenn on his freynde and maisterr Geoffrey Chaucer.*

The poem itself reads:

> Con I yn rythms thilke clerke's fame make knowen,
> Hondlynge so poorlee thys my quille

> As rathere makes me hys fame kille;
> Unless yt bene that gratefull minde alone
> Con trumpe hys praise; since butt for hym I owne
> Endless indeede had bene the travaile untoe mee
> Ryghte praisse and thankes to offerr thus yn poesie.[9]

Clearly, William-Henry was attempting to mimic medieval orthography. But the second title is, in my opinion, the original title to the work. My opinion is based on two observations: (1) the first title seems to be a preliminary introduction, (2) the second title is specifically linked to the piece in its stylistic principles, namely its use of pseudo-Chaucerian spelling. This second title is all but redundant to the first except that it does not pretend to be in the style *of* John Lydgate but actually is *by* John Lydgate.

Though there is no record of William-Henry having tried to pass the poem off as authentic, there is no doubt the piece represents an important crossroads for the future Shakespeare forger. His later Shakespeare forgeries display the same curious neo-Middle English spelling. Both this early piece and the later forgeries are said to be by long-dead writers. However, Chaucer and Shakespeare were centuries apart. William-Henry obviously thought that if a writer were dead for a long period of time his writing must be much of a muchness in relation to other dead writers. Despite owning both Medieval and Reniassance books and reading them, William-Henry Ireland evidently thought that Middle English was the same as Elizabethan!

But the poem is important for its thematic as well as its stylistic facets: William-Henry/Lydgate's acrostic is an admission that fame through forgery can damage the reputation of Chaucer ("thys my quille / As rather makes me hys fame kille . . ."). Outweighing the penalties of damaging the dead were the benefits to the living. The dead writers have saved the living writers from starting all over again. The modern writer owed a debt to the dead writer. Chaucer had served as a role model; a cast into which William-Henry shaped ideas. The implication is that an original style is either impossible or unnecessary. While such imitation is common in an apprentice period, William-Henry used imitation as an art form unto itself. He became an artisan who could produce two literary *Mona Lisas* a day.

But if William-Henry needed a role model for writing, he also needed a role model for forgery. Again, his father's evening readings were his source of inspiration. These after-dinner readings consisted of Shakespeare, Shakespeare, Shakespeare. However, on rare occasion, Samuel Ireland varied his after-dinner readings. One night, instead of Shakespeare, Samuel read from Herbert Croft's novel, *Love and Madness*. The book in part explores the genius of the boy-forger and suicide, Chatterton. After the reading came discussion:

> I perfectly well remember that the conversation turned upon Chatterton; and, from the circumstances then curiously mentioned, I was prompted to peruse the above [mentioned] work. . . . the fate of Chatterton so strongly interested me, that I used frequently to envy his fate, and desire nothing so ardently as the termination of my existence in a similar cause.[10]

As with Chaucer, William-Henry penned an acrostic to his hero, but this piece was not from a contemporary, nor did it share in Chattertonian spelling:

> Comfort and joy's for ever fled:
>   He ne'er will warble more!
> Ah me! the sweetest youth is dead
>   That e'er tun'd reed before.
> The hand of Mis'ry bow'd him low;
>   E'en Hope forsook his brain:
> Relentless man contemn'd his woe:
>   To you he sigh'd in vain.
> Oppress'd with want, in wild despair he cried
> 'No more I'll live!' swallow'd the draught, and died.[11]

The poem is no great work. What is interesting is that he takes the facts (starving writer, suicide) and turns it into a fiction, complete with emotional depth and monologue. Once again, William-Henry was in his Chaucerian world, augmenting known facts with his own Chattertonian fantasies.

He admits that from the time he read *Love and Madness* only "the lapse of a few months was to hold me forth to public view as the supposed discoverer of the Shaksperian manuscripts."[12] William-Henry's poems to Chaucer and Chatterton were more than just bad juvenilia. They are his versified essays on art, originality, fame, and fraud.

WILLIAM-HENRY IRELAND'S EARLY FORGERIES

From the theoretical, William-Henry soon worked out the practical difficulties of forgery. Before collectors, scholars, and enthusiasts were to know him as the discoverer of the Shakspeare Papers, they were to know him as the discoverer of a lost book owned by Queen Elizabeth, and a lost masterpiece by the sculptor Simon.

His father, Samuel, was a collector of art, of books, of Shakespeariana and other curiosities. It is reasonably common for a boy to emulate, or imitate his father. It is equally normal for a boy to wish to please his father. William-Henry began collecting books. But his emulation of and respect for his father was not of a common sort. Indeed, the forger readily confessed that his first forgery was presented to his father to both please and fool that same gentleman:

> Having one day purchased a thin quarto tract of the time of *Elizabeth,* illuminated and bound in vellum, with her arms on the cover, I determined on trying an experiment with it, and for the purpose wrote a letter (in imitation of the hand of that period) as from the author of the book, making it the presentation copy from himself to the queen.[13]

This first forgery was done with ordinary ink, weakened with water. William-Henry Ireland showed it to a bookbinder named Laurie, who remarked that "it was well done, and might deceive many."[14] It was good enough to fool his father, Samuel, who was delighted to accept his son's present.

William-Henry continued to follow the curious path of pleasing and deceiving his father. He studied the signatures published in a Malone 1790 edition of Shakspeare, but with no malicious or material intent, but only for "a little mirth, [to] . . . shew how far *credulity* would go in search for antiquities."[15]

In the meantime, Laurie demonstrated how to create the impression of aged ink. William-Henry watched closely as Laurie

> mix'd a few drops of acid with some other liquid (used in marbling the covers of books) in a vial; then writing a few words on paper, held it up to the fire to shew its effect, when the letters turn'd completely brown.

This time the presented forgery was not simply a practical joke but a commercial transaction. It was exchanged for a book in his father's library. Later, when he had written a great deal of the Shakespeare manuscripts, he sneaked into his father's library and destroyed this "first attempt, so badly executed."[16]

His next forgery would be of a higher quality. William-Henry purchased a statue, modeled in terra-cotta. It was the work of a young artist, who had died in a "putrid fever." To the back of the statue William-Henry attached a piece of paper upon which he wrote "a label, intimating that the head in question had belonged to Cromwell, and was a gift from himself to Bradshaw, whose signature I affixed to the superscription."[17]

He showed the head to his father, who in turn showed it to some experts who "pronounced it as their firm opinion that the head in question *must have been modeled by Simon,* the justly celebrated artist who lived during the protectorship."[18] He states that it is merely curious that his autograph of Bradshaw matched perfectly with Bradshaw's real autograph.

William-Henry is perfectly frank as to why he perpetrated this fraud:

> . . . if the model had been produced as the performance of the young man who really modeled it, a slight commendation would have been passed upon his merits by the very persons who attributed it to Simon, and there the matter would have terminated.

William-Henry believed, perhaps justly, that only famous artists could create famous works of art. The new artist was permanently excluded from an old-boys' network designed to keep the up-and-coming down-and-out. He understood the situation, but he was not happy with it:

> Now let me submit a simple proposition. The workmanship was produced as from the hands of Simon. Either it possessed merit, or it did not. If it did possess merit sufficient to entitle it to the name of that sculptor, the young artist was certainly a rising genius as a modeler: if it did not possess sufficient spirit, it was the name of Simon being annexed which made it pass current.[19]

Just to hammer home the message, William-Henry added a quatrain reaffirming that time alone can make an artwork great and that a modern artist could only receive praise if he worked under the name of an established artist:

> So purblind, so unfeeling, is mankind,
> That living genius vainly boasts its mind;
> But, 'ray'd in Time's *erugo,* sages praise,
> And give a modern Simon, SIMON's bays.[20]

It was some time after these forgeries that William-Henry claimed "the idea first struck me of imitating the signature of our bard. . . ."[21] Yet this is at odds with the notion of William-Henry's spontaneous need to please his father and his lack of formal planning. Indeed, contemporaneous documents make it clear that it is possible, even probable, that William-Henry worked long and hard to perfect his Shakespeare-hand. As evidence, I cite the diary of the landscape painter Joseph Farington, who recorded that in the early months of 1794 he had attended a party with William-Henry Ireland. While intoxicated, William-Henry boasted that he "had been employed in writing a Copy of all Shakespeares [sic] plays."[22]

The story is an odd one. Why would the boy need to copy out Shakespeare's plays when he might simply purchase a cheap edition? If the story is authentic, William-Henry must have been doing something other than copying the plays, or perhaps he was copying the plays, but not in his hand. Perhaps William-Henry had been forging, or at least practicing, Shakespeare's hand for almost a year before he presented his first Shakespeare forgery.

He says that the forgeries were done to please his father but this cannot account for the pre-Shakespearean forgeries. His father never fantasized about a writer sending an autographed copy of his book to Queen Elizabeth. Let us remember that this forgery from some unnamed writer to Queen Elizabeth was not impulsively executed. The Elizabethans had a far different lettering pattern from our own. We call everyday Elizabethan script "secretary-hand." One does not learn to read it in a day, nor write it in an hour. It might take days to become familiar with the hand, weeks—maybe even months—to manage a forgery that was passable and/or professional. This was no child's scrawl which William-Henry presented to his father. It had to fool a man whose very business consisted of buying and selling authentic, collectible books.

This forgery of a general Elizabethan hand was followed by a forgery of a specific Cromwellian hand: Bradshaw's note on the Simon statue. This is perhaps the most damning piece of evidence when judging William-Henry's early forgeries. He claims that it was very strange that his signature matched Bradshaw's. There was nothing strange about it. It is simple proof that William-Henry checked Bradshaw's signature, studied it, practiced it, faked it perfectly, and executed it with ink and paper good enough to fool both his father and the experts. In other words, William-Henry had already bought the special ink and watermarked paper and seals he would need long before the Shakspeare Papers were executed. How else could he convince his father (a collector) and various experts that the paper (and subsequently, the statue), dated to the time of Cromwell? And then there is the curious matter of the Chaucer acrostic, written as a forgery, and his deep affinity for Chatterton, a forger whom William-Henry confesses was a role model.

Were the forgeries premeditated? You bet they were. His father had shown an interest in three things: money, Shakespeare, and books. William-Henry says that he forged to make his father happy, and yet he deceived his father on all three counts: the signatures were phonies, the money generated was fraudulent, and as for the book traded, William-Henry double-crossed his own father. He traded the letter to Elizabeth for a book and then stole back the letter and destroyed it. The father lost not only the book but also the letter. William-Henry got something for nothing, and cheated his father at the same deal, twice.

THE TRIP TO STRATFORD

The last preparatory phase for the Shakspeare Papers came during Samuel's trip to Stratford. The dutiful son who had already cheated his father in selling him a book with a bogus letter to Elizabeth and a phony Simon statue was with him. But William-Henry was an amateur forger and he knew it. If he did not know it when he arrived in Stratford, he definitely knew it when he left.

Father and son hired a guide to show them around the town and environs. William-Henry described him as a "very honest fellow" and as a "civil inoffensive creature."[23] This honest, civil, inoffensive creature was John Jordan: carpenter, failed poet, conman, and Stratford's most successful forger.

The three wandered around Stratford, visiting the tourist sites. As William-Henry recalled, "not one hour was spent but in the favorite pursuit; . . . the immortal and divine Shakspeare."[24] They went to Trinity Church. Samuel made some sketches and asked if he could make a plaster casting of the bust. Trinity declined the honor.

But Jordan's job was not just to guide them around Stratford. Jordan was a businessman, a fraud, a confidence man, and it seems in Stratford the confidence men worked together for their mutual benefit. If William-Henry could not spot Jordan, he was more discerning with Jordan's associates.

The first stop was a gift shop where articles were made from the wood of a mulberry tree Shakespeare is reputed to have planted. William-Henry knew that the pieces were forgeries. "I much fear," he wrote, "a dozen full-grown mulberry trees would scarcely suffice to produce the innumerable mementoes already extant." Either he did not communicate his suspicions to his father or his father refused to listen. Samuel Ireland bought a goblet "for which he gave an adequate price" to "this manufacturer of Shaksperian relics. . . ."[25]

Jordan took the Irelands to the birthplace. William-Henry was unimpressed. He called it a "lowly mansion." Jordan conducted a tour and pointed out the hearth in which was found John Shakespeare's Profession of Faith.[26] Jordan was an expert on the subject of this document. He had forged it. Later, this very document would serve as a model for one of William-Henry's forgeries.

Meanwhile, Samuel had been talking to other people:

> He was at length given to understand, by some of the oldest inhabitants . . . [that] some manuscripts having been conveyed for safety, at the time of the fire at Stratford, from New Place . . . to Clopton House, situated at a little distance from the scene of the conflagration.[27]

Let's examine this statement as a gauge of Samuel's credulity. People had looked for Shakespeare's papers for years. No one remembered a thing about them, that is, until the great fire. As half the town went up in flames someone suddenly remembered where the sacred relics lay. Instead of fighting the fire with sand and buckets of water from the nearby river, the inhabitants entered burning buildings, with no regard for their own safety. Despite the smoke, they were able to find the papers, and recognize the hand. People died, buildings collapsed, children ran naked in the streets but all was well. Shakespeare's papers were safe. Then came the solemn march, Stratford burning as a backdrop, as the guardians of the sacred scripts marched across the river to deposit the treasures in a temporary place of safekeeping. But in all the rush, no one remembered to take the papers back after the fire had been extinguished. Even John Jordan, whose livelihood depended on finding Shakespeare memorabilia, did not hear about or think about rediscovering these precious papers. Only a moron would believe this story. Samuel, we are told, believed this story.

Whether we should believe William-Henry's assessment of his father's intellect is a point discussed in a later chapter. Certainly William-Henry goes out of his way to present his father as a near imbecile. When father, son, and Jordan arrived at Clopton House, they met the tenant, Mr. Williams. William-Henry describes Williams as a "gentleman-farmer; rich in gold and the worldly means of accumulating wealth, but devoid of every polished refinement."[28] Yet this Midlands hillbilly would have no problem in fooling Samuel

Ireland, artist, writer, book collector. Samuel asked him if he had any papers with Shakespeare's signature on them.

> The gentleman's answer was, that having some young partridges which he wished to bring up, he had, for the purpose, cleared out a small apartment wherein these papers lay, and burnt a large basket-full of them. . . .[29]

Mr. Williams said that most of the papers in question were rotten as tinder but on many of them, he could plainly perceive the signature of William Shakespeare, and turning to his wife asked, "Don't yon [sic] remember it my Dear?" Her answer was, "Yes, perfectly well, and you know at the time, I blamed you for destroying them." Samuel swallowed the bait hook, line, and sinker. "Good God, Sir! you do not know what an injury the world has sustained by the loss of them."[30] A search of the house was conducted, but no documents were found. Samuel must have cursed the day God created the partridge. As Williams later admitted to another Stratfordian, he was only joking. William-Henry must have marveled how easily an educated man like his father could have been fooled.[31]

Jordan must have been holding back the giggles as well. He had to—the tour was not over. William-Henry, and his father Samuel, with his goblet, had one more stop to go: Anne Hathaway's place. There, Samuel bought a bugle purse—a gift from William to Anne—and an old oak chair—not just any oak chair but Shakespeare's very own one-of-a-kind courting chair.

Once again this evidence turns on William-Henry Ireland's claim of spontaneity. He had executed forgeries, many of which he had passed off to the public. He had seen Jordan and the mulberry tree manufacturers in action. He knew, as did Jordan, that an artist could reach fame and fortune with relative ease by using an established name. The Simon statue, the tract given to Elizabeth, and Jordan's own miserable tales proved this. Like a good commercial artist, William-Henry simply gave the public what it wanted.

William-Henry noted that Samuel was willing to pay generously for a Shakespeare document:

> My father would often lavish his usual praises on *Shakspear,* and frequently add, that he would give all his curious books to become possessed of a single line of his hand writing.[32]

In his various confessions, William-Henry says that he explored legitimate means of securing a Shakespeare signature for his father. He writes that on his return from Stratford, he "was more partial than ever to the pursuit after antiquities of every description, and more particularly to every thing that bore the smallest affinity to our bard."[33] He says (in a chapter entitled "A Fruitless Hunt") that he looked high and low in his office for an autograph of Shakespeare. He couldn't find one. Eventually the hunt extended beyond the confines of his desk and filing cabinets. No doubt the closets and pantries were searched. A bold idea to visit a few bookshops ensued. This hunt was equally fruitless.

Why should his law office have Shakespearean documents lying around? And how does one search for Shakespeare's signature in a bookseller's? ("Excuse me sir. Have you any signatures of Shakespeare in any of your books?" "Sure do, just look in the Elizabethan bargain bin.")

It seems perfectly obvious that William-Henry never searched the law office or the bookstalls. He was too clever to be as stupid as his father, knocking on doors and asking shop owners and farmers if they had any priceless papers lying on the floor. He had already begun forging and his trip to Stratford had shown him who to forge and how to market. There was no need to search for Shakespeare documents. William-Henry and his magic ink could make them appear as easily as a magician pulls a rabbit out of a hat.

THE SHAKSPEARE PAPERS: RELEASE DATES AND WHAT THEY TELL US

On 22 November 1794, the Shakspeare Papers began in earnest. According to Samuel's own diary for that day, "my Son was invited to dine at the house of our mutual friend Mr. M.—— where amongst other Company- he met a gentleman from —— of considerable property."[34]

William-Henry told his father the following story concerning this "gentleman":

> I had, by mere chance, formed an acquaintance with a gentleman, and being one day at dinner with him, expressing my partiality for old books, as well as the autographs of great personages, I said, the gentleman appointed me to meet him, and told me I might rummage over a large quantity of old deeds and papers which had descended to him from his father, who had practised the law, and acquired a great fortune;

I added, that for some time I neglected calling according to my promise, alledging [*sic*] that as he was a young man, he had only meant perhaps to laugh at me. . . .[35]

However, on 2 December 1794,

being near the place, curiosity prompted me to call; the gentleman, I said, was rather angry at my remissness and breach of promise, but having made an apology, he permitted me to go into the next room, where I saw a great quantity of papers tied up in bundles. . . .[36]

How carefully constructed this story was! Whereas Chatterton simply found his papers in an old trunk, Ireland had created an entire history of recent experiences, vague enough to be filled in, detailed enough to be believable. The details to be added were clear: What was the gentleman's name? Where did he live? But these mysterious vagaries were built upon a solid foundation of details: the meal, the dutiful son's disbelief, their difference in social stature, their equality in age, all leading to a room where the treasures of the literary world had lain hidden for centuries and guarded by a mysterious gentleman.

William-Henry had planned well. But there were questions to be answered. Some questions could be answered later; others had to be answered immediately. Why had these documents not come to light sooner? Where was the young gentleman? Why was he reluctant to show himself? Ireland would need to explain why he had to shield his imaginary friend while adding plausibility to his own trusting, honest, good character. Ireland was protecting him, from whom, for what? What could a boy who was only a law clerk do? Ireland was smart enough to go with his strengths. The answer would be logical and legal:

I added the following story: that in searching among my friend's deeds, I had found one which ascertained to him some property, long a matter of litigation and dispute; upon this he promised me every thing I should find appertaining to *Shakspear,* and further, to stop all enquiries as to his name, &c., I added, that being a man of large fortune, he did not choose to undergo the impertinent questionings of the world, for which reason, he had bound me on oath, to secrecy, and better to strengthen this, I hinted, that his father perhaps might have detained the papers illegally in the course of his practice, and should his name be known, it would undoubtedly lead to a discovery, and throw a slur on the honour of his family; by such means, I for some time stopped all enquiries.[37]

A man of fabulous wealth no one knew, a gentleman who dined with clerks, a lawyer who never looked at papers, family honor threatened by a scandalous secret—and at the center of this drama was our young hero, law clerk by day; stalwart friend of the super-rich by night.

William-Henry had covered all the angles. For curiosity's sake he had found the documents, for his father's sake he had brought one home, for the world's sake he searched for more, and for the gentleman's sake he had saved his land and protected his reputation. William-Henry Ireland had painted himself as a retardedly altruistic boy.

On Tuesday, 16 December 1794, William-Henry brought home the first of the Shakspeare Papers, the Fraser Deed.[38] This first major Shakespeare forgery was a facsimile of the Blackfriars deed, which he found in a modern edition of Shakspeare. With this as his guide, he made out a deed, written apparently "At the Globe by Thames" and dated 14 July 8 Jam[s]. The deed itself referred to "Willam Shakespeare of Stratford on Avon in the County of Warwick Gent but now residynge in London and John Hemynge of London Gent of thone Pte and Michael Fraser and Elizabeth hys Wife of the othere Pte." Turning to a facsimile of Shakespeare's will, William-Henry then forged the Bard's signature. Having no model for Heminges's signiture, William-Henry made one up. As for the wax seals, the forger hit upon a method of using a hot knife to cut away an old seal from an authentic document. He then used fresh wax to attach the authentic seal to his forged document. He then carefully rubbed the seal with soot and ash to cosmetically mask any differences between the new and old wax.

It was more than good enough to fool his father, who offered William-Henry any book in his collection for it. The previous offer had been the entire library but be that as it may, William-Henry says he gave his father the book for nothing. He was a generous boy. He had made his father happy. He was happy. All was well. William-Henry says he never meant the deception to go any further. But his father had told his collector friends about his son's discoveries. On Thursday, 18 December 1794, Samuel took the deed to the Herald Office for identification. On 20 December he showed it to Sir Fredrick Eden, "a cultivated dilettante" who studied seals as a hobby.[39] The deed was validated by Eden.

William-Henry used his youth as an excuse for the forgeries. Yet he was nineteen years old, no longer a child. He had received a college education in France. He had been working at a law firm for over two years. When Alexander was seventeen, he had conquered the known world. Are we to believe that William-Henry Ireland did not realize the legal and commercial ramifications of forging literary documents? He was a law clerk and book collector!

Even if he were ignorant, even if he had never intended to go further than the first forgery, why had he continued to forge after the literary world was notified of the early forgeries? His excuse is that most of those who saw the first Shakspeare Paper agreed that the document was indeed original and that "wherever it was found, there must undoubtedly be all the manuscripts of Shakspear so long and vainly sought for. . . ." His father was sure that his son "knew of many more" documents.[40] In William-Henry's eyes, he had no choice:

> and being thus urged forward to produce what really was not in existence, I then determined on essaying some composition in imitation of the language of Shakspeare. I must, however, solemnly affirm, that had not such incitements been used, I never should have attempted a second document. . . .[41]

According to the forger, this document was a profession of Shakespeare's religious faith.

But according to his father's diary, it was William-Henry himself who first mentioned the possibility of there being more documents.[42] And the Profession of Faith was not the second document William-Henry delivered, but the third. One week before, on 17 December, he had presented his father with a receipt from Shakespeare to Heminges.[43] It read:

> One Moneth from the date hereof I doe promyse to paye to my good and Worthye Freynd John Hemynge the sume of five Pounds and five shillings English Monye as a recompense for hys greate trouble in settling and doinge much for me at the Globe Theatre as also for hys trouble in going downe for me to statford Witness my Hand
> Wm Shakspere
> September the Nyth 1589[.]
> [One Month from the date hereof, I do promise to pay to my good and worthy friend John Heminge the sum of five pounds and five shillings, English money, as a recompense for his great trouble in settling and doing much for me at the Globe Theatre as also for his trouble in going down for me to statford. Witness my Hand
> Wm Shakspere
> September the Nith 1589.]

Strange that "Shakspere" should misspell the name of his own town. Accompanying Shakspeare's evidently clerk-like bookkeeping was the following note from "Jnº Hemynge":

Received of Master Wm Shakspeare
the sum of five Pounds and five
Shillings good English Money thys
Nynth Day of October 1589[.][44]

Never mind that the Globe wouldn't be built for another ten years, Samuel and his followers validated the document as genuine.

On 24 December 1794, William-Henry presented his father Shakespeare's Profession of Faith.[45] His father's happiness was no longer his paramount concern. William-Henry's new excuse for forgery was the enhancement of Shakespeare's reputation:

I heard him [John Shakespeare] much censured for the invocation to the Saints, and the superstitious manner in which it was composed, I resolved on writing the son's perfectly simple, wishing thereby to prove *Shakspear* a Protestant, that having been often a matter of doubt.[46]

Yet earlier in this account he says he wrote this document for "mere frolick and diversion."[47] Which is it? The idea of the document being created off the top of his head for diversion is a difficult one to conceive. For one, he took care as to the paper used.

In the Profession of Faith, as with the first forgery, William-Henry was careful in his technical details. His *Confessions* adds the revelation that he was at this point unfamiliar with Elizabethan watermarks. He chose two half-sheets that bore no mark whatsoever. However, on the reverse of the phony Profession of Faith, were several other real Professions of Faith, the earliest dating from the reign of Charles I. The inference to be gathered was that the paper had been reused for the same purpose by generations subsequent to Shakespeare. The Profession of Faith is written by a man on his deathbed, eager to unburden his soul:

I beynge nowe offe sounde Mynde doe hope thatte thys mye wyshe wille atte mye deathe bee acceeded toe as I nowe lyve in Londonne ande as mye soule maye perchance soone quitte thys poore Bodye it is mye desire thatte inne suche case I maye bee carryed to mye native place ande thatte mye Bodye bee there quietlye interred wythe as little pompe as canne bee ande I doe nowe inne theese mye seyriouse Moments make thys mye professione of fayth. . . .

[I being now of sound mind do hope that this my wish will at my death be accedded to. As I now lie in London and as my soul may

Letter from Shakspeare to Heminges and receipt. Reprinted with permission of The Folger Shakespeare Library.

perchance soon quite this poor body, it is my dear desire that in such case I may be carried to my native place and that my body be there quietly interred with as little pomp as can be. And I do now in these my serious moments, make this, my profession of faith. . . .]

And on the Bard wanders, writing of "Synne," "Pittye," his "wretched pillowe," and "colde Deathe." But he finds solace in the Lord. His poetic simile is striking:

Forgive O Lorde alle oure synnes ande with thye grete Goodnesse take usse alle to thye Breaste O cherishe usse like the sweete Chickenne that under the coverte offe herre spreadynge Wings Receyves herre lyttle Broode and hoveringe oerre themme keepes themme harmlesse ande in safetye

Wm Shakspeare[.]

[. . . Forgive, Oh Lord, all our sins and with thy great goodness take us all to thy breast. Oh cherish us like the sweet chicken that under the cover of her spreading wings receives her little brood and hovering over them keeps them harmless and in safety.

Wm Shakspeare.]

William-Henry said that the text of the forgery was "altogether unstudied"—that he wrote simply "just as the thoughts arose in . . . [his] mind."[48] Yet William-Henry admitted that he kept facsimiles of Shakespeare's autograph before him and "formed the twelve different letters contained in the Christian and sir names of William Shakspeare as much as possible to resemble the tracings of his original autograph." But above even this, William-Henry was "particular in introducing as many capital *doubleyous* and *esses* as possible."[49]

This was William-Henry's third Shakespeare forgery and it certainly marks a new development. Hopkins's cross rhymes are certainly a difficult challenge to any poet but composing an entire, coherent letter depending as much as possible on twelve letters is a near impossibility. Trying to make us believe that this tremendous achievement was reeled off the top of his head is fatuous. I question whether any writer, particularly a young, inexperienced one, could write as quickly as is here claimed. It is far more probable that the Profession of Faith had been the labor of some days, if not weeks.

And certainly the document he presented was the culmination of many drafts. Years later, George Steevens bought a folio of William-Henry's forgeries that included the Profession of Faith. He noted that the forgeries in his possession "were Ireland's experimental pieces done before those handed to the father."[50]

Shakspeare's Profession of Faith. Reprinted with permission of The Folger Shakespeare Library.

This is also supported by his admission of being unable to write quickly. He says of the later forgeries:

> I began to consider what would be the best expedient to accomplish this end [a quantitative increase in the papers] without much labour of the brain; for . . . my muse was not so very prolific as to 'spin and weave' poetry as fast as it was required. . . .[51]

So we may safely assume he is lying when he says he wrote the Profession of Faith off the top of his head.

William-Henry had written forgeries concerning Shakespeare's financial and theatrical interests and his personal, religious convictions. Aside from their orthography, the papers were all quite plausible. Indeed, they were just the sort of documents one might expect to find—uniformly historical, convincingly factual. The papers had been authenticated by experts who believed that where one authenticated document rested, all other documents culled from the same source must be equally authentic; in for a penny, in for a pound.

VORTIGERN APPEARS

On 26 December 1794, only ten days after the presentation of the first forgery, William-Henry told his father he had discovered the original manuscript to an unknown play, based on a chapter in Holinshed's *Chronicles,* entitled *Vortigern and Rowena.* Samuel was told that this play was assuredly by Shakespeare since the manuscript "had many interliniations-and additional Notes in it-to which Shakspeare has frequently added- the initials of his name W.S. and in some places his name written at length. . . ."[52]

On 31 December 1794, William-Henry presented his father with a promissory note from Shakespeare to the actor Lowine.[53] Days later, William-Henry gave his father more information on the unknown play. Samuel recorded the following information in his diary:

> The play that has never been performed is taken from Hollinsheds [*sic*] Chronicle Vol. 1: p: 109- History of England- The story is the dethronement and murdering of Constantius King of Britain by Vortigern- and the consequent espousal of the latter with Rowena

daughter to Hengist a Saxon General- The Characters in the play are written by Shakespeare in the first page as follows:

Constantius-King of Britain
Vortigern- King of Britain
Aurelius Ambrose
            +   } Sons of Constantius
Uter Pendragon
The two Tutors to the Sons
Hengist General of the Saxons
Vortigerns three Sons
Two Murderers
The Wife of Vortigern
Rowena-daughter to Hengist
A Princess—Soldier + Attendants.[54]

To explain why the play had remained unknown, William-Henry later forged a series of letters between Shakespeare and a printer, in which neither could accept the other's financial terms for publication.[55] The first letter, from Holmes to Shakespeare, read:

Goode Master Willim
    Itt grieves me muche thatte I cannott give thee thatte whiche thou doste aske forre thye playe ande as I doe alsoe Knowe thou nere before didste gette soe muche forre any onne lette me begge thee therefoure toe lowerre a littell inne thye demandes forre though I doe like thy playe yett I doe like mye moneye
                                        thine trewelye
                                        William Holmes
[Good Master William,
    It grieves me much that I cannot give thee that which thou dost ask for thy play and as I do also know thou never before did'st get so much for any one. Let me beg thee therefore to lower a little in thy demands. For though I do like thy play, yet I do like my money.
                                        Thine truly,
                                        William Holmes.]

But *Vortigern* was a special play, worth more to Shakespeare than any of his other works. The Bard held firm:

Deare freynde
    I doe esteeme muche mye Playe havynge takenne muche care wrytynge of itte ande I doe thynke thatte care hathe notte beene toe a very lyttelle purpose thereforre I cannotte ithe leaste lowerre mye pryce
                                        Thyne trewlye

June 12   Wm Shakspeare

[Dear friend,
    I do esteem much my play, having taken much care writing of it and
I do think that care hath not been to a very little purpose. Therefore I
cannot in the least lower my price.
Thine truly,

June 12   Wm Shakspeare.]

And so the correspondence continued. In the next letter
"Holmes" offered a raise of £4. "Shakspeare" wanted more.
"Holmes" raised his offer to £3 more than "Shakspeare" had ever
received for any other play, plus a bonus of £5. On 22 June 1604,
"Shakspeare" wrote "Holmes" one last time:

Goode freynde
    Thou myghtste as welle turne the Currannte othe Sea asalterre thatte
whiche I ha sayde whenne I knowe itte toe bee ryghte wele speake
noe moure onne thys matterre therefore thys Evenynge sende mee
backe mye writtenne Playe ande mye Letterres whyche I ha sente thee
if thou haste notte burnte themme
farewelle thyne trewlye

22 June   Wm Shakspeare
1604.[56]

[Good friend,
    Thou myght'st as well turn the current of the sea as alter that which
I have said when I know it to be right well. Speak no more on this
matter. Therefore, this evening send me back my written play and my
letters which I have sent thee if thou hast not burnt them.
Farewell. Thine truly,

22 June   Wm Shakspeare
1604.]

It was now clear why the play had remained unknown, but also
that Shakespeare himself considered it to be his finest work, the
play he had labored on the most, the play he had negotiated on
hardest, the play for which he wanted the most money, the play of
which he was proudest. Greater than *Macbeth,* greater than *King
Lear,* greater even than *Hamlet, Vortigern* was the greatest play
of all and William-Henry must have known his father would pester
him unceasingly for it. Any papers delivered after 26 December
1794, like the letters from Holmes, were done so as to clear the
way for *Vortigern.*

Goode freynde

    Thou myghtste as welle turne the
Currunnte othe Sea as alterre thatte
whiche I ha sayde wheune I knowe itte
toe bee ryghte wele speake noe moure
onne thys matterre therefore thys Evenynge
sende mee backe mye writtenne Playe
ande mye Letterres whyche I ha sente
thee if thou haste notte burnte themme

          farewelle thyne trewelye
             Wm Shakspeare

22 June
16 04

        Forre mye Masterre
          Holmes the
            Prynterre

Letter from Shakspeare to his printer. Reprinted with permission of The Folger Shakespeare Library.

Though the fraud was still in its early days and the manuscript *Vortigern* had yet to be presented, William-Henry had already begun affixing a commercial value to the papers. On 26 December 1794, the very same day he told his father about the *Vortigern* manuscript, he also told his father that according to Mr. H.'s own estimates, the papers might well prove to be worth over £20,000.[57] On 5 January, a mere two days after giving his father the list of characters for the play, he said that the gentleman had refused offers of £2,000 on the papers. A counteroffer of £2,500 was similarly refused.[58] Why should William-Henry sell the papers for £2,500 when the gentleman had valued them at ten times that amount?

On 19 January 1795, William-Henry brought home yet another discovery: a small portrait in ink of Shakespeare standing before his house on Henley Street. On one side of the portrait was an ancient "W." and on the other side an "S." His coat of arms was displayed in another corner. In the background were inscribed the following plays:

> Asse you lyke itte
> Othello-Hamblette
> Kynge John
> Kynge Henry the fyfthe
> Romeo ande Julyette
> Tempeste
> Rycharde the Seconde.[59]

Samuel had his doubts about this portrait.[60] The very next day, William-Henry produced a letter from Shakespeare to Cowley in which the portrait was mentioned. One document validated the other; Samuel was satisfied.

THE EXPERTS ARE FOOLED

On 1 February 1795, Samuel invited two Shakespeare experts to inspect the papers: Drs. Parr and Warton, two highly regarded men of letters. Joseph Warton was a critic respected by Cowper and a friend of Johnson, Burke, Garrick, and Reynolds. His dubious claim to literary fame was his *Essay on the Writings and Genius of Pope,* which Malone thought "an abominable peice of scholarship."[61] Samuel Parr was a clergyman, a classical scholar and student of lapidary verses, headmaster and author of a number of political tracts and epitaphs.[62] He was a writer of educational and religious tracts and had a library of 10,000 volumes. He also claimed he was a descendant of Catherine Parr, sixth wife of Henry VIII.[63] Though Parr was later described as someone who "sometimes overcharges a picture," there is no doubt that they were both deeply moved by the papers.[64] Both Parr and Warton were particularly impressed with the Profession of Faith, the document that compares God's love of man to the paternal instincts of poultry. They remarked, "Mr. *Ireland,* we have very fine things in our *church service,* and our *litany* abounds with beauties, *but here is a man has distanced us all.*"[65] After inspecting the papers, they questioned the boy and concluded saying:

> Well, young man; the public will have just cause to admire you for the research you have made, which will afford so much gratification to the literary world.[66]

To this panegyric William-Henry bowed his head, and remained silent.[67] William-Henry claims that it was only after Parr's praises

> when vanity first took possession of my mind, to which every other consideration yielded: fired with the idea of possessing genius to which I had never aspired, and full of the conviction that my style had so far imitated Shakspeare's as to deceive two persons of such allowed classical learning as Drs.P*rr and Wh*rton . . . and thus implicitly yielded myself to the gilded snare which afterwards proved to me the source of indescribable pain and unhappiness.[68]

But this is an outright lie. Three weeks before Parr and Warton had even seen the papers William-Henry had given his father the name of the play, its source, and the cast of characters.

And the forgeries kept on coming. On 10 February 1795, ten days after Parr and Warton's visit, William-Henry presented his father with a love letter from Shakespeare to Anne Hathaway. The letter included a five-stanza love poem. The first stanza is indicative of its overall quality:

> Is there inne heavenne aught more rare
> Thanne thou sweete Nymphe of Avon fayre
> Is there onne Earthe a Manne more trewe
> Thanne Willy Shakspeare is toe you[?]

> [Is there in heaven aught more rare
> Than thou, sweet nymph of Avon fair;

Is there on earth a man more true
Than Willy Shakspeare is to you?]

The letter also included a locket of the poet's hair.[69] The latter, no doubt, was of special significance, considering the poet's scalp condition. Shakespeare even instructed his wife on how to treat the lock:

> perfume thys mye poore Locke withe thye balmye Kysses forre thenne indeede shalle Kynges themmeslves bowe and paye homage toe itte I doe assure thee no rude hande hathe knottedde itte thye Willys alone hathe done the worke[.][70]

> [perfume this, my poor lock, with thy balmy kisses for then indeed shall kings themselves bow and pay homage to it. I do assure thee no rude hand hath knotted it. Thy Willy's alone hath done the work.]

By mid-February, both the *King Lear* and the *Vortigern* were on display at 8 Norfolk Street. When rewriting *King Lear*, William-Henry did his homework. The forger studied the 1608 quarto and subsequent folio editions. William-Henry maintains that he uniformly used the 1608 quarto as a copy text, to which, he says, he had access by "being at liberty to resort to his [Samuel's] library whenever . . . [he] thought proper," for instance, when nobody was around.[71] William-Henry did not just recopy the printed quarto text of *King Lear* in Shakespeare's hand but also made numerous additions, alterations, and omissions.

In the seventeenth century, Nathum Tate had rewritten *King Lear*, but William-Henry allowed Shakespeare to rewrite Shakespeare:

> As it was generally deemed extraordinary that the productions of Shakspeare should be found so very unequal, and in particular that so much ribaldry should appear throughout his dramatic compositions, I determined on the expedient of rewriting, in the old hand, one of his most conspicuous plays, and making such alterations as I conceived appropriate.[72]

Kent's closing "I have a journey, Sir, shortly to go, / My master calls, and I must not say no" was expanded upon:

> Thanks Sir butte I go toe thatte unknowne Land
> Thatte Chaynes each Pilgrim faste within its Soyle
> Bye livynge menne mouste shunnd mouste dreadedde
> Stille mye goode masterre thys same Journey tooke

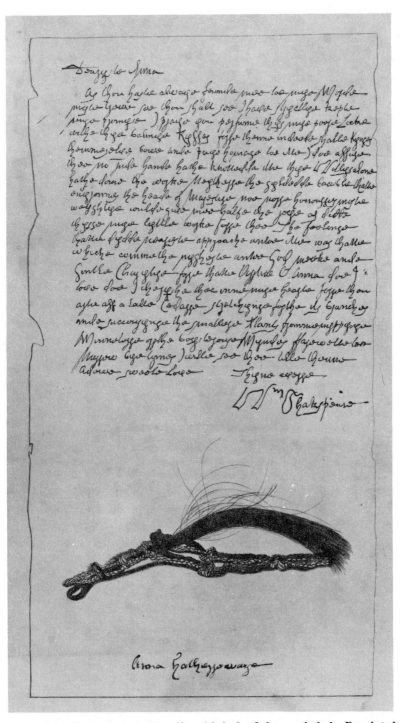

Letter from Shakspeare to his wife, with lock of the poet's hair. Reprinted with permission of The Folger Shakespeare Library.

He calls mee I amme contente ande strayght obeye
Thenne farewell Worlde the busye sceane is done
Kent livd mouste true Kente dyes mouste lyke a Manne[.]

[Thanks sir, but I go to that unknown land
That chains each pilgrim fast within its soil:
By living men most shunned, most dreaded.
Still, my good master this same journey took.
He calls me. I am content and straight obey.
Then farewell world, the busy scene is done;
Kent lived most true, Kent dies most like a man.]

William-Henry did not see these revisions as vandalism but as enhancement. Many considered these lines an improvement on the original. With this new information, Shakespeare was judged "a much more pure and even writer than before."[73] He says that he did it all for Shakespeare. This is his familiar argument in another guise: I did it for my father, for the scholars, for Shakespeare; never for myself. But there is no doubt that even if he did do it for Shakespeare, one of the chief spin-offs was that it served as a mini-apprenticeship period; a perfect training ground for composing and perfecting the "new" Shakespeare.

3

Why *Vortigern*?

W_{HY} did William-Henry pick this subject, what research did he do in writing the play? The story, as usual, is a complex one, filled with half-truths and full-blown lies. According to his confessions, William-Henry, with his "usual impetuosity made known to Mr. Ireland the discovery of such a piece, before a single line was really executed."[1] This is probably a lie, for we have seen that William-Henry was seldom impetuous. Yet the author would have us believe that he was largely ignorant of even the fundamental aspects of Shakespeare's plays:

> I was really so unacquainted with the proper length of a drama as to be compelled to count the number of lines in one of Shakspeare's plays, and on that standard to frame the Vortigern; and the play I had chosen happening to be uncommonly long, mine consequently became so: when completed, it contained, to the best of my recollection, two thousand-eight hundred lines and upwards.[2]

True to his character, William-Henry is probably lying. His father had read him excerpts from Shakespeare for years; they had visited the theater often; William-Henry had been involved in amateur theatricals; and Samuel's library was piled with both modern editions and rare first quartos of Shakespeare's work. Are we to believe that this boy, who had heard Shakespeare recited, seen the plays in performance and read them at his leisure, was unaware that *King Lear* is longer in line count than *Macbeth?*

What is certain is that the subject matter and construction of *Vortigern* were extremely well thought-out. The actual starting date of the play's composition is unrecorded. In early February 1795, William-Henry started to present sections of *Vortigern*.[3] By 12 February 1795, *Vortigern* was on display with the other Shakspeare Papers.[4] He had been "unceasingly tormented for the manuscript" which he brought forward in small portions, as he found time to compose it, in own handwriting, "pretending to have copied it from the original. . . ."[5] By March, the play was finished and Shakespeare's supposed original manuscript was brought forward.[6] William-Henry said he took two months to write the play but we cannot be sure.[7]

LITERARY MATERIALS FOR *VORTIGERN*

As for literary materials William-Henry had used when composing his play, he had certainly read Shakespeare's plays, though there is no reason to assume that he limited his readings to just the Bard. There is no doubt that *Vortigern* tries to be unashamedly Shakespearean, often to the point of nauseous repetition. But it is interesting to note that a copy of Holinshed's *Chronicles* was listed as among the books in the Irelands' library. Since it is clear he read his Shakespeare, it is no great leap of logic to assume he read Holinshed, especially since it is a well-known Shakespeare source.

The history of Vortigern's reign appears in Holinshed's *Chronicles* (1: 553–65) although it differs in some ways from Ireland's play. According to Holinshed, Constantius had three sons—Constantius, Aurelius Ambrosius, and Uter Pendragon. Constantine was poisoned by a Pict, and Vortigern persuades the nobles to elect the king's eldest son, Constantius, to succeed him. The nobles agree. But Constantius was not his father's choice. In fact, the king thought his eldest was too stupid to succeed him, thus sending the boy away to be a monk.

With this dull-brained monk now as king, Vortigern rules the kingdom in all but name. This is not enough for him, and he hires the Picts, Britains, and Scots to kill Constantius, which they do. Vortigern, pretending to avenge the king's murder, then attacks and destroys his former allies. For these acts, he is crowned king. Vortigern has three sons—Vortimer, Catagrinus, and Pascentius.

Soon after, Vortigern is threatened on two fronts: the two remaining brothers of Constantius begin to gather arms, and the Picts, Britains, and Scots reinvade the country. To offset these forces, Vortigern makes a pact with the Saxons, led by Hengist and Horsus. The Saxons defeat Vortigern's enemies and soon after Vortigern falls in love with Hengist's daughter, Rowena.[8] Vortigern divorces his wife and marries the Saxon princess. Hengist now rules over Vortigern's kingdom, love having made Vortigern as dim-witted as his former victim.

Vortigern's male heirs are not pleased by this. Vortimer is elected to succeed his father and make war on the Saxons. His brother, Catagrinus, and Hengist's brother, Horsus, kill each other in a long and bloody conflict. Vortimer continues to deal his enemy several harsh defeats before being poisoned by his stepmother, Rowena. During this time, Vortigern has stayed with the Saxons out of his love of Rowena. He is now ransomed back to the English.

But Vortigern's days are numbered. Uter and Aurelius have come back to avenge their brother's death. Uter is made king. Vortigern retreats to Wales, and by some reports, sleeps with his own daughter in the hopes of a male heir. Why Vortigern would do this, considering Pascentius is not dead, remains a mystery. Finally, Uter attacks Vortigern's castle and kills the king.

William-Henry combines elements of this storyline with a hodge-podge of Shakespearean motifs catalogued at the beginning of this book. Clearly, much of the play does correspond to the tale found in Holinshed and other histories, but William-Henry may have consulted more than one source or more than one playwright. Indeed, an apocryphal Shakespeare play, *The Birth of Merlin,* actually draws upon the history of Vortigern and Rowena. If William-Henry was looking for the subject matter of a lost Shakespeare, he might have done so by reading not only canonically accepted Shakespeare, but also his apocryphal works.

I think it almost certain he read many of the works of Shakespeare's contemporaries. While we may accept that Shakespeare's plays and one of his known sources were consulted by the forger, there is reason to suspect his source material included other avenues of research. Indeed, much of the plot material is not definitively Shakespearean. True, the outlines of the story appear in Holinshed, but Shakespeare was not the only playwright to consult that source. Though incest figures prominently in *Hamlet* and *Pericles,* it seems a subject more associated with Ford, or Beaumont and Fletcher, than Shakespeare. Vortigern's instant love for Rowena has much of the wonder Marlowe's Faustus displays for Helen. And plays such as Greene's *James the Fourth* make it clear that long-suffering queens, fickle kings, and civil wars are not necessarily proto-Shakespearean devices. The Ireland family's library did include poems by Drayton and Daniel, plays by Robert Greene, Ben Jonson, Beaumont and Fletcher, Rowley, Dekker, Ford, and Massinger, as well as Shakespeare imitators such as Killigrew, Dryden, Rowe, Otway, and Kenrick.[9] In addition to Samuel's sizeable collection, William-Henry was a book collector in his own right. Works of many or all of these playwrights and poets, and many more besides, might have been in his personal collection.

John Hamilton Mortimer, *Vortigern and Rowena.* **Photo obtained from Witt Library, Courtauld Institute.**

THE MAIN SOURCE FOR *VORTIGERN*: THE MORTIMER PICTURE

While it is irrefutable that William-Henry read his Shakespeare, carefully culling what he thought were the Bard's best parts, and his Holinshed, and perhaps even Shakespeare's contemporaries, he was careful to choose a subject that his public would perceive as being appropriately Shakespearean. Oddly, this process had more to do with eighteenth-century art than sixteenth-century prose. William-Henry has told us that it was inspired by a large picture of Mortimer's concerning Vortigern and Rowena. This picture hung in the Ireland house.

At first glance, his story concerning the Mortimer painting reads like a lie, and a poor one. It seems very unlikely that no visitor nor member of the family noticed that the subject matter of this forged play corresponded to a Mortimer picture that hung in the house! However, there is evidence to suggest that despite the unusual details of his story, William-Henry Ireland may be telling the truth, though he is not telling the whole truth. I have found evidence the forger was a better scholar than he was a liar. The Mortimer was not the only picture he consulted, nor was the Holinshed the only history he read.

There was indeed a John Hamilton Mortimer, and his life intersected with that of the forger's father, Samuel Ireland. John Hamilton Mortimer was born in 1740 and died in 1779. His life was short but prolific. In 1762, he held an exhibition at the Society of Artists.[10] Later he would become president of this same organization, as well as an associate of the Royal Academy.[11] In 1775, Mortimer married Jane Hurrell. They lived at 33 Norfolk Street. The Irelands lived at 8 Norfolk Street.

William-Henry Ireland might have found features in Mortimer's work with which he might have identified. Although acclaimed for his talent, Mortimer was something of a copier. Horace Walpole called Mortimer a mere "imitator" of Salvator Rosa.[12] Ireland and Mortimer even had similar literary tastes. Mortimer's best known work is a series of twelve etchings of Shakespeare characters.[13]

In the year of Mortimer's death, his picture *The Meeting of Vortigern and Rowena* was exhibited at the Royal Academy.[14] The picture remained in his wife's hands until she auctioned it in 1808. The picture was sold twelve years after the 1796 presentation of *Vortigern*.[15] How had William-Henry Ireland become aware of the picture? Had he seen it on exhibition at the Royal Academy? If so, he was only four years old at the time. It is possible that as a nearby neighbor, Ireland had access to Mrs. Mortimer's house.

There is no information concerning this point. More likely, the forger never saw Mortimer's original picture. However, William-Henry Ireland did see a copy based on Mortimer's picture. Moreover, this copy was executed by his father. According to Jane Mortimer, *The Meeting of Vortigern and Rowena* was never engraved but a copy of the picture had been made by Samuel Ireland.[16]

The date of this duplicate is not specified. However, there is evidence of a long working relationship between John Hamilton Mortimer and Samuel Ireland. Samuel had etched many of Mortimer's pictures, including *Fantastic Vases, Captain of the Bandetti and his Gang, Death of Sir Philip Sidney,* and *An Obese Man.*[17]

Indeed, Samuel Ireland's domicile was something of a storehouse for Mortimer drawings, paintings, etchings, and prints. In a detailed Sotheby's catalog compiled after Samuel Ireland's death, page after page itemizes the extent to which Samuel collected—and was connected to—John Hamilton Mortimer. Samuel owned a first impression of Mortimer's *Twelve Characters in Shakespeare,* one hundred and nine etchings and prints based on Mortimer's originals, eleven copper etching plates of various scenes by Mortimer, as well as various impressions printed from each plate, a sketch of the head of Mortimer, fifteen prints, and a variety of sketches and various drawings done "after" or in the style of Mortimer.[18]

SPECULATION ON SOURCES: OTHER VISUAL MATERIALS

However, in a house that might have had a starling taught to say nothing but "Mortimer," the picture *The Meeting of Vortigern and Rowena* is not listed among Samuel Ireland's possessions. Moreover, there is a very real possibility that *Vortigern* was inspired by other pictures not by or after Mortimer. In a manuscript version of the play, William-Henry Ireland added not one but two pictures of Vortigern and Rowena.[19] The problem is that neither of these pictures is by Mortimer!

John Sunderland has catalogued Mortimer's works for the Walpole Society.[20] His volume contains a copy of Mortimer's *The Meeting of Vortigern and Rowena.* It does not correspond to William-Henry Ireland's two pictorial insertions. One of the prints Ireland includes is by Francis Hayman, one-time president of the Free Society of Artists.[21] It appears in Smollett's *A Complete History of England.*[22] The other is almost certainly by Richard Westall. It appears in an edition of Rapin's *The History of England* (vol. 1).[23] Elizabeth Einburg of the Tate Gallery, believed the print might be by Hamilton, Barry or Singleton. John Sunderland of the Witt Library, suggested an additional possibility of it being by Smirke or Westall. I picked Westall, as two of his pictures, *Helen at the Scalean Gate* and *Lady Jane Grey Pleading for her Children,* bear strong resemblances to the picture in Rapin. Sunderland, upon examining these two prints, agreed with my attribution. Both pictures have led me to believe that William-Henry Ireland consulted many histories of Vortigern and Rowena and their accompanying pictorial sources before composing the play.

VORTIGERN'S SIGNIFICANCE

It is not possible that William-Henry Ireland confused either of these two prints with the work of Mortimer. However, they do

VORTIGERN AND ROWENA

RAPIN Hist Vol.I Book.II Chap.94

Richard Westall, *Vortigern and Rowena*. Photo obtained from Witt Library, Courtauld Institute.

Richard Westall, *Helen at the Scalean Gate.* Photo obtained from Witt Library, Courtauld Institute.

Richard Westall, *Lady Jane Grey Pleading for her Children.* Photo obtained from Witt Library, Courtauld Institute.

Angelica Kauffman, *Vortigern and Rowena*. Photo obtained from Witt Library, Courtauld Institute.

signify that the tale of Vortigern and Rowena was one often handled by British painters and historians. The subject was familiar to any eighteenth-century Englishman interested in history, and available for study to anyone with access to a decent library.

Although the story is obscure to us, eighteenth-century historians—and consequently the illustrators for their editions—considered the meeting of Vortigern and Rowena as among the most important events in early Anglo-Saxon history. In 1725, the French historian Rapin called it "a very fatal Moment for *Britain*."[24]

The earliest illustration of Vortigern and Rowena for inclusion in a history occurred in the midcentury. In 1751–52, Knapton and Dodsley published six prints (three by Francis Hayman and three by Nicholas Blakey). According to Edward Edwards, these prints were run off from "the first attempt to produce a regular suite of engravings from our national history."[25] Dodsley described them as "Representing the most memorable Actions and Events, from the landing of JULIUS CAESAR to the Revolution."[26] One of Blakey's three prints was "The Saxons obtaining a Settlement in England. The subject, Vortigern falling in Love with Rowena the

William Hamilton, *Vortigern and Rowena*. **Photo obtained from Witt Library, Courtauld Institute.**

daughter of Hengist, at a Feast to which her Father had purposely invited him."[27]

In 1770, Angelica Kauffman painted *Vortigern and Rowena*. The picture was displayed at the Royal Academy in 1770.[28] Other pictorial versions of the meeting of Vortigern and Rowena appeared in many of the major histories of Great Britain published during the eighteenth century. These histories went through many editions and revisions. Aside from the previously mentioned Rapin and Smollett editions, the forger might have studied Parson's 1793 pocket edition of Hume's *History of England*. This edition included Thomas Stothard's interpretation of the story.[29] William Hamilton painted his version of Vortigern and Rowena in 1793. This piece was not published until 1806, as part of yet another edition of Hume's history, this time entitled *Illustrated History of England*.

Although the Hayman and Westall pictures were added to William-Henry Ireland's annotated manuscript after the premiere of *Vortigern*, there is no real reason to assume that the forger was ignorant of the existence of any of these other pictures when he wrote the play. Certainly his father, as a book collector, art dealer, and engraver, was aware of at least some of the recent historical and pictorial treatments of Vortigern and Rowena.

If William-Henry was aware of these pictures, which seems to me very likely, he might have selected Vortigern and Rowena for the subject of his play, not only because it was a famous, important event in history that had been illustrated many times, but also because of who had executed these very same illustrations. Hayman, Westall, Kauffman, Stothard, Mortimer, and Hamilton had all executed very famous and widely published scenes from Shakespeare.[30]

Thus, if—or perhaps, when—William-Henry saw these pictures, he could not help but notice their "Shakespeareanness" since these artists were in part famous for their pictures based on the works of Shakespeare. *Vortigern* had the natural makings of an eighteenth-century Shakespeare forgery because Shakespeare's principal artists during the period were already drawing it. The play's subject matter was not accidental or incidental but deliberately informed by the literary and artistic life of the eighteenth century.

4

More Forgeries: The Authentication of
Vortigern Continues

KEEPING the eighteenth-century's preoccupation with Shakespeare and English history in mind might explain how and why so many respected critics were fooled. William-Henry created a play that passed all contemporary paleographic tests, and gave the public what it wanted. But William-Henry still had to convince one of the finest critics of the day, and find a way to collect the royalties for the "new" Shakespeare play.

Vortigern was by no means the last of William-Henry's forgeries. Indeed, William-Henry must have been a forging machine. Again, these additional forgeries only served as fortification for the lost play. It may seem surprising that even as the sheer number of the forgeries proliferated, so too did the support for the papers. The most respected supporter was James Boswell.

BOSWELL ENDORSES THE PAPERS

On 20 February 1795, James Boswell inspected the papers. This was the biggest test yet. Boswell's breeding and learning were unquestioned. His father, Alexander Boswell, was the eighth laird of Auchinleck, and a distinguished jurist. James Boswell had succeed his father in title and outstripped him in fame. He had completed a degree in Scottish law, and despite a modest London practice, his title and education allowed him to move among the highest intellectual circles. He was a friend of the historian Edmund Burke, the painter Joshua Reynolds, the economist Oliver Goldsmith, the actor David Garrick, and several Shakespeare editors, including Samuel Johnson and Edmond Malone. He was also a distinguished prosodist and somewhat of an expert on both Shakespeare and forgery. In 1785, he published his *Journal of a Tour to the Hebrides With Samuel Johnson, LL.D.,* a work that helped ultimately to expose the forgeries of James Macpherson. Boswell helped Malone with 1790 edition of Shakespeare. In 1791, he published his monumental *Life of Johnson,* a work celebrating the life of Shakespeare editor and lexicographer Samuel Johnson. Boswell was more than just a gifted academic with land. He was a link in an Shakespeare editorial tradition stretching back forty years.

William-Henry must have held his breath in dread as Boswell, ill (and though only fifty-four, in his last year) entered the room.[1] The renowned scholar touched the papers, examined the inks and watermarks. Being satisfied as to their antiquity, as far as the external appearance would attest, Boswell proceeded to examine their style and language from the fair transcripts.[2] Upon the completion of his examination, he requested a tumbler of warm brandy and water.[3] Having nearly finished his drink, Boswell could no longer contain himself. He fell to his knees and cried out, "how happy I am to have liv'd to the present day of discovery of this glorious treasure-I shall now die in peace."[4] And then he kissed the papers.[5]

Boswell refers to the papers in the singular. It is possible he saw all the papers as a single treasure, or he might have referred to just one. It is possible Boswell referred to the treasure William-Henry brought home that very day.[6] It was addressed, "For Master William Shakspeare atte the Globe bye Thames" and read:

Wee didde receive youre prettye Verses
goode Masterre William through the hands
off oure Lorde Chambelayne ande wee doe
Complemente thee onne theyre greate excellence
Wee shalle departe fromme Londonne toe
Hamptowne forre the holydayes where wee
Shalle expecte thee withe thye beste Actorres
thatte thou mayste playe before oureselfe toe
amuse usse bee notte slowe butte comme toe
usse bye Tuesdaye nexte asse the lord
Leicesterre wille bee withe usse

Elizabeth R[.]

[We did receive your pretty verses,
good Master William, through the hands
of our Lord Chamberlain, and we do
compliment thee on their great excellence.
We shall depart from London to
Hamptown for the holidays, where we
Shall expect thee with thy best actors,
that thou may'st play before ourself to
amuse us. Be not slow but come to
us by Tuesday next as the lord

Leicester will be with us.

Elizabeth R.]

On a small paper attached to the letter, a helpful note read:

Thys Letterre I dydde receyve fromme
mye moste gracyouse Ladye Elyzabethe
ande I doe requeste itte maye bee
kepte with alle care possyble

Wm Shakspeare[.]

[This letter I did receive from
my most gracious lady, Elizabeth,
and I do request it may be
kept with all care possible

Wm Shakspeare.]

MORE FORGERIES

William-Henry had also started to bring home Shakespeare's library—rare books from the period that he had annotated in Shakespeare's hand.[7] On 3 March 1795, William-Henry brought home what he maintained was Shakespeare's copy of *Churchyard Worthiness of Wales.*[8] On 22 March 1795, he brought home *A Brief true Relation of what hath happened unto the Princely Excellence Counte Maurice of Nassau, since the taking of Rynberk etc etc 1601.*[9] On 27 March 1795, he brought home *A true discourse of the whole occurrences in the Queen's voyage from her departure from Florence until her arrival at the Cite of Marseilles etc etc.*[10] Over the next few months, this library would swell immensely. On 1 February 1796, the *Oracle* reported that the library might consist of up to eleven hundred volumes.[11] Evidently, Shakespeare had owned a very large trunk.

These books were also a cohesive part of the authentication of *Vortigern.* For instance, in the play, the Fool swears that if he is not telling the truth he'll go "to Paul's, and there i'the presence of Bonner be whipp'd for a slanderer" (2.5.49). Was there a Bonner and if so, how would Shakespeare know of him? William-Henry's Shakspeare library answered such questions. The library included an annotated copy of Fox's *Book of Martyrs,* with a poem in Shakespeare's hand dedicated to Bishop Bonner.[12]

And still William-Henry found more in the trunk. He brought home a fragment of *Hamlet.*[13] He also brought home a record of a

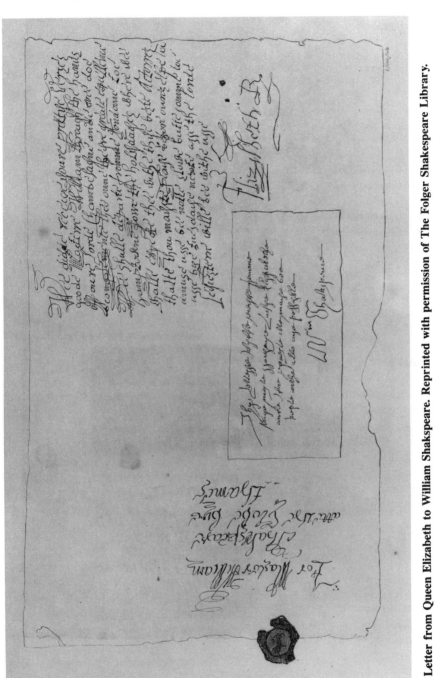

Letter from Queen Elizabeth to William Shakspeare. Reprinted with permission of The Folger Shakespeare Library.

performance before Lord Leicester.[14] He even brought home a portrait of Shylock, with a reverse portrait of Shakespeare, claiming it had once hung in the Globe's Green Room.[15]

SAMUEL IRELAND AND THE MONEY MACHINE

Meanwhile, Samuel had converted his house into a museum open to the public. On 4 March 1795, Samuel printed and released a statement concerning the discoveries and the first of his many money-making schemes:

> Any Gentleman, on sending his address in writing, or being introduced by a Subscriber, may view the MS. at No. 8, Norfolk Street, on Mondays, Wednesdays, and Fridays, between the hours of Twelve and Three. . . .
>
> Mr. Ireland informs the Public that with the above papers was discovered an Historical Play, founded on the story of VORTIGERN and ROWENA, taken from Holingshed [*sic*], and which is in the handwriting of Shakspeare.- This play being intended for theatrical representation, will not be printed till the eve of its appearance on the Stage.[16]

Entrance charge: two guineas! One visitor, Revd. Wesson, looked at the Leicester document and informed Samuel that the letter, supposedly in Leicester's hand, was dated three years after Leicester's death. The next time the document was shown, the date had either been "expunged" or was torn off.[17]

Soon after, the Irelands unleashed their latest cash grab. The Irelands published the documents, increasing both the public's interest and their own income. The book was entitled *Miscellaneous Papers,* and William-Henry is quite clear as to why the papers had been published:

> Mr. S. Ireland conceived, that, if published, they would give infinite satisfaction to the public, and prove a source of benefit to his family. . . .[18]

Translation: Samuel knew he could make a buck. In fact, Samuel thought the book would be "productive of a fortune to" William-Henry and presold it at the substantial price of four guineas.[19]

The book was released on 24 December 1795: 368 copies were printed, of this amount, 122 were sold, ten were given away and six were claimed by copyright libraries. The rest were destroyed after William-Henry's confession of 1796.[20] *Miscellaneous Papers* included all the major Shakspeare documents found thus far, except *Vortigern*.

Samuel was careful when it came to financially overexploiting *Vortigern*. At first he thought of publishing the play before the performance. On 9 November 1795, Samuel had mentioned in a letter to a Mr. Byne, a bookseller in Dublin, that the play would be printed sometime in December

> in a volume in folio the Same size as the Lear- containing Richard 2, Private letters and MSs: papers relative to the Theatre from Shakespeares [*sic*] own Mss. the price 1G. and a half.[21]

Indeed, had he gone for the quick buck, his short-term profits would have been considerable. Mr. Barker, a local printer, stated that:

> had Mr. Samuel Ireland applied to me ten days previous to the night of the performance of the piece, and desired to know what I would have given for the manuscript of Vortigern, I would have bound myself under any penalty not to have made one copy public before the hour of *four* on the night of its representation; and, under such a restriction, I would have gladly have paid him one thousand guineas for the copyright, taking every risk upon myself as to the future sale of the production.[22]

Miscellaneous Papers also excluded another newly discovered play, called *The Devile and Rychard*.[23] This play, however, was not by Shakespeare:

> Having perused several curious interludes and sacred mysteries, from the pen of Bayle, &c., I determined on producing a performance of the same nature, and selected the subject of the Devil and Richard the Third. . . .[24]

Bayle had been a source for Shakespeare's *Richard III*. Surely the point of forging an original manuscript by Bayle was to "discover" that Shakespeare had also been a collector of sorts; that he possessed not just the printed versions of the sources he used, but unknown manuscripts on the same subject. Perhaps the point was to expose Shakespeare as a forger?

The play was finished, and resides in the British Library Manuscripts Collection (BL MS 30348, 198r-311r). Another version, written in his archaic hand, was prepared. This is yet another proof that William-Henry's plans extended beyond *Vortigern*.

Still the family had found yet another way of making money from the forgeries. Aside from the display of and lecture on the documents three days a week for three hours a day, there were added funds gained from the treasured lock of hair included in Shakespeare's letter to Anne Hathaway. Never mind that it seemed odd that Shakespeare should have the very letter he sent to his wife! Here, for the picking, were hairs from the crown of that immortal, balding genius. Several hairs were distributed, like religious relics, to the Believers. Some of the hairs were inlaid in gold rings. The Irelands had gone into the jewelry business.[25] And, of course, there remained the biggest potential moneymaker of all, *Vortigern.*

ROYALTY PROBLEMS

When *Vortigern* was completed, Samuel entered into negotiations with the theaters. Covent Garden was very interested, although Samuel favored Drury Lane. But William-Henry was shocked to hear he would receive no money for his work.

Nobody paid royalties on Shakespeare's plays. His family line was dead. The plays were part of the public domain. William-Henry thought quickly. What if he became a relative of Shakespeare's, if not genetic, then legally adoptive? Then he would collect the money. But what if a real relative of Shakespeare's were found? Then he would lose all the money from *Vortigern* and the rest of the papers he had produced. He would have worked day and night to make someone else rich. He needed a document that would validate his collection of any money generated by the papers while protecting the family from any rival claimant. The result was the most audacious of all the forgeries. It was called the Deed of Gift. It seems that William-Henry Ireland was the direct descendant of an Elizabethan named William-Henry Ireland, who was a friend of Shakespeare's. But not just any friend, but the very man who had saved a drunken Shakespeare from drowning.

The Deed of Gift was presented to Samuel on 12 June 1795.[26] Accompanying the deed was a letter from Shakespeare to William-Henry Ireland:

> Givenne toe mye mouste worthye
> ande excellaunte Freynde Masterre
> William Henrye Irelande inne
> Remembraunce of hys havynge

Savedde mye life whenne onne
Thames

William Shakspeare[.]

[Given to my most worthy
and excellent friend, Master
William-Henry Ireland, in
remembrance of his having
saved my life when on
Thames.

William Shakspeare.]

The incident to which the Bard refers is further detailed within the
long, disjointed narrative of the deed itself:

mye goode freynde Masterre William Henry Irelande ande otherres
taene boate neare untowe myne house afowresayde wee dydd purpose
goynge upp Thames butte those thatte were soe toe connducte us
beynge muche toe merrye throughe Lyquorre they didd upsette oure
fowresayde bayrge alle butte myeselfe savedd themselves bye swim-
myng for though the Waterre was deepe yette owre beynge close nygh
toe shore made itte lyttel dyffyculte for themm knowinge the fowresayde Arte Masterre William henry Irelande notte seeynge mee dydd
aske for mee butte oune of the Companye dydd answerre thatte I was
drownynge onn the whiche he pulledd off hys Jerrekynne and Jumpedd
in afterre mee withe muche paynes he draggedd mee forthe I beynge
then nearelye deade and soe he dydd save mye life. . . .

[. . . my good friend, Master William-Henry Ireland and others taken
boat near unto mine house aforesaid, we did purpose going up Thames
but those that were to conduct us being much too merry through liquor,
they did upset our foresaid barge. All but myself saved themselves by
swimming for though the water was deep, yet our being close nigh to
shore made it little difficult for them knowing the foresaid art. Master
William-Henry Ireland, not seeing me did ask for me but one of the
company did answer that I was drowning on the which he pulled off
his jerkin and jumped in after me. With much pains he dragged me
forth, I being then nearly dead, and so he did save my life. . . .]

In recompense, Shakespeare bequeathed to Ireland and his de-
scendants the rights to *King John, King Lear, Henry IV,* and
Henry V as well as an unknown play, *Henry III.* The document
itself was dated 1604. Yet it mentioned Shakespeare's play *King
Lear,* written years later. This was not an oversight. William-Henry
used this earlier date as corollary proof that an earlier *King Lear*
existed, the one he had written weeks earlier.

And then he found a previously unknown will, entitled the Deed of Trust. In 1795, Shakespeare's real will—uncovered only in 1747—had been a worry to Shakespeare scholars.[27] In it, Shakespeare made no references to his shares in the playhouses, nor any arrangements for his manuscripts. Worse still, he seems to have disliked his wife, leaving her only his second-best bed. Malone and other scholars had poured much ink pondering Shakespeare's seemingly unhappy marriage. But William-Henry's new will would make all well:

> Firste untoe mye deare Wife I doe orderr as folowithe thatt she bee payde withinne oune monthe afterre mye dethe the somme of oune hondrythe and fowre score Pounds fromm the moneys whyche be nowe layinge onn Accompte of the Globe Theatre inn the hands of Master John Hemynge Alsoe I doe give herr mye suyte of greye Vellvett edged withe silverr tog[r] withe mye lytelle Cedarr Trunke in wyche there bee three Ryngs oune lyttel payntyng of myselfe in a silverr Case & sevenn letterrs wrottenn to her before oure Marryage these I doe beg herr toe keepe safe if everr she dydd love me[.]

> [First unto my dear wife I do order as folow'th: that she be paid within one month after my death the sum of one hundred and four score pounds from the monies which be now laying on account of the Globe Theatre in the hands of Master John Heminge. Also, I do give her my suit of grey velvet, edged with silver, together with my little cedar trunk in which there be three rings, one little painting of myself in a silver case and seven letters written to her before our marriage. These I do beg her to keep safe, if ever she did love me.]

To his "lovynge Daughterr" ("Shakspeare" does not specify whether he is addressing Sussana or Judith), the poet left twenty pounds and seven shillings, money from the sale of two houses near the Globe, a suit of black silk and "the Rynge whyche I doe alwaye weare givenne toe mee bye hys Grace of Southampton thys I doe beg herr as she dothe love mee neverr toe parte fromm." It also made provisions for a bastard child to receive the royalties from eight plays, including one called "Kynge Vortygerne."

The puzzle was now complete. The Deed of Gift and this new will insured that William-Henry would collect profits from among Shakespeare's most celebrated plays. Further, it validated the existence of at least two lost plays, among them *Vortigern*. Moreover, it was now completely clear why Mr. H. had given William-Henry all these documents. Two hundred years ago, William-Henry's great-grandfather had saved Shakespeare's life on a boating holiday. It was only decent that now, two hundred years later, the descendant of that same Ireland reap the benefits. The Shakspeare Papers were not given to William-Henry just to clear up a legal problem, or to honor a promise, but because he was a descendant of *the* William-Henry Ireland, savior of Shakespeare. Mr. H. had providentially restored the rightful papers to the Ireland family.

The potential revenues from these documents were enormous. William-Henry could legally claim a share in any production or printing of *King Lear* for the past two hundred years! This was not the amassing of wealth for wealth's sake. There were bigger plans in the works. After all, how much longer could the present fraud go on? The idea that all the forgeries came from one trunk was ludicrous. Every trunk has its bottom. But William-Henry soon came up with a simple enough temporary solution to explain why he had continued finding new papers for over a year: he had found a second trunk of treasures. This second trunk yielded another unknown Shakespeare play, *Henry II,* a "Tragedy, the subject of which is the insolence of *Becket,* and the misfortunes of Fair *Rosamond.*"[28]

He even supplied the Believers with a list as to this second truck's contents. It must have whetted their appetites considerably:

Full Dramatic Manuscripts
Richard II
Henry V

Partial Dramatic Manuscripts
62 leaves of *King John*
49 leaves of *Othello*
37 leaves of *Richard III*
37 leaves of *Timon of Athens*
27 leaves of Julius Caesar
14 leaves of *Henry IV*

Newly Discovered Works in Manuscript
Henry II
verses to Queen Elizabeth
     "   Sir Francis Drake
     "   Raleigh
     "   Lord Howard
autobiography [!]

Annotated Books from Shakespeare's Library
Books relative to Queen Elizabeth

Bible
Bochas' works
Barcley's *Ship of Fool*
Euphues
Chaucer
Holinshed's *Chronicles*

Legal Documents
Shakespeare's deed of partnership in the Curtain Theatre

Paintings, Drawings, Etc.
two drawings of the Globe on Parchment
Full length-oil portrait of Shakespeare

Jewelry
miniature of Shakespeare set in silver[29]

BUYING THE BIRTHPLACE

William-Henry knew this second trunk was just a temporary solution. If the game was to go on, a new playground was required. And William-Henry was looking into it. He was going to buy a place where he could forge more Shakspeare Papers without suspicion. Indeed, the location would only confirm the authenticity of any newly found documents. William-Henry planned on buying Shakespeare's birthplace![30]

Samuel Ireland began enquiries on the price of John Shakespeare's house in Henley Street. On 3 September 1795, a Mr. Hunt sent Samuel a plan of the premises and grounds. He wrote that the house might be purchased for as little as £350, but that John Jordan was claiming he could raise the price to £500.[31] On 1 December 1795, Samuel received a note from John Byng concerning the house's more recent history and of New Place.[32] Perhaps Samuel was hoping to buy both properties. But the papers were exposed before they could generate enough money. Malone had not just saved the day, he had done it without a moment to lose. For William-Henry had begun making the Shakspeare Papers he was to "find" under some birthplace lodestone.

Indeed, William-Henry had already made a list of documents to "find." Once William-Henry decided to confess, he stated that he turned over "the remains of my ink used in the fabrication, as also . . . various other documents, as collateral proofs of the veracity of my confession."[33] This included "the written outlines of dramas on some few of our monarch's reigns which had not occupied the genius of our Bard."[34] These projects included *Henry II, William the Conqueror,* and a play on Elizabeth.

THE NEW FAERIE QUEENE

But inventing the private world of Shakespeare was not enough for young William-Henry. Shakespeare's friends and their past were to be detailed as well. If Shakespeare's plays and poems might come from his pen, why not the works of others? William-Henry had planned to become the spirit of Shakespeare's age, not just for his generation, but for all generations. I have paraphrased Ben Jonson's monody of Shakespeare. William-Henry went one better, he forged a new one in Jonson's hand.

Actually, he does not admit to this forgery. He simply says he once owned a first folio which included an unknown poem in Ben Jonson's hand. And though he no longer owned the book, he still reprinted the text. It is more likely that he never owned this missing poem. He simply forged it:

> Behold this face; and, if thou read'st aright,
> His eyes should beam Apollo's radiant light:
> Deep penetration should his look impart,
> And Pity's touch, to thrill the feeling heart.
> Or wouldst thou Mars behold, thou still mayst find
> The rugged soldier's daring dauntless mind.
> Philosophy, religion, vice, and wit:
> Of passions here the mastery is writ.
> Envy in vain, with pois'nous Slander's breath,
> Would on his temples blast to verdant wreath:
> For long as Fame shall sound th'applauding blast,
> So shall his blooming crest for ever last.[35]

This was not the first attempt William-Henry made at forging Ben Jonson. He admits that he forged a Ben Jonson poem to be attached to the Shylock portrait but that he was unhappy with the piece and so erased it. Was the original implication to be that Jonson painted the picture, or worked in conjunction with Inigo Jones on the portrait?

Other forgeries that had been made ready for release included eighty-odd signed and/or annotated books, and pamphlets from Shakespeare's library.[36] Like many of the other forgeries, the library also interlinked with Shakespeare's literary contemporaries.

For instance, Spenser's *Faerie Queene* was annotated in Shake-speare's hand and released. An offer of £60 was made on the two volume work before his confession. Source materials for some of Shakespeare's legitimate plays were similarly provided, such as Carion's *Chronicles*. Other books, such as an account of Guy Fawkes's execution, interlinked the forgeries with established history. As a crowning touch, a note in Shakespeare's hand was added:

> Thatte hee . . . hadd beene intreatedd bye hys freynde John Hemynges to attende sayde executyonne, butte thatte he lykedde notte toe beholde syghtes of thatte kynde.[37]

> [That he . . . had been entreated by his friend, John Heminges, to attend said execution, but that he liked not to behold sights of that kind.]

Poor, delicate Shakespeare! The episode apparently upset him so much he had to refer to himself in the third person.

Apparently this Guy Fawkes book was a favorite of Shake-speare's, for William-Henry bought it twice and annotated the second copy thus: "Thys lytlle booke I ha hadde ownce befoure."[38] But why would Shakespeare inform himself of a fact of which he seems fully aware?

Original works that William-Henry had produced but not yet told the public about included an "Epitaph on Eleanor Rummin"—an alewife described in Skelton's works—lines on beauty, and a full manuscript of acrostics to be entitled "A Crown Garlande daintyile besette with costlye Gemmes." This work included acrostics on Richard II, Mary, Queen of Scots, Queen Elizabeth, Henry, Prince of Wales, Dudley, Earl of Warwick, Robert Dudley, Southampton, and Earl Rivers and an acrostic to Shakespeare, so banal it's not worth reprinting. Besides, why would Shakespeare write an acros-tic to himself? Also, he promised but never delivered two uncut first folios, though how Shakespeare would have collected two cop-ies of a book that was only published seven years after his death must remain a mystery.[39]

From another source we also learn that William-Henry had be-gun a collection of portraits owned by Shakespeare. Only one of these portraits was executed: the earl of Cumberland.[40] Yet the only original picture William-Henry executed, the pen and ink drawing of Shakespeare, was amateurish in the extreme. It's hard to believe that William-Henry executed this forgery by himself.

William-Henry, it seems, was a perpetual forger. But he was also a sloppy one. If one reads the confessions closely, comparing conflicting statements against verified facts, hidden truths begin to emerge. William-Henry did not work alone.

5

Talbot and Wallis: Two Cases of Blackmail?

THERE was another reason why the forgeries had to be enlarged: blackmail. William-Henry had created a little world into which he might happily have retreated. But his little world soon became very crowded. The first to intrude was a fellow law clerk, Montague Talbot.

TALBOT'S INVOLVEMENT: PRANK OR BLACKMAIL?

They had met at the New Inn, and seemed to have been genuine friends. But Ireland did not tell Talbot about his forgeries. Nonetheless, Talbot had doubted the validity of the Shakspeare Papers and thought that William-Henry had forged them. In fact he even told William-Henry of his suspicions. He denied Talbot's accusations. Ireland could rest easy, Talbot had no proof, until that one fateful day "he caught me in the fact; no longer able to deny the charge, I bound him to secrecy, alledging [*sic*] the anger of my father should he know the truth. . . ."[1]

According to William-Henry, Talbot did not wish to expose his friend. He merely wished to join in the fun. William-Henry had little choice. By 3 October 1795, the *Oracle* was referring to Talbot as the codiscoverer "of the Shakspeare MSS." Very soon after confronting William-Henry, Talbot left the study of law to become a minor actor. One critic saw him in Home's *Douglas*. According to the commentator, Talbot was "too much in the Operatic manner" and unintentionally played his part "with very whimsical effect."[2] That being said, Talbot was pleased with his new work. On 9 June 1796, Talbot wrote to William-Henry, informing him that "I am going very well in my profession."[3]

William-Henry says that his "friend" Talbot suspected him. He even caught him in the act of forging. But he did not expose him because his father would be angry. Why would Talbot care if Sam-

96

uel was angry with William-Henry? What had that to do with Talbot? William-Henry says that he agreed to keep Talbot informed. I believe this. Talbot's secrecy could only come at a price: a financial price. It is true that Talbot later boasted to Samuel that he did not rely on the stage for his livelihood.[4] But the fact remains that Talbot had left his secure law job for the uncertain success of the theater. He may well have needed additional financial security. The forgeries may not have been his meal ticket, but he might have relied on them for an occasional snack. He was certainly interested in the money that the forgeries might generate when he heard that *Vortigern* was to be staged.

In his *Confessions,* William-Henry tells us that two conventional letters were exchanged before Talbot recommended that they write in code so the letters would be:

> unintelligible to any other person but ourselves, should any letter be by chance mislaid or miscarry. The *talisman* adopted on this occasion was a sheet of paper having several pieces cut from different parts of it; which, when desirous of writing, was placed on a sheet of post paper; when the communication to be made was written on the parts of the post paper appearing through the holes so made in the mutilated sheet; after which the blanks left were filled up with any words, so as to render the whole unintelligible . . . [except to] Mr. Talbot and myself, having each a sheet of paper cut precisely the same. . . .[5]

But William-Henry never informed his "friend" about *Vortigern.* We are told that when Talbot did find out about the play, he wrote to William-Henry, informing him that he was leaving Dublin that very night.[6] Talbot had kept a careful watch on his "friend," and when left in the dark he returned to straighten out their relationship. Talbot returned on 4 November 1795 to confront William-Henry. Remember, we are not referring to the 1990s but the 1790s. One did not return from Ireland in a day. Talbot's trip took ten days. Why would Talbot jeopardize his job by temporarily leaving the theater he worked for to travel across the sea—travel many hundreds of miles over land—just because William-Henry did not tell his best friend about his newest game? Talbot was willing to risk his job. Surely he could only be so prompt to leave his livelihood and travel so far because he himself had an important stake in the forgeries—and no doubt it was a financial stake.

Talbot had also written a letter concerning the finances of the play, but it was not addressed to William-Henry. It was addressed to Samuel Ireland. He informed Samuel that as co-discoverer of the papers, Mr. H. had promised him half of any money generated from the papers. However, he was willing to settle for one-third of the profits *Vortigern* might generate from dramatic presentation and publication.[7] Clearly, he came back to pressure William-Henry in person. And he wrote to Samuel to show William-Henry he meant business.

We are told he returned to Dublin only after he had received an apology from William-Henry and a promise that Talbot would be a "party in the story."[8] In William-Henry's *Confessions,* Talbot is said to be "a friend of the Muses . . . anxious to add a portion of his own composition . . . to the production of the *Vortigern.*"[9] "Anxious" means Talbot was going to spill the beans unless he got what he wanted. Maybe Talbot did want to contribute a written piece to the play, an extra bit of insurance to go along with his letters from William-Henry. Talbot had not come for friendship or for collaboration but for extortion; for a slice of the profits. William-Henry had no choice. Talbot was in.

Covering up Talbot's Involvement

Or was he? William-Henry told Talbot he was in but in his *Confessions,* he says that he had decided to write the play himself.[10] He was lying, as we shall see, but there is no evidence that Talbot had a hand in the play. On the other hand, is the reader to believe that Talbot traveled ten days from Dublin to see William-Henry, and left immediately after getting what he wanted without following through on their agreement?

Perhaps the forger doth protest too much. William-Henry's *Confessions* have no less than ten chapters devoted to Talbot, all denying his involvement. He appears in FIRST ACQUAINTANCE WITH MR. TALBOT, and in MR. TALBOT'S SHREWD SURMISE, MR. TALBOT'S DISCOVERY OF THE FORGERY and in MR. TALBOT'S MYSTERIOUS METHOD OF CORRESPONDENCE, etc, etc. The last four of these ten chapters are solely devoted to proving that Mr. Talbot had nothing to do with the writing of *Vortigern.* They prove nothing of the sort. All they prove is (1) Talbot was publicly acknowledged as a friend of Mr. H. and (2) that William-Henry is a liar.

In a letter to Samuel Ireland, Talbot explained that he knew the mysterious gentleman and had been present at the discovery of the Shakspeare Papers.[11] Both had something to gain by this maneuver. Talbot could now openly blackmail William-Henry by publicly revealing who Mr. H. was/was not and William-Henry had now openly implicated Talbot. Talbot was now sharing in the fraud. They would either rise or fall together.

William-Henry admits that on Talbot's return from Ireland they "mutually destroyed every letter which had previously passed between us; so that no one document then existed to prove the fact respecting the fabrication of the papers by myself."[12] And yet he quotes from a letter dated 6 January 1796 as proof that Talbot had nothing to do with the forgeries.[13]

Reexamining the William-Henry Ireland/Montague Talbot Correspondence

How can he quote from a letter which he admits he destroyed? Furthermore, if it was a real letter from their correspondence, why wasn't it in code? There is no reason why William-Henry should have lied about his Captain Midnight decoder method. It hardly enhances the story. Such a detail can only have been added because it was true. And it does not make sense that they destroyed all past communication. After all, that's why they invented the code, so that no one would understand the letters but themselves. They might have been paranoid, and destroyed the letters on the off chance that the letters would be found with the code papers, or that some Sherlock might crack the code, but then we return to the original problem: if the letters were destroyed how can the forger be quoting from them as evidence? The answer is quite simple: William-Henry was a forger. He forged his own evidence.

As with the Shakspeare Papers, William-Henry forged the evidence badly. The thing that really gives it away as a fake is its date: 6 January 1796. Here William-Henry made the same mistake as he did with the Leicester document. William-Henry says that Wallis caught him forging *Vortigern* in November 1795. But the play had already been finished and was on display seven months earlier, in March 1795. Clearly, the date would have to be refalsified by several months if we are even to entertain thoughts of its authenticity.

It is true that on 23 December 1796, the *Herald* reported that *Vortigern* had actually been written by "a gentleman of Dublin."[14] But Talbot himself never objected to William-Henry's statements of sole authorship. Indeed, on 15 April 1796, Talbot wrote to Mrs. Freeman stating that he felt the play was probably genuine, though no doubt "one of Shakespeares [*sic*] first Essays at dramatic writing."[15] On 1 July 1796, he again wrote to Mrs. Freeman, confessing that he had never seen *Henry II*, nor the manuscript of *Vortigern* until his return to London in November of the previous year.[16]

Why should he confess any authorship? Talbot "had the goods" on Ireland and could ask what he liked as long as the secret remained a secret. When the forger eventually confessed, William-Henry took away Talbot's only weapon. Talbot could no longer threaten William-Henry, but William-Henry could threaten Talbot. Talbot had written to Samuel Ireland. He had told Samuel that he had met the mysterious gentleman. He had implicated himself. He was an accessory to fraud. He had blackmailed a minor. He was publicly known as the coauthor of a play that caused a scandal. I will deal with what happened during *Vortigern*'s premiere in due course. For now, I merely wish to point out that this was not a good position for a third-rate actor to be in. Had William-Henry implicated Talbot in the slightest regarding any of these charges, Talbot's career would have been over.

TALBOT TRIES TO STEAL THE SHAKSPEARE PAPERS

On 21 May 1796, desperate that the controversy not touch him, Talbot took matters into his own hands. Samuel recalled that on that evening, a woman arrived, claiming all the Shakspeare Papers as her property. Samuel demanded an explanation. She told him that the papers had been stolen from her, and, moreover, that she had written them all. He then recalled who she was and where he had seen her:

> about two years ago when Mr. Talbot called on me-and asked me if I would go with him to see a Curious character-in Newman Street who had seen 2 Moons-and had sworn to seeing Men and horses galloping over them. . . .

Samuel sent her over to Wallis's office and he never saw her again.[17] Clearly, Talbot knew her. Is it possible that he had arranged this attempted theft? Perhaps it was sheer coincidence that Wallis knew of this woman. But if sheer coincidence, we might ask what the lady in question hoped to gain for herself? I don't want to jump ahead of the story, but by this time the papers had been exposed as forgeries. They were worthless. Only Talbot, who lived under threat of collusion, had anything to gain.

Having failed in this attempt to steal the papers, Talbot did the smart thing: he said nothing. Samuel tried to get him to reveal the identity of Mr. H., even threatening to have the Lord Lieutenant of Ireland bar him from performing in Ireland.[18] In November of the same year, a Mr. Coles questioned Talbot as to his involvement.[19] In both cases, Talbot remained silent. As it was, William-Henry never exposed Talbot. Perhaps it was nobleness of character, but more likely, William-Henry expected his own exposure to bring fame and he wasn't about to share it with anyone, especially someone who had blackmailed him for nearly two years.

ANOTHER COLLABORATOR: ALBANY WALLIS

In at least one other instance William-Henry lets slip that he worked in collaboration. The unintentional admission comes when he describes a nearly disastrous episode and his very lucky escape:

> Now it unfortunately happened that some person inspecting one of the deeds suffered the same to fall from his hands upon Mr. Samuel Ireland's mahogany writing-desk: on which occasion, such was the brittle property of the wax, that the front side of one of the seals severed from the back part, which had held it to the strip of parchment appending from the deed; by which any shrewd observer would have instantly recognized the difference in the colour of the wax:- However, this circumstance being communicated to me, I instantly advised the binding of the two together with black silk.[20]

William-Henry told his father that Mr. H. wanted to look at that document for an hour or so, took it to chambers and fixed it.

Who told him the seal had broken? William-Henry worked at chambers. His day ended at three o'clock. The tours at his house were from twelve to three o'clock, Mondays, Wednesdays, and Fridays.[21] Someone in the house had to have noticed the broken seal and either gone to William-Henry for instructions or sent someone else to receive instructions. Either way, William-Henry did not work alone. The question is, who did he work with?

It might have been Albany Wallis. It seems certain that their involvement started on 30 December 1795. It was the very day that Samuel Ireland had been invited to display the papers before the prince of Wales.[22] Just as Samuel was about to leave, Wallis walked in and declared all the documents to be forgeries.

Wallis was no stranger to Shakespeare sleuthdom. Years before, he had found Shakespeare's mortgage deed. Wallis had given it to the Shakespeare actor Garrick, who in turn had given it to Edmond

Malone. Wallis had made no money. Perhaps he was jealous of the Irelands. In any case, Wallis had found a real document with John Heminges's signature and it did not resemble the document produced by Mr. H. And yet, nothing was made of it. Wallis did not go to the press after showing the document to Samuel. There is no record of their conversation and Samuel kept his meeting with the prince, making no mention of the damning proofs against the papers. Still, the prince was no fool:

> His royal highness, I perfectly well remember, made numerous objections, and particularly to the redundancy of letters apparent throughout the papers. . . . the doubts which arose in his royal highness's mind were obviated by Mr. Ireland.[23]

William-Henry arrived home at 3:00 P.M. He was told what had happened. He went with Samuel to Wallis's office, saw the document and knew he was in serious trouble. He said that he had left both his father and Wallis to seek the "supposed gentleman during the morning, and acquaint him with the whole event."[24]

He then ran to his office and with the authentic signature committed to memory, forged a new Heminges signature and rushed back.[25] He reported that this exercise took one hour and fifteen minutes:

> This remarkable expedition was afterwards alleged as a convincing proof that the documents could not be other than original, as it was affirmed to be out of all human probability that such a succession of events could have taken place in so limited a space of time.[26]

This, however, did not solve the problem but compounded it. Now there were three extant John Heminges signatures, only two of which matched. In reply to this, William-Henry explained that there were two John Heminges: one tall at the Globe, the other short and at the Curtain. He stated that he later added even more John Heminges signatures that passed as perfect facsimiles.[27] Wallis was satisfied and never again questioned the papers' authenticity, or so William-Henry would have us believe.

Unfortunately, there are several details that are hard to believe: (1) How could William-Henry be present at the meeting with the prince when he only found out about the other Heminges signature on returning home; (2) why did Wallis say nothing more to anyone about his discovery; (3) how could William-Henry run from his house on Norfolk Street to his office, get his materials, and calmly forge a signature he had seen only minutes before; (4) why would Wallis accept a cock'n'bull story about a short and tall Heminges?

Even the chronology is suspect. If William-Henry did go with Samuel to see the prince, he would have had to do so after Wallis showed him the document. Therefore, he could hardly have raced off to do the forgery. Of course, he might be lying. He might not have accompanied Samuel. Here, still, we have problems: If William-Henry was home by 3:00 P.M., and returned in one hour and fifteen minutes, the entire episode should have been over at 4:15 P.M. Yet he says he only set out for Mr. H.'s house the next morning!

What seems to have happened is that William-Henry has conflated two different visits to conceal his involvement with Wallis. We know that on 18 November 1795, William-Henry did accompany his father when the documents were displayed before the duke of Clarence and his mistress, the actress Mrs. Jordan.[28] This explains William-Henry's account of a Royal perusal of the papers but gets us no closer to solving the Heminges mystery. I do, however, have a theory.

We know that William-Henry forged documents in two ways: with models and without. For Bradshaw's, Elizabeth's, and Shakespeare's signatures, he worked with facsimiles in front of him. For Lydgate's, Southampton's, and short Heminges's signatures, he worked creatively because he did not know of any existing models. If possible, William-Henry preferred to work with models, models that he had constantly before him. We know that Wallis possessed such a model and had shown it to him. But William-Henry had never shown any signs of a photographic memory, a gift so rare that it is always remarkable. Therefore, it was only possible for William-Henry to forge Heminges's signature if Wallis had given it to him. Yet Wallis was not going to give this young criminal an invaluable, authentic document connected with Shakespeare. If the forger ripped it up in order to preserve the legitimacy of his Shakspeare Papers, it would simply be one man's word against the other. And yet Wallis must have given William-Henry the signature to copy. So the question that remains is: Why?

WALLIS'S BACKGROUND: DISREPUTABLE AND WELL-CONNECTED LAWYER

If ego, nationalism, hatred, and greed are among the prime motives of forgers, certainly the motives of their accessories can be no different. In the case of Albany Wallis, greed seems to be the most likely motive. It was not that Wallis needed the money. He was a very successful lawyer, representing, among others, some of the biggest names in theater. He had represented Garrick as the executor of his will, represented Sheridan in negotiating the purchase of Drury Lane and continued to serve as that theater's legal council. He was often entrusted with large amounts of money. For instance, he was named a co-trustee for securing payment of £12,000 to one Andrea Gallini in 1781.[29]

Nevertheless, there were instances where the observer might have objected to Wallis's ethics. He had represented Garrick when selling the actor's shares to Sheridan. The problem was that he was also representing Sheridan in the very same deal![30] He negotiated for both sides. Today, we would call it conflict of interest.

In November 1789, Wallis was apparently working against Sheridan, for the dramatist wrote to one James Ford that "those *Law demands* of Mr. Wallis's shall be satisfied immediately."[31] In June 1792, Wallis was working with Sheridan in validating the patents for a new Drury Lane.[32] But they were very soon pitted against each other. In a letter to Wallis, Sheridan writes:

> I find that Mr. Taylor pretends that his only objection to executing the regular assignments of the other two Boxes which belong to me at the King's Theatre is that you oppose it. I am confident this cannot be the case. . . .[33]

Of course, there seems nothing illegal in this, but it does show that theirs was not an entirely amicable relationship. Yet their business continued. In May 1793, a theater settlement was signed. Representing Sheridan and Drury Lane was Albany Wallis.

Wallis's services were not cheap. The Drury Lane Theatre General Abstract lists the following debts to him: £22,000 as Garrick's executor, plus £5,972.14s, 8d in interest and £325 for costs. Linley also owed Wallis £8,900, with £895.18s interest.[34] And sometimes Wallis was not honest. Sheridan notes with contempt "the detected villainy of two lawyers [Troward and Wallis] and one banker [who] stole £30,000 from the [theater] fund." Another note claims to have paid over £27,000 to these two lawyers in legal expenses.[35]

Understandably, despite working together for many years, there was no love for Wallis on Sheridan's part. On 5 September 1800, Sheridan wrote to his wife:

> Old Wallis died on Wednesday Night- I am curious to learn how He has bestow'd his ill-gotten hoards. If He had a living conscience in his

Bosom when He made his will He will have restored me some thousands.[36]

I have no evidence to suggest that Wallis ever had a conscience. He was a good lawyer, that is clear. Why else would Sheridan stay with him? But he was a thief. He was also a friend of Samuel's, and in yet another conflict of interest, represented both Sheridan and Samuel in the negotiations for *Vortigern.*

If the point of this information about Wallis is to make him more of an Edmund than an Edgar, such disguises were matter-of-fact for William-Henry. It is certain that William-Henry needed and received some legal advice. One visitor, John Taylor, noted that after seeing the documents, he awaited William-Henry, who had promised to explain the origin of

> these valuable reliques. At length he appeared, and after some private conversation between him and Mr. Albany Wallace, an eminent solicitor at that time, the latter addressed the company, and told them that Mr. Ireland, junior, had not been authorized by the person from whom he had derived the matters in question. . . .[37]

Unfortunately, Taylor does not record the date of his visit, but it is clear that Wallis and William-Henry had already been discussing the legal aspects of the papers. And more legal advice was soon required, for William-Henry noted that:

> When the multiplicity of the papers became an object of wonder, it was stated, by some of the visitants at Mr. Samuel Ireland's house, that, if a descendant of Shakspeare could be found, he might lay claim to all the papers which I had produced.-Astonished at this information, I began to think of some method which might obviate any such step being put into effect, even should a claimant appear. . . .[38]

Yet this cannot be the case. It would be far too coincidental for William-Henry to suddenly create a convenient document giving him all the money. But if Wallis was privately allowed into the conspiracy on 30 December 1795, William-Henry would have had six months to prepare for this worst-case scenario. Perhaps it was not Wallis who suggested the need for such a document, but there are no other lawyers mentioned in any of the letters. If not Wallis, then who was supplying William-Henry with this much needed legal advice?

There is yet another reason to suspect Wallis's involvement. William-Henry stated that:

> towards the termination of the business, when doubts ran very high respecting the authenticity of the manuscripts, I destroyed an infinite number of unfinished papers then in my possession, that no document might appear in evidence against me.[39]

Yet, if this is so, how is it that he had so many pieces to show both Wallis and Byng when he confessed? It is possible that he reforged the pieces from memory, but I think there is another explanation. He confessed and gave some documents to Wallis. If my theory pertaining to Albany Wallis is correct, then there was no need for a confession in 1796. Wallis already knew the whole story. Wallis might have had some documents for safekeeping. William-Henry simply destroyed the rough drafts in his office. But Wallis had other documents, perhaps as part of his bargain of silence.

DID WALLIS DOUBLE CROSS THE IRELANDS?

But if he had promised silence, there is evidence to suggest he broke the bargain. In Malone's *Inquiry,* the book which discredited the papers once and for all, the Shakespeare editor noted that he had seen some of the forged poems entitled "Shakspeare's Pretty Verses to the Queen." The papers had come into Malone's hands through "a Gentleman" intimately acquainted with the "possessor of these treasures. . . ."[40] This can be no one other than Wallis, since these poems had not yet been released. Therefore, these poems were among the papers Wallis had for safekeeping. But since Malone's *Inquiry* came out before William-Henry confessed, Wallis must have had the papers while the fraud was still in progress.

However, if Wallis was in possession of certain papers and unofficially showed them to Malone, officially he remained silent. He never revealed Mr. H./William-Henry Ireland. Again, we must ask the question: Why? Why did Wallis keep this secret? Did he think the entire episode would blow over? Surely Wallis knew better. As a discoverer of authentic Shakespeare documents, Wallis realized the significance of William-Henry's "findings." He knew the controversy would not just go away. His silence was not an attempt to let the entire case fade into oblivion, but a stonewalling attempt. Perhaps their enemies would destroy themselves. After all, no concerted scholarly attack had yet been mounted. And if one were mounted, it might be as easily refuted. All they had to do was stick to their story and there would be plenty of money for everybody.

If my theory is correct, William-Henry must have approached 1796 with confidence. He now had a legal expert who would not only fight off Talbot but would also ensure that no one else could claim the benefits of his labor. But his staff must have included at least one other person, the one who had torn off the date from the Leicester letter and informed him of the broken seal. Wallis could not have torn the date before presenting it to the public, as we have no indication whatsoever that William-Henry ever gave the documents to Wallis first. They always went to Samuel first. In the case of the broken seal, it is possible that Wallis was present and did notice the broken seal. And it is possible that Wallis might easily have slipped out of the room and rushed to chambers to tell William-Henry. But if it was Wallis, William-Henry had been very lucky. Though Wallis might well have spent a vast amount of his free time at the Irelands'—after all it was suddenly filled with rich and interesting people—Wallis had his own livelihood to worry about. He had his job. He had to attend to affairs. He had to make a living. No, Wallis was now a conspirator, but there was someone else helping William-Henry.

CONSPIRACY?

But as logical as Wallis's and Talbot's nefarious involvement seems to be, many riddles remain: How is it that Samuel did not see his son's presentation of the forgeries as a clear case of wish fulfillment? How is it that an expert in collectibles was so easily fooled? Who told William-Henry about the broken seal? Who told him the date of Leicester's death? Who painted the Cumberland portrait? Why did Samuel go to his meeting with the prince when Wallis had just exposed the documents as fakes? Why is it Samuel did not even recognize the handwriting of his own son? Is it possible that Samuel was a fool or is it possible that Samuel was a very smart businessman? Is it possible he approved of his son's forgeries, even abetted in them for personal profit? Surely Samuel knew more about Shakespeare than William-Henry. Is it possible that William-Henry and Samuel were in it together from the start? Is it possible that William-Henry took the fall, while his father saved what was left of his reputation and business by pleading ignorance? The ultimate question is: Did Samuel Ireland know that the documents his son gave him were forgeries?

6

Lies and More Lies: The Truth About the Ireland Family

This chapter deals with the private lives of the Ireland family. This type of study often descends into tabloid journalism, a shadowy area in which people are condemned on the basis of mere rumor and slander. Nevertheless, this is an enquiry that must be made for two reasons: (1) to demonstrate that Samuel Ireland was dishonest enough to have aided and abetted his son, perhaps even masterminded the forgery operation, and (2) to focus on William-Henry's anxieties concerning his legitimacy, and how these anxieties might have played a role in the creation of the Shakspeare Papers.

We have seen that William-Henry's Shakspeare Papers were not the result of a sudden, unforeseen opportunity. William-Henry had forged other writers and artists before he attempted to imitate Shakespeare. Fundamentally, he was the same person he had always been. It was only the subject matter that had changed, the artist had not. The same, of course, could be said of Samuel Ireland. Either he had been fooled by his son, in which case we must believe he had always been a fool, or he had always been a thief. There is enough evidence to convince me that Samuel was not a fool.

DID SAMUEL FORGE THE PAPERS?

Even before *Vortigern* premiered, the shadow of suspicion was cast upon Samuel Ireland. Over four months before the play was even staged, the *Tomahawk* journal suggested that Samuel deposit the papers "in THE MUSEUM, for a *certain given* time, and invite all THE CRITICS to comment upon them. . . ."[1] His failure to do so seemed to satisfy many that Samuel was guilty of fraud. Less than a month later the *Herald* was openly lampooning the whole case with reports that "*Old trunks* have been in great demand ever since the discovery of the Shakespeare Manuscripts. . . ."[2]

Similarly, the great Shakespeare scholars of the day imperiously regarded the situation, and like Zeus hurled their verdict: Samuel Ireland had forged the papers. George Steevens, a forger in his own right, and later a purchaser of many of the papers, believed that William-Henry's confessions were nothing more than a son's attempt take the blame for his father.[3] Edmund Malone, who had written a book exposing Chatterton, thought that a group had participated in the forgeries. In reference to the Shakspeare Papers, Malone criticized the knowledge of the "artist, or rather artists" involved.[4] He notes that some of the papers read like the work of "a young lady of fifteen, after reading the first novel that has fallen into her hands"—a possible reference, as I shall explain, to one of William-Henry's sisters, Jane or Anna Maria.[5] He notes that the Shylock portrait has features easily recognizable to anyone who has "visited Holland" and the letters are so picturesque, they might have been written by an editor of Hogarth.[6] Malone also notes that one forgery has "the miserable scrawl of a . . . man of fourscore . . ."—three obvious references, as we shall see, to Samuel Ireland.[7] As for William-Henry, Malone merely notes that his name appears on the Deed of Gift out of accident or "zeal to do honour to the son of the editor."

The scholarly consensus was that Samuel alone had the learning required to write the papers. Scholars and much of the informed world assumed William-Henry lacked the knowledge, experience, and intelligence to plan and to perpetrate such a crime.

WAS WILLIAM-HENRY CAPABLE OF FORGING THE PAPERS BY HIMSELF?

The reason why Samuel, and much of the critical world, refused to believe William-Henry had forged the papers himself is pretty clear: Everyone thought the boy was a half-wit. Despite his good education, his future was not thought to be promising. His teachers thought him a dullard and this opinion was shared by many of the family. In his *Confessions,* William-Henry includes a short chapter entitled, "Stupidity When a Child." The forger confesses:

When at Mr. Shury's academy, at Ealing, I was so very backward, that once, on going home for the vacation, I was made the bearer of a letter from Mr. Shury, wherein he acquainted my father, Mr. Samuel Ireland, that I was so stupid as to be a disgrace to his school, and that, as he found it impossible to give me the least instruction, he would much rather I should not return after the holidays, as he (Mr. Shury) conceived it was no better than robbing Mr. Ireland of his money.[8]

One contemporary referred to William-Henry as "a lad of no parts."[9] His father was of a similar opinion. Schoenbaum describes William-Henry's relationship with Samuel as one "Eager to win approval from a parent who regarded him at best with indifference, at worst as a simpleton. . . ."[10] There was little hope that William-Henry would be the next literary light. One day, during an excursion up the Thames, Samuel pointed to Pope's villa, patted his son on the head and sighed, "I fear you will never shine such a star in the hemisphere of literary fame."[11] Of course not everyone can be a famous writer, but as a portrait of a father-son relationship, it is not heartening or endearing.

Mair states that after William-Henry returned from his further schooling in France, "Samuel sadly noted his son's lack of useful talents, complete indifference to sensible ambitions, and obvious inclination for the life of a cultivated waster."[12] If Samuel was blamed for the forgeries, it was his own fault. He had portrayed his son as an imbecile.

Reexamining the Letters and Affidavits Protecting Samuel Ireland

Samuel's innocence rests on the double assurance of both the public confessions of father and son, and the private letters between the two. As Mair wrote, "William[-Henry]'s confession was doubted until long after his death, and only his father's correspondence, here extensively quoted, has finally proved that he did, after all, speak the truth."[13] I do not share his certainty.

Questions remain: I have listed them at the end of the last chapter. Many people did think that Samuel was the forger, and his son a useful stooge. Were they all wrong? Do the confessions of father and son and their private letters prove anything? I believe that there is both external and internal evidence to suggest that they do not.

The first paper marshaled in evidence to protect the father was an affidavit, drawn up on 17 January 1796 by Wallis, swearing that Samuel knew nothing about the origins of the papers. But this paper does not prove that Samuel was ignorant of the forgeries.

This affidavit had been drawn up months before *Vortigern* was staged. As such, it only proves that William-Henry and Wallis thought that they had to protect Samuel against this very charge, months before it was needed. In other words, it is very possible that they were covering their tracks.

In the latter part of March 1796, mere days before *Vortigern* was staged, William-Henry made another affidavit protecting his "innocent" father:

> [William-Henry Ireland] maketh Oath that he this Deponents [*sic*] father the said Samuel Ireland hath not nor hath any one of the said Samuel Ireland's family other than save and except this Deponent any Knowledge of the manner in which he this Deponent became possessed of the same Deeds or Manuscript papers aforesaid or any part thereof or of any Circumstance or Circumstances relating thereto.
>
> W.H. Ireland.[14]

SAMUEL'S CORRESPONDENCE WITH MR. H.

If we cannot believe William-Henry's affidavit when we know he has lied in the past, what else can be submitted as proof of the old man's innocence? Sadly, there is little else but still more letters from William-Henry to Samuel. However, these letters are interesting in themselves because they are not from son to father and back again but from William-Henry's persona, Mr. H.!

Why would Mr. H. and Samuel communicate? The reason was money. Samuel wrote to Mr. H., his son acting as carrier, to thank him for his generosity, to ensure this generosity would continue, and requesting permission to publish the papers. William-Henry wrote back in his normal hand. If we are to believe these letters to be genuine, then this bizarre correspondence was surely yet another outlet for what Schoenbaum describes as William-Henry's "megalomaniac fantasies."[15] Certainly the first response from Mr. H. smacks of flaunted lies and inflated ego:

> It may appear strange that a Young Man like myself shou'd hase [*sic*] thus form'd a friendship for one whom he has so little knowledge of, but I do assure you *Dear Sir* without flattery he is the young man after *my own heart.* . . .
>
> As he seems to speak much of the *Lear* for *you* and for which I still esteem him *more and more* You shall in a short time have it not from

me but through his Hands. . . . Pray excuse my familiarity but I cannot write otherwise to the Father of one whom I esteem. . . .[16]

On the following day Mr. H. wrote again with a great idea: "your Son shou'd take on himself one of the parts in the new play."[17] Samuel decided against this, but wrote to Mr. H. informing him of his decision to allow William-Henry to introduce all the characters in a pageant after the play.[18] Mr. H. then wrote to Samuel, complaining that his son should grow his hair long if he so wished.[19] Samuel decided not to answer. But Mr. H. clearly was not to be put off. In another letter he actually confides to Samuel that his son is a genius:

> I often talk with him and never before found one even of triple his age that knew so much of human nature do not think this flattery for I again vouch to the truth of my assertion *No man* but your *Son* ever wrote like *Shakespeare* This is bold I confess but it is true.[20]

On 3 March 1796, Samuel resumed the correspondence, asking him for permission to publish the papers. This time it was Mr. H. who refused to answer. Samuel wrote again, asking not only for more information on the gentleman, and permission to publish the papers but also for the rest of the treasures promised.[21] Mr. H. promised even more treasures: a deed showing that Samuel's ancestor had been knighted by Henry V and a leather-covered writing desk.[22] Still he dodged the question of publication. Perhaps William-Henry sensed that the forgeries had been successful only because the experts had not had a chance to study them at their leisure. Publication would change that.

By November 1795, Samuel had been informed by Talbot that the reason why Mr. H. was hesitant about publishing the Shakspeare Papers was that he was ashamed to publicly admit he was a descendant of someone who had worked with Shakespeare.[23] One would think Mr. H. would have been proud to acknowledge such a connection. But William-Henry and Talbot were not thinking clearly. They were desperate. But so was Samuel, who already set the book up for press. As he told Mr. H. in a letter:

Dear Sir
    The delicate predicament in which I now stand-being about to Commit myself to the Public, in my preface to the Shakspeare Papers-will I flatter myself plead in apology for my troubling you again on the Subject of this letter. As I find I have a host of unbelieving to Combat with-who are now laying in wait, for my publication- and to Catch at

any point to serve their purposes- I will esteem it a very particular favor if you will oblige me with a few lines relative to the nature of the discovery of the papers.[24]

That commitment was first made in Samuel's book, *Picturesque Drawings of Stratford*. Its preface included an advertisement for the publication of the Shakspeare Papers. The book was to be called *Miscellaneous Papers*. Now the book was held up because Samuel wanted more proof before risking his own cash. Of course these objections had not stopped him from charging admission to the Shakspeare Papers, or from selling the Shakspeare hairs or negotiating to stage *Vortigern*.

Finally, William-Henry gave his father a verbal agreement to publish the papers, but at his own risk.[25] It really did not matter. By this time the book had already gone to press, and it did not mention Mr. H.'s approval or identity. Nor were any qualms raised about the papers.[26] There was cash on the line and no one was going to buy a book entitled *Miscellaneous Dubious Papers*.

According to William-Henry, at one point he asked his father, "Suppose . . . the gentleman . . . should resolve on saying he knew them [the papers] all to be forgeries[?]" Samuel replied, he would see it as "a premeditated scheme to ruin an innocent Family in which he had made his own. [*sic*] son the chief Instrument."[27] The next day he mused again over this statement but came to the same conclusion. He wrote in his diary, "I wou'd never believe such a Villain cou'd exist upon the Face of the Earth."[28]

QUESTIONING SAMUEL'S CHARACTER

If these letters are genuine, this statement must have thrown William-Henry into unutterable despair. But what if none of these letters are real, or more exactly, what if they were merely as real as the Shakspeare Papers? It may seem that I am looking for conspiracies in each corner. After all, I have already explored the possibility of two conspiracies—one concerning Talbot, the other concerning Wallis. But it must be remembered that either Samuel or William-Henry forged the Shakspeare Papers. If one or both forged all those documents, is it not equally possible that they also forged these correspondences after they were sure to be exposed? The purpose that such a cover-up would serve is clear: it would vindicate the father at the expense of the son—something William-Henry was apparently all too willing to do. Still, merely coming up with a theory to validate another theory is like building one airy castle on top of another—complexities of dreams do not necessarily make them real.

What I am able to do is alert the reader to the evidence leading me to this conclusion. I must show that Samuel was not quite the upstanding businessman and artist that William-Henry would have us believe, and that William-Henry and his father had both falsified documents and rewritten or hidden episodes of their lives. Since I can present proofs for these allegations, I find it perfectly possible, even reasonable, to conclude that they both hid or rewrote the truth concerning each other's involvement in the Shakspeare Papers and the staged play, *Vortigern*.

The only information presented to the reader thus far concerning Samuel Ireland has come from William-Henry. By his various accounts, Samuel was a pillar of society, a friend of the theater, a fine artist, a knowledgeable and cunning collector with "a marked tenacity respecting adherence to the truth. . . ."[29] Indeed, others were of a like mind. Francis Webb called Samuel, "a gentleman, in all respects, [of] worthy credit."[30] Dr. Spence, M.D., confided to Samuel that "from his [Samuel's] public Character" alone, "some might almost make a favorable decision" on the authenticity of the papers.[31]

But Samuel's public character was not perfect. Indeed, one contemporary, the painter Joseph Farington, when told of the discoveries, noted in his diary that "The story He [Malone] told [concerning the discoveries of the Shakspeare Papers] does not engage confidence when a man of Sam Irelands [*sic*] character is to support it. . . ."[32] Farington's suspicions rested on the impropriety of Samuel Ireland's domestic and business dealings.

He was not alone in his low regard for Samuel Ireland. Farington's friend, the painter Richard Westall, had known Ireland years before this notoriety. According to Westall, Samuel Ireland was the nephew of a bricklayer, from whom he received a small dependence. When Westall knew him, Samuel was not a book or art collector. At that time he was a weaver in Spital Fields. "In this business he failed."[33] Soon after, however, things improved. He received a medal from the Royal Academy in 1760, and exhibited there in 1784, though his work was considered amateurish.[34]

These later public successes seem to have made little impact, or more correctly, these successes were vitiated by Samuel's private life. When Steevens was accused of helping Samuel Ireland, a charge I will deal with at a later point, Steevens remarked snubbingly that were he to forge such documents, it would "not be in

Samuel Ireland, failed weaver with aristocratic airs. Photo obtained from the Shake-speare Birthplace Trust.

conjunction with Samuel Ireland."[35] Samuel Ireland was too low even to commit a crime with! Malone, too, had a low opinion of Samuel Ireland. Samuel Ireland had once called on Malone, and asked if he could see Malone's casting taken from Shakespeare's grave monument in Stratford-upon-Avon. Malone, who had never met Samuel Ireland, icily declined to show one of his most precious, personal possessions to a stranger. Samuel Ireland, as far as Malone and his friends were concerned, was as common as the hills, a man who, according to Westall, could not "trace [his heritage] back to a great grandfather."[36]

Imagine their upper-class reaction when they heard that this rude, intruding, business failure; this weaver, nephew of a bricklayer; this piddling, pretentious artist who could not trace his lineage to a great grandfather, now claimed that his ancestor had been a friend of Shakespeare and that he was now in possession of a collection of his priceless papers, mementos, lost poems, and even lost plays! But it was not simply bad manners or a common background that made Samuel Ireland odious. His own life was riddled with vice.

In reading William-Henry's accounts, one would think that he was an only child, and that the mother had passed away as there is no mention of any others in the household except the housekeeper, Mrs. Freeman. William-Henry was hiding the truth, and the truth may well have been hidden from him. There is a sleazy underbelly to this story, one the tabloids would have relished to print. Samuel was not the only one to have a questionable family tree. There was also the complicated past of Mrs. Ireland.

The Ireland household included a housekeeper named Mrs. Freeman. But Mrs. Freeman was not merely the housekeeper. She was Samuel Ireland's mistress. Farington wrote in his diary that he was informed:

> Mrs Freeman who lives with Ireland and is the mother of the Children, had, it is said a fortune of £12000, and is of a good family. Her Brother is now living in London in great circumstances, but disowns Her. . . . Ireland behaves very ill to her.- The Children for many years bore the name of Irwin; and it was at the birth day of one of them, when many persons were invited . . . that it was signified by Mrs. Freeman that the young people were to be addressed by the name of Ireland. They had passed as her nieces.[37]

There is, I assure the reader, a very good reason for alerting you to this intimate family matter. William-Henry's legitimacy is of little interest to me. What does concern me is the hiding of such basic facts as name and parentage. Despite the details of the family Bible, it is entirely possible that William-Henry was not even Samuel's son. Certainly William-Henry was unresolved as to his parentage. According to Grebanier, author of *The Great Shakespeare Forgery*, Mrs. Freeman's maiden name was Anna Maria de Burgh.[38] The reason her brother disowned her was not merely because she lived in sin with Samuel Ireland. Compared to her recent past, her arrangement with Samuel Ireland might have been deemed the beginning of her discreet period. According to Malone, she had been married but had separated from her husband, surnamed Coppinger.[39] Worse yet, this Mrs. Freeman (alias Anna Maria de Burgh Coppinger) had been mistress to the earl of Sandwich, a man known for his debauched lifestyle. Somehow, Samuel Ireland became involved with Sandwich's ex-mistress.

If Samuel's contact with Mrs. Freeman (or whatever she called herself at that point) was "improper" by the day's standard, it is a detail that fits in with other details of Samuel's life gleaned from his books, the first of which was *Picturesque Tour through Holland, Brabant and Part of France* (1789). His highlight of the tour is a visit to a Dutch brothel.[40]

WILLIAM-HENRY'S POSSIBLE ILLEGITIMACY: AN IMPETUS TO FORGE?

Perhaps the annotated family Bible is yet another forgery? Is it not possible that one or all of the children living with Samuel were Sandwich's? Is it not possible that the £12,000 came from Sandwich as a payoff to Samuel for taking one of his old mistresses off his hands? Perhaps I am being overly dramatic, recreating in Sandwich Middleton's roving Sir Walter Whorehound (*A Chaste Maid of Cheapside*). There is no record of Samuel's marriage to "Mrs. Ireland," nor are there any baptism records for any of the children.[41] Furthermore, we may also infer that there was little love in the relationship, for he treated her badly. We do not know if this treatment was physical, but we do know it was psychological.

Remember William-Henry told us his obsessive father used to read Shakespeare most every night, except when he read from Croft's *Love and Madness?* The book is not only about Chatterton's life. Accounts of Macpherson's, Defoe's, and Dodd's careers are also supplied.[42] The book is a veritable *Who's Who* of forgery. Chatterton and company are but part of its subplot. Principally, the book is a nonfiction account of the murder of Martha Ray by

James Hackman. Martha Ray was a former mistress of the Lord Sandwich.[43] Mrs. Freeman was forced to listen to her lover read, in front of her illegitimate children, a story closely connected to her former lover. These constant reminders of her past in front of her children must have made for perverse and cruel treatment. And what of the children? Surely puzzled looks passed between them as double *entendres* went over their heads.

Or *did* they pass over their heads? William-Henry's forgeries created an alternate father figure. James Hackman is referred to within Croft's book as Mr. H. [44] Is it a coincidence that Mr. H. is also the name of William-Henry's imaginary patron? In terms of his own legitimacy and possible bastardy, Mr. H. does become a kind of surrogate father, communicating with Samuel, providing for William-Henry's future. And then there is the matter of "Shakspeare's" will, which leaves a provision for a bastard child. Can this have been anxiety concerning his own origins rising to the surface?[45] It does seem overly formal to refer to his father almost constantly as Mr. Ireland. It seems that despite the family Bible entry, William-Henry always thought that Samuel Ireland was not his father.

This might explain William-Henry's impetus to forge. As the boy forged Shakespeare's life, he believed that he, too, came from a union of half-truths and outright lies. Certainly after his exposure and his "father's" rejection, William-Henry began to openly question his parentage. In a letter dated 3 January 1797, he demands of Samuel point-blank: "If you are really my Father I appeal to your feelings as a Parent."[46] Later in the same letter he notes that he often told Mrs. Freeman "that you did not think me *your Son*." He also recalls "you have frequently said that when of Age you had a Story to tell me which would astonish and (if I mistake not) much shock me."[47] Can this story be anything else but the truth concerning his mother's lurid past and his own bastardy? Perhaps Samuel told him the truth, or maybe the boy figured it out himself. A letter on 13 December 1796, from William-Henry to Samuel, made it clear that the schism was complete. The letter is signed W. H. Freeman.[48] Almost a year later, William-Henry was keeping thoughts of his paternity uppermost in his relationship with his father. On 1 December 1797, he wrote to Samuel concerning a rumor that he, William-Henry, was keeping a mistress, and that this news was an insult to his dignity.[49]

Even his name must have been a constant reminder of his birth. Samuel almost always addressed William-Henry as Samuel Jr. This would usually be seen as an affectionate appellation. But William-

Henry states that he had an elder brother, named Samuel.[50] This statement is corroborated by the family Bible, which states that Samuel Jr. was born 15 June 1773. Apparently this Samuel died early in life, though there is no record in any parish register of his baptism or burial. The records for this era are far from complete. Assuming there was another child named Samuel, is it merely a coincidence that Samuel Ireland often addressed William-Henry as "Sam"? Perhaps the loss of Samuel Jr. was part of the impetus to accept Mrs. Freeman and her bastard brood. Perhaps William-Henry was a counterfeit for the son Samuel lost or once hoped to have. Even if the family Bible can be trusted, Samuel still preferred the thought of Samuel, rather than William-Henry as his son and William-Henry did not believe he was Samuel Jr.—that is, a copy of Samuel.

The psychoanalytic implications of this situation might have been at least some of the agents motivating William-Henry to forge the identity of his father's idol, Shakespeare. A fraud is an imposter whose identity is self-made. William-Henry's forgeries created a new genealogy that effectively bypassed his father for Shakespeare. Thus, while William-Henry may have had logical reasons for forging his play, outlined in the opening chapter, psychoanalytically, his impetus to forge may have been an aberrant fear of his own legitimacy.[51]

It wasn't just William-Henry who grew up with these unresolved questions and open lies. William-Henry had two sisters, Anna-Maria (named after her mother of the same Christian name) and Jane.[52] We know only a few details concerning these daughters: one is that at the height of the Shakspeare Papers on 15 December 1795, Anna-Maria married a man from the import-export firm India House.[53] The other is that Jane dabbled in oil painting, engraving, and etching. She even had exhibitions of her work at the Royal Academy in 1792 and 1793.[54] Among Samuel's possessions at the time of his death were several miniatures by Jane Ireland of Shakespeare and Ben Jonson, and six copper plates by Jane depicting scenes in various Shakespeare plays.[55] Samuel's obsession with Shakespeare had carried over to other members of his family as well. Need we look further for the painter of the Cumberland portrait? Samuel himself recorded an interesting detail that also implicates Jane in the forgeries. On 5 July 1796, both Samuel and Jane visited Albany Wallis. Samuel confided in Wallis that he might lose as much as £400 on his *Miscellaneous Papers,* at which point Wallis looked directly at Jane and responded that the forgeries would "fetch their full value some time hence."[56] I grant that there are

Misses Anna Maria & Jane Ireland drawn from the life by Mr Samuel Ireland.

William-Henry's sisters, Anna-Maria and Jane Ireland. Picture by Samuel Ireland. Reprinted with permission of The Folger Shakespeare Library.

other reasons for looking at a young woman, and it is possible that Jane might have contributed to the forgeries without Samuel being a party. Furthermore, it might have been Jane who tipped off William-Henry about the broken seal.[57] Is there any other reason to suppose that the letters between father and son, or father and adopted son, and father and Mr. H. might be part of a carefully orchestrated cover-up?

LIKE FATHER, LIKE SON: SAMUEL WAS A FORGER

There are more facets of Samuel's life that establish a penchant for forgery, fraud and mass deception. William-Henry might be forgiven for not mentioning his parentage. It is, one feels, a personal matter. But his father's previous shady business dealings are another matter. Samuel was not exactly in rivalry with Sotheby's. His more natural affinity might be with P. T. Barnum, whose motto was "There's a sucker born every minute." Among Samuel's collection, always open to offers, lay: Sir Philip Sidney's jacket, a pocketknife used by Addison, a mummy, hair from the beards of Edward IV and Louis XVI, a bit of Wycliff's vestment, Cromwell's leather jacket, Charles I's cloak, and James II's garter, Anne Boleyn's purse, a pair of gloves given to Queen Elizabeth from Mary, Queen of Scots, one pink, leather shoe belonging to Lady Lovelace, and perhaps most significant in terms of the later forgeries, a purse of glass beads given by Shakespeare to his eldest daughter.[58]

Even more suspicious were Samuel's literary dealings. In 1787, Walpole (whose books had inspired Chatterton) made a reference to Samuel Ireland. Apparently Samuel had bribed Walpole's engraver for a printing of a frontispiece and pirated the pamphlet. In 1794, as the Shakspeare Papers controversy was just beginning, Samuel put together a book of Hogarth prints from his collection. Some experts claimed that some of the prints included were forgeries and others claimed that Samuel forged them.[59]

But pamphlets and prints weren't Samuel's only unscrupulous literary dealings. He also stole a play. In early 1778, Samuel submitted *The Flitch of Bacon* to Drury Lane. Samuel waited for word of acceptance. He wrote to Thomas King, who had promised to read it but did not. Samuel asked for the manuscript back. After some delay, it was returned. He submitted it again on 19 September 1778, this time to Sheridan. He wrote to Sheridan in late November and December, asking for a decision.[60]

Of course any first-time author is anxious about his work, and Drury Lane did seem very slow in responding, but Samuel had an added reason for wanting the manuscript back. Someone might realize he had stolen it. On 1 January 1779, Sheridan wrote to Samuel, asking to "keep your Piece for a few Days longer-when you shall certainly receive it and my sentiments as far as they are worth while communicating to you."[61] On 8 February 1779, Samuel wrote to Sheridan, asking for the return of his manuscript. Sheridan did not reply. He tried again on 16 March; no reply. Finally, on 15 April, Samuel had a meeting with Sheridan. The piece had been accepted and he was told that "the piece shou'd certainly be brought out next season."[62]

But by August of the same year, Samuel had asked for the manuscript's return, saying he did not wish it performed. Sheridan was mystified:

> Sir,
> There appears to me to be some mistake relative to the Dramatic Piece of yours in my Hands . . . . When I met you some time since I mentioned to you that the Piece should certainly be performed-and I do not recollect that you wish'd to have it returned. . . . But if you have changed your intention about the Piece or wish to have it back to do anything to it I'll trouble you for a Line-and it shall be left as you shall appoint,/ I am, Sir/ Your obedient Servant/ R B Sheridan. [63]

On 1 September 1779, Samuel Ireland wrote back to Sheridan, requesting the return of the manuscript, this time saying that the play was three years old and was in need of revision.[64] More letters were exchanged but in the end the play was returned to Ireland, unperformed.[65] Ireland blamed Sheridan.

But Sheridan might have done Samuel Ireland a favor, since *The Flitch of Bacon* was not by Samuel Ireland at all! The play was actually written by Henry Bate Dudley and was published in 1779.[66] How Samuel Ireland got his hands on it, or hoped to collect the royalties on the stolen copy without raising the ire of Dudley remains a mystery.[67]

I am not claiming that Samuel Ireland stole the Shakspeare Papers from anyone. And certainly the fact that he stole a play, rather than wrote one himself, might support his innocence concerning the Shakspeare Papers, were it not for the fact that he had already forged those Hogarth prints and had all those odd collectibles for sale. And Samuel was a writer of some note: a travel writer, but so were Dickens and Twain for parts of their careers. And like Dickens and Twain, Samuel Ireland did not confine his literary ambitions to travel writing. After William-Henry's death, Puttick and Simpson issued a catalog of his book collection and collectibles. Among the items for sale were two manuscript plays by Samuel Ireland, "Bretville, or the Mysterious Son," and "The Double Intrigue, or It's Ne'er Too Late to Mend."[68] The man had literary talent, though not great talent. Never mind, *Vortigern* isn't a great play.

Samuel wasn't the only writer in the house. His mistress, Mrs. Freeman, had modest literary talent. In 1771, she had published *The Doctor Dissected,* a rhyming attack on a Dr. Cadogan, who had prescribed outdoor exercise and teetotaling as a cure for gout.[69] She also tried her hand at a play, which was rejected.[70]

Both Samuel Ireland and his mistress had reasons to lie about their past and reasons to protect their child, William-Henry—and Jane, who I suspect helped William-Henry with the Cumberland portrait. But this is only a theory. I am creating motives that might explain why the idea persisted that Samuel, and possibly the whole family assisted William-Henry. The parents would have us believe that they had nothing to do with the creation of the Shakspeare Papers and the play, *Vortigern*. But when it came to negotiating with the theaters for the play's premiere, *Vortigern* became very much Samuel's play.

7

Negotiations and the Rewriting of *Vortigern*

BY March 1795, the play was put on exhibition with the other papers and often read aloud. The lucky listener would settle himself in the Shakespeare courting chair, which Samuel had bought in Stratford, to heighten the effect of listening to the new play. John Taylor recorded that on his visit he was "requested to sit in Shakespeare's chair, as it might contain some inspiring power to enlighten my understanding, and enable me the better to judge [the play]."[1]

William-Henry watched the listeners, as they sat

to hear the perusal of the papers; and their settled physiognomies have frequently excited in me a desire for laughter which it has required every effort on my part to restrain.[2]

While on exhibit, the play went through alterations, some on the suggestion of visitors. John Taylor's diary records a visit to 8 Norfolk Street. Seated in the courting chair, Samuel read the play aloud and asked for comments. Taylor noted:

During the reading there appeared to be passages of great poetical merit, and of an original cast, but occasionally some very quaint expressions. . . . Mr. Ireland observed, that it was of course the language of the time, and that many of the words which were then probably familiar and expressive, had become obsolete. One passage, however, Mr. Ireland admitted to be so quaint and unintelligible, that it would not be suitable to the modern stage.[3]

Samuel then asked if Taylor could suggest any alterations, to which Taylor replied, "God bless me, shall I sit in Shakespeare's chair, and presume to think I can improve any work from his unrivalled muse?"[4]

Covent Garden or Dury Lane?

Samuel watched and gauged his market and planned to adapt the play to suit his audience. When he was satisfied with his survey, he began negotiations with Covent Garden and Drury Lane. The latter had only recently reopened and was trying to reassert its preeminence over Covent Garden as London's principal theater, a position it had held since the days of Garrick.[5] On or about 24 May 1795, Sheridan read about four hundred lines of the manuscript and said "he would come and read the remainder on his return from Winchester which would be about Wednesday."[6]

The Bidding War for the Lost Shakespeare Play

In the meantime, Covent Garden had made some attractive offers. Mr. Harris, then manager of Covent Garden, "naturally conceived that . . . a newly discovered play of Shakspeare's must prove a source of great profit to the theatre. . . ."[7] Harris visited the Irelands on 30 March 1795, and was "particularly anxious to see and read the *Vortigern*." Samuel offered to show him the four hundred lines he had shown to Sheridan. An appointment was made for the following Friday.[8] However, the very next day Mr. Wallis called at about twelve o'clock to say that he had been commissioned by Harris to negotiate terms for *Vortigern*, sight unseen. Harris was not interested in the merits of the play. He simply did not want Sheridan to get it. *Vortigern* may not have been a masterpiece but it was a piece by a master and thus worthy of production, and capable of producing profit. William-Henry says that Harris offered Samuel *carte blanche*.[9] But Samuel's own diary reveals that he expected a better offer from Sheridan. Harris's offer was contemplated and then rejected.[10]

Samuel preferred Sheridan's Drury Lane. The choice is surprising. Harris had made concrete offers, Sheridan only promised to read the play. It's true that Samuel did know Sheridan and Linley. He had attended a few parties with them. His son had been in an informal children's play that they had watched. But that was years ago. And certainly Samuel had not forgotten the shabby treatment they had afforded "his" *The Flitch of Bacon*, nearly fifteen years before. Had they not taken months to read it, and then put him through countless delays before he withdrew the play altogether?

Despite all this, Harris was turned down. It was a dreadful mistake, and years later William-Henry bitterly regretted the decision: "had my father acquiesced [to Harris and Covent Garden], as that theatre was favoured by the King and the Court, there would have been great probability of its success. . . ."[11] Perhaps the play would have been a failure at Covent Garden but certainly William-Henry was right in accusing Sheridan and others of doing less than their duty in preparing and presenting the play.[12]

Sheridan Not Keen on the Play

Any reluctance to stage the play had nothing to do with its aesthetic merits: everyone knew how low they were. Sheridan had also read the play as it had been delivered sheet by sheet.[13] When the play was complete, he read it once again from beginning to end from a fair copy.[14] Sheridan also came many times to look at the manuscript.[15] And the more Sheridan read *Vortigern*, the less he liked it:

> There are certainly some bold ideas, but they are crude and undigested. It is very odd: one would be led to think that Shakspeare must have been very young when he wrote the play.[16]

Perhaps he looked right at William-Henry as he made this remark. Sheridan might have suspected the truth but he had no evidence. "As to the doubting whether it [the play] be really his [Shakespeare's] or not, who can possibly look at the papers, and not believe them ancient[?]"[17] Sheridan was right. The papers were ancient. It was the writing that was new. Still doubts plagued Sheridan. "This is rather strange," he remarked, "for though you are acquainted with my opinion as to Shakspeare, yet, be it as it may, he certainly always wrote poetry."[18]

Actually, Shakespeare did not always write poetry. Most of his low-life figures speak in prose, not verse, and one play, *The Merry Wives of Windsor,* is almost completely in prose. What Sheridan was commenting on was not the lack of metrical lines, but the lack of poetry in the lines. William-Henry had composed with a slide rule, not a muse. Sheridan decided to judge it by the same rule: the judgment of art by mathematics. The "purchase of the play," Sheridan decided, "was at any rate a good one, as there were two plays and a half, instead of one."[19]

WALLIS BEGINS TO NEGOTIATE

The weighty art of playwriting soon gave over to the nimble art of negotiation. Samuel Ireland turned to his neighbor, Albany Wallis, for representation. Wallis was very likely all too happy to take the job. In all probability he was already blackmailing the family. Sheridan, too, must have welcomed Wallis. Had not Wallis represented the considerable interests of both Sheridan and Drury Lane for many years? No doubt Wallis was collecting a kickback from both ends: from Samuel to continue the fraud, from Sheridan to keep the price low. Both got what they wanted. Formal negotiations began on 9 June 1795:

> The Proprietors of Drury Lane Theatre wish to deal in the most liberal Manner with Mr. Ireland and are ready to leave to Mr. Wallis's arbitration the terms on which the play of Vortigern should be produced. They conceive that the fairest and most honorable grounds to proceed on will be to assign to Mr. Ireland a proportion of the first forty Nights receipts. The compensation will then be contingent on the success and if that answers present expectation it will be [a] most considerable sum/ RBS[.][20]

But Samuel was not so quick to sign. Seven days later, he issued his own counterproposal:

> Five hundred Pounds to be pd down with one Month-and Six clear nights vis: 2nd. 4th. 6th. 8th. 10th. 12fth. subject to such deductions as have been usually made by Authors who have read their 3 nights according to the usual custom of settling for a New Play. . . .[21]

Samuel wanted it both ways: the rights given to every contemporary playwright, plus the extra status he felt should be accorded to a lost classic.

Sheridan countered on 10 July 1795, with the offer of

> £200 down and 3rd, 6th, 9th, 20th, 30th, 40th Nights deducting the established charge of £220 or Receive 200£. down in Lieu of the Moiety of the Receipts of the 1st Night after deducting 350£ and a moiety of the receipts after deducting the same for a run of 40 nights after.[22]

According to Sheridan's own projections, if *Vortigern* ran forty nights, it would generate for Samuel £1,280. But Samuel wanted the same proportion of money for the early nights. He obviously suspected the play would fail to run for forty nights, and he wanted the early box-office profits while interest was high. His own diary reflects this anxiety. Again and again, Samuel worked out the projected profits, adding three new points to be brought into the negotiations. He stated his fear about the "immediate payment of each nights produce," that the play was to be "brought on the stage on or before the 1 Dec. 1795" and most importantly, that "The Copy right of the original Manuscript and of the Alter'd Copy both to remain the Sole property of Ireland."[23]

SHERIDAN STALLS THE NEGOTIATIONS

Meanwhile, negotiations fell into the same rut that characterized Samuel's negotiations with Sheridan on *The Flitch of Bacon.* Sheridan let Samuel sweat it out. Why not? Samuel had already agreed to give the play to Drury Lane, Sheridan could afford to wait. Samuel could not, and Sheridan knew it. Again and again, Sheridan made and broke appointments with Samuel, even when it came to basic concerns such as the text:

10 June 1795

Wansted

Wednesday Night.
    My Dear Sir
    I fear I must put off to Saturday the Pleasure of hearing Vortigern but I will take my Chance of finding you in the course of tomorrow in Norfolk-St./Yours Truly/ RBS.[24]

Two more typical examples are Sheridan's letters to Samuel on 8 and 13 July 1795. The first reads:

Dear Sir
    As I must dine out of Town tomorrow and am particularly engaged in the morning I will call on you at ten this evening as I have miss'd you now/ Yours/ RBS.[25]

The second reads:

Dear Sir
    By some mistake I was not met on the road and so am come to this Place and cannot be in Town till wednesday [*sic*]—the moment I come I will call or send to you/Yours truly/ R B Sheridan.[26]

No doubt Sheridan was a busy man and some of these delays were excusable. However, such delays were not the exception but the rule. In a letter to Samuel dated 24 July 1795, Sheridan says that "There has been no delay on my Part."[27] But there is no doubt that negotiations and details were going slowly and that Samuel was getting very upset. The very same day Samuel had stated his feelings in the strongest terms:

> Such frequent disappointments render it necessary now to be informed what are really your intention with regard to signing the agreement for the play- as I am waiting in Town on that matter alone-and my Son is prevented from going into the Country- on a very material business both to himself and to me- I therefore request the favor of an immediate answer as it will admit of no longer delay-
> July 24:95   I am etc.[28]

Direct tactics seem to have had little effect on the unpunctilious Sheridan. Two weeks later, he failed to attend another meeting:

> My Dear Sir,
>   I have been disappointed this morning, but I am confident I shall not fail tomorrow when I will be with you by one./ Your's [*sic*] truly/ RB Sheridan.[29]

It became a kind of game and Sheridan easily countered Samuel's repeated complaints:

> My Dear Sir,
>   I find we are so circumstanced here that it must be at twelve tomorrow that we must meet and the money will be ready. I assure you I have returned to Town on the business so don't accuse me of unpunctuality.
>   I will be exact tomorrow. Kemble is come./Yrs truly,/ RBS.[30]

During these delays, Samuel had not been idle. In lieu of his pending negotiations and contract, he had done some research into Drury Lane box-office receipts. What he found could not have pleased him. He notes that *A School for Scandal* earned the author, Sheridan, £648.56 for the third, sixth, ninth, and twentieth nights of its recent run. For the night of 21 April 1794, Drury Lane had sold out, with cash on the door at £648.2.

From this figure Samuel then began deducting overhead costs. Everything was taken into account. He writes a note to himself:

> What may the Expense of bring out [or up] the price be estimated at in addition to the Nightly Charge?

> This Question must be ascertained by the Manager when the Scenes, Drapes, Decorations and Properties are determined or necessary to the price.
>
> Forty Nights being in succession last season have averaged £313.[31]

Samuel wanted a lavish production but only if it didn't eat into his profits. And if his play only averaged £313 a night, those profits would not be considerable. Once the deductible expenses of £220 had been subtracted, Samuel would be left with only £93 a night. Assuming this as a constant, and multiplying the figure for the nights of the third, sixth, ninth, twentieth, thirtieth and fortieth, as Sheridan had proposed, Samuel would earn £558, much less than Sheridan's projection of £1,280!

The Contract is Signed

Sometime in September 1795 (the exact date is left blank), a contract with a performance date of no later than 15 December was signed.[32] It began promisingly enough:

> Whereas the said Samuel Ireland is possessed of a certain ancient Manuscript play called or intitled Vortigern and sign'd as supposed to be written by William Shakspear. . . .

But the actual numbers, in lieu of Samuel's calculations, were not heartening. Samuel was given £250 for signing and one-half the profits for receipts tallying over £350 a night. This was no deal at all since the theater's average was only £313.

One might argue that Samuel was innocent of any fraud and only wanted what was best for Shakespeare, no matter if he received slight remuneration. But the contract goes on to crush this argument, for it is all too clear that the genius of Shakespeare was the last concern of either party:

> And whereas the said Samuel Ireland hath a [sic] delivered to the said Richard Brinsley Sheridan and Thomas Linley a copy of the manuscript of such play It being agreed between the said Parties that no use whatever is to made of the said Play by the said Richard Brinsley Sheridan and Thomas Linley other than to represent the same at the said Theatre in Drury Lane having power nevertheless to make alterations or cause to be made such alterations therein, and Additions thereto as they shall think fit And it is further agreed that the copy right of the said manuscript with all such Additions and Alterations as

shall be made and the right of printing and publishing and selling the same and all vantage to arise by the Sale or publishing thereof shall belong to the said Samuel Ireland[.]

Samuel wanted the publishing rights to both the foul papers and the prompt copy. The text itself was to have no special protection. Indeed, the point is stressed, underlying Sheridan's lack of faith in the play in its present form:

> Theatre Royal Drury Lane shall and lawfully may from time to time Exhibit represent and perform the said Play called Vortigern or cause or procure the same to be Exhibited represented or performed at or in the said Theatre Royal Drury Lane in such way and manner and with such Additions or Alterations as they the said Richard B. Sheridan and Thomas Linley or either of them their or either of their Executors Administrators or assigns or any persons appointed by them shall think proper. . . .

In other words, anyone but the janitor was allowed to rewrite this lost play by Shakespeare. To all this, Samuel acquiesced. The cash was on the table. And the cash was the only thing they haggled over. The same collection that houses this contract also houses the original draft.[33] There are differences, but only concerning money. Ireland was completely unconcerned that Shakespeare might be tainted by a Tate, or a Shadwell, or a Dryden before anyone had even had a chance to see the original play. Why should he be? As we shall see, his whole family had already had a hand in improving Shakespeare. The only thing Samuel negotiated on was the cash.

REWRITING *VORTIGERN*

The contract signed between Samuel and Drury Lane had, as we have seen, extensive clauses allowing changes to the manuscript for the purposes of staging. It was a clause that was to be invoked often. Samuel Ireland admits:

> After the play was contracted for, some alterations were deemed necessary to fit it for representation. It was much too long, and consequently many passages were expunged . . . it underwent some further alterations; but excepting these particulars, it stands nearly as in the original.[34]

But he is painting too rosy a picture. After it was sold for representation to Drury Lane the entire play was rewritten. But if Samuel downplayed the extent to which *Vortigern* was rewritten, William-Henry overplayed the extent to which he rewrote the play for the requirements of the cast. William-Henry stated "that every leading character introduced in the Vortigern was positively written for some certain performer. . . ."[35] As William-Henry tells it, he rewrote the play, taking especial care to highlight his friends. For instance, Mrs. Jordan, with whom he spent much of the opening night talking, must have been a favorite of William-Henry. They had met when William-Henry and Samuel showed the papers to the duke of Clarence, who had bought several copies of *Miscellaneous Papers*. The duke had decided to come to the play, and William-Henry wanted to ensure Mrs. Jordan was justly recognized:

> As the native sweetness of Mrs. Jordan's voice had so invariably excited public approbation, I conceived that by writing a ditty expressedly for that lady I should in great measure benefit the piece when represented. In consequence of this supposition, I composed the annexed verses, which were ably set to music by William Linley, esq. and were received with unabounded plaudits. . . . *that . . . ditty was expressedly composed for Mrs. Jordan.* . . .[36]

Soon after he added, Mrs. Jordan was "to assume the male attire" because those were the roles that suited her best.[37] Therefore, according to William-Henry, the play was rewritten to allow for the addition of a song for her character.

William-Henry may well have been on cordial terms with Mrs. Jordan, and the song might have gone down well, but he certainly did not rewrite the play or even her part. The song appears in MS 1, an early version of the play that predated any negotiations with Drury Lane, much less changes due to casting. In fact only two manuscripts bear William-Henry's hand: MS 2 and MS 5. In the former he is responsible for only the occasional revision; in the latter his hand is only one of many involved.

Despite Samuel's assertions, major changes were made, and despite William-Henry's self-proclaimed flexibility, in private at least, William-Henry was none too happy with the changes to his play. When he finished his second play, *Henry II*, he delivered it directly to Mr. Harris at Covent Garden, to avoid his father "cutting out and making alterations."[38]

The rewriting process had begun in the autumn of 1795. On 4 October 1795, the *Observer* reported that "The Manuscript Play of *Vortigern* . . . is committed to Mr. Sheridan's care, for revision and alteration. . . ."[39] However, a letter from Samuel to Francis Webb, on 12 October 1795, informs us that "Mr. Sheridan has had the Vortigern in his hands about a month. . . ." Samuel goes on to account Webb with Sheridan's opinion of the play:

[Sheridan] has expressed to me the necessity of *very material alterations* to be made in it before its representation-principally on account of the want of measure in the poetry- To these *material* alterations I greatly object- wishing only to have it so shortened as to bring it within a reasonable time for representation- It at present consists of about 2500 lines, when 17 or 1800 is quite long enough for the Stage. I have therefore desired to have it returned and that I will fit it, or cause it to be fitted for that Purpose. This I need not say is a bold undertaking. I wish therefore to have the aid of some friendly hand-to further the undertaking, and one that is not immediately an avowed hireling or Author . . . as I do not intend any name shall be affixed to the play when alter'd and published.[40]

The manuscript was returned in late October or early November, untouched. Sheridan saw the manuscript on one, further, but important occasion. On 7 December 1795, a very curious letter was sent to Sheridan by Jane Linley, daughter of Thomas Linley, key shareholder in Drury Lane, and brother to William Linley, the musical composer for *Vortigern*. It read:

Dear Sir,
Mr. I. was here yesterday and had your note he was in so great a hurry that he said little excepting that the Play should certainly be brought out with the greatest Expedition after the Pantomime. But my Mother desires me to say that she most particularly wishes you to send the Play to Mr. Kemble. She says she has reasons for it which she will explain to you when she sees you

Yours sincerely
M. Linley.[41]

If the play was sent, it was probably at this time that Malone and Kemble worked out the strategy they would use during the play's premiere.

None of the manuscripts show any signs of material alterations by Sheridan. Clearly, if the play was to be readied for the stage Sheridan was going to be of little help. The very next week, the manuscript was returned. But it did not stay in the Irelands' possession for very long. By 15 December 1795, Samuel's daughter Jane had lent the play to Mrs. Byng for her opinion.[42] Very soon after, the play was in Francis Webb's hands. Webb reread the play, and agreed with Sheridan's recommendations: For *Vortigern* to succeed, major alterations were necessary.[43]

And alterations there would be. Soon, the entire family began reforging Shakespeare. William-Henry's original Shakespeare-hand version has been lost, as has his transcription on display at Norfolk Street. Still, no less than seven manuscripts and two printed texts reveal an unbroken chain of recopying and revision dating from 1795 until 1832.

A Discussion of the Various Extant Manuscripts and the Rewrites Involved

Of the seven extant manuscripts, the longest and clearly earliest is probably in Anna-Maria's handwriting. In a cover letter to this MS, William-Henry identifies this hand as Anna-Maria's, although there is reason to suspect his identification of the various hands involved, as we shall see. At any rate, I have not been able to locate any other sample of Anna-Maria's hand. MS 1 has 2,421 lines. It is most probably a transcription of the Shakspeare-hand manuscript. Certainly it is the most literary.

The manuscript itself retains several distinguishing features that indicate it came from an early, literary version. The manuscript retains William-Henry's Chattertonian spelling, includes transcriptions of letters from Shakspeare and his "publisher" Holmes, a prefatory note from Shakspeare apologizing for diverging from his source, a note in the margin from Shakspeare which reads:

Thys Lyne hath appearredde ownce before ande therefore I dydded soe Marke itte

W.S.

and a closing note from Shakspeare which reads:

Thus endeth mye Chronycle Playe of Kynge Vortygerne inne
    the whyche Vice dothe falle ande Virretewe meetes its
    properre Rewarde

Wm. Shakspeare[.]

MS 2 is a transcription of MS 1. It is was written by Mrs. Ireland/ Freeman. After transcription, 431 lines were cut from MS 2, 34 lines were inserted, and 727 lines were tampered with in some way, either insertion, deletion, or transposition. A variety of hands are involved in these revisions. I have identified the hands of Mrs. Ireland, Francis Webb, and William-Henry. In its finished form, the play is 2,024 lines long. Other notable changes are the silent omission of the letters from Shakspeare and Holmes as well as Shakspeare's marginalia. More importantly, MS 2 modernizes spelling, adds punctuation, inserts and/or substitutes, or crosses out many passages.

Like MS 2, MS 3 has a variety of hands involved. In a note accompanying MS 3, William-Henry states that the manuscript is in the hand of his sister, Jane. However, its scribal history is more complicated than William-Henry would have us believe: 1.1 to 2.1 is copied by Samuel Ireland, 2.1 to 5.2 is copied by Charles Marsh, and 5.2 to the close of the play is in the same hand as MS 1, probably William-Henry's other sister, Anna-Maria. Why William-Henry would lie about the identities of the hands involved is a mystery. Even a brief study reveals more than one hand at work. Moreover, a comparison with a letter written by Jane Ireland to her brother, in 1803, shows no resemblance to any of the hands on MS 3.[44] After recopying the new readings into a fair state, MS 3 was then rewritten by the same process of insertions, substitutions, and cross outs. This stage of revision was completed by Mr. and Mrs. Ireland. The changes include 144 lines deleted by cross outs, 135 lines inserted, and 436 lines tampered with. In its finished state, MS 3 is 1867 lines long. It was at this stage that the incest scene was cut, because the original was "thought too gross for the public ear. . . ."[45]

MS 3 was recopied twice, once into MS 4, and once into MS 5. So the Irelands were used to working with multiple manuscript versions at the same time. The original MS 4 was written by Mrs. Ireland and has corrections by her and her husband. These various revisions included 79 newly inserted lines, 477 lines that were tampered with in some way, and 292 lines deleted by cross out. In its finished form the MS is 1,636 lines long. It does not include any prologue or epilogue. MS 4 follows the pattern of the previous manuscripts in that it began as a fair copy and was then used as a basis for further insertions.

MS 4 and MS 5 do have a major change necessitated by problems with the Drury Lane cast. For example, in MSS 1–3, Edmunda sings in 3.6. But in MSS 4 and 5, the song was transposed to an attendant because the actress playing this minor role, Miss Leake, had a fine voice.[46]

MS 5 has 1807 lines, 17 inserted lines and 63 tampered lines. This overall number does not include 139 lines deleted by cross out. It is written in four different hands. The first hand is William-Henry's. His hand is the most difficult to identify, as he has at

Act. 1. Sc: 1.

A large Hall discovers Constantius, Vortigern
Vortimerus, Catagrinus, Pascentius & attend.ᵗˢ

Con: Good Vortigern! as Peace doth bless our Isle,
And the din of War, no more affrights us
And as my Soul hath plac'd thee near herself,
'Tis our desire, that you deny us not,
That, which anon we crave you to accept.
For though most weighty be our proffer'd task,
yet do we We trust, thy goodness won't refuse;
we have always found thee soft by Nature,
And like the Pelican, e'en with thy blood,
Ready to succour, and relieve the wretched.

Vor: Gracious Prince! it is ever thine to command,
And subject-like, always to obey —

Con: Such was the answer we did here expect,
And farther now we do explain our meaning;
As frozen Age we find doth fast approaching,
And

Vortigern

Act 1st Scene 1st

A large Hall discovers Constantius, Vortigern
2 Vortemerus, Catagrinus, Pascentius & Attendants.

Constantius — Good Vortigern! as Peace doth bless our Isle,
And the dread din of war no more affrights us,
And as my soul hath plac'd thee near herself
'Tis our desire that thou deny'st us not,
That, which anon we crave thee to accept
Nor though most weighty be our proffer'd task
We trust thy goodness will not refuse —
For we have always found thee cast by Nature
And like the Pelican, e'en with thy blood
Ready to succour & relieve the wretched.

Vor. — Most gracious Sovereign! it is thine to command,
And Subject as mine always to obey.

Con: — Such was the answer we did here expect,
And farther now we shall explain our meaning:
As frozen Age we find doth fast approach
And the great & weighty affair o'th' State

Lee

Sample of MS 4. Reprinted with permission of The Folger Shakespeare Library.

least four distinct handwriting styles: his natural hand, his scribal hand, his Mr. H. hand, and his Saraphina hand, details I will return to in a later chapter.[47] MS 5 shows an example of his scribal hand, identical to the affidavits he wrote to clear his father of any responsibility concerning the forgeries. Acts 1, 4 and 5 are in William-Henry's hand. Acts 2 and 3 are in a formal, scribal hand, probably that of a professional copyist employed by the theater. The manuscript is corrected throughout by Mr. and Mrs. Ireland. It is the only manuscript to bear a date: 4 February 1796. It also includes a prologue and two epilogues, only one of which has ever been printed. Both prologue and epilogues are copied by Mrs. Ireland.[48]

MS 5 is housed in the Huntington Library in California as part of the Larpent Collection, so named because it is a collection of plays inspected by John Larpent, the Lord Chamberlain between 1778 and 1824. Each playwright was required to send the Lord Chamberlain one copy of the play for his approval. This was not a rubber-stamp process. In Shakespeare's time a play he had collaborated on, *Sir Thomas More,* was banned by the Lord Chamberlain. And in 1796, there was talk of banning *Vortigern.* Indeed, if William-Henry had written a Shakespeare play customized for 1796, he had grossly misjudged his own age. Firstly, there was the issue of regicide in the age of the French Revolution. The *Oracle* queried whether "the licenser [would] allow a Royal Murder in the present times."[49] John Larpent allowed the scene, albeit in a cut fashion. The murder scene would have to be rewritten. The king could die, but not on stage. Reluctantly, the family began working on the play yet again. On 20 February 1796, Powell wrote to Samuel requesting, "with all possible speed . . . the copy of *Vortigern* (as alter'd by the Lord Chamberlain) with your alterations, for the purpose of representation[.]"[50]

The Irelands were apparently struggling with this revision, for by 2 March 1796, they had yet to deliver the new version. Powell wrote to Samuel informing him that if the new version was "longer withheld it will be impossible it can be acted with any new Alterations, but must be produced with Such Amendments as the Lord Chamberlain has thought proper to make."[51]

The family hurried through a rewrite, not even bothering to produce a new, fair copy. Later that same day the play was delivered with the following note:

Sir
    I send with this the play of Vortigern with the alterations of the Lord Chamberlain- It is much underlined-yet I presume you will be able to

read it, at least I hope so for the time will not permit its being copied-
The Prologue and Epilogue you will likewise receive with this, and the
original Epilogue to the which I have now determined shall by [*sic*]
spoken by the fool.[52]

The play was changed again to such an extent that it was necessary to send it back to John Larpent.[53] Samuel was not in charge
of all these alterations. On 5 March 1796, he wrote to Powell,
asking if the MS of *Vortigern* was "to undergo any further alteration before representation. . . ."[54] So MS 5 was copied from
manuscript 3, sent to and edited by John Larpent, and returned.
These new cuts were then copied into MS 4. New readings were
added to manuscript 4 to accommodate the new cuts. MS 5 was
then updated with fresh readings from MS 4 and resubmitted for
Larpent's approval. The play was recopied at least two other times,
both by William-Henry, but after *Vortigern*'s premiere, a point I
will return to in a later chapter.

Somewhere along this complex trail (clarified in Table 1) Samuel
put the play into the hands of Thomas Caldecott. According to
Caldecott, his task was to "weed of superfluous & improper matter
& to give some body & form to the loose disjointed, skimble skam-
ble stuff, which, it was pretended, was the original state of all of
Shakespeare's versification. . . ."[55] This account, written more
than a year after *Vortigern*'s failure, may belie Caldecott's original
support for the piece. Nonetheless, his hand is not evident in any
of the manuscripts. He did not, for whatever reason, agree to the
rewrite, although I admit it is possible that he helped select any
number of lines to be cut. And still the rewrites were not at an
end. Had Samuel Ireland had his way, the collaborative process of
family and friends would have spread to include both John Kemble
and R. B. Sheridan. In the preface to the printed, 1799 version of
Vortigern, Samuel reflected bitterly that:

> In this state [cut, edited of incest, altered in speeches and with song
> additions] it [MS 4] was delivered to the Theatre, with a request, or
> rather *intreaty,* that all further alterations, deemed necessary, should
> be made by the acting manager, or any other person competent to the
> business. . . .[56]

Samuel had evidently expected the acting manager, in this case
Kemble, to make further changes. Kemble refused.[57] Samuel also
resubmitted the play to Sheridan, reminding him that he had been
thus far inattentive. Samuel therefore requested that Sheridan
"look it over- *and make or come to be made such alterations as*

you may think proper."[58] As on the previous occasion, there is no indication that Sheridan complied with this request. He simply wrote back to Samuel that "the play would be acted faithfully from the copy sent to the theatre."[59] Samuel tells us that Sheridan was good to his word, for "it was accordingly acted, literally from the manuscript delivered to the house."[60] And for this Samuel should probably have been grateful. Sheridan did not improve *Vortigern,* but his statement implies that he did not allow Kemble to worsen it either. It was a small but rare favor afforded to Samuel Ireland. The play was ready, but so too were its enemies.

Table 1.
Diagram of Manuscript and Printed Text Progression.

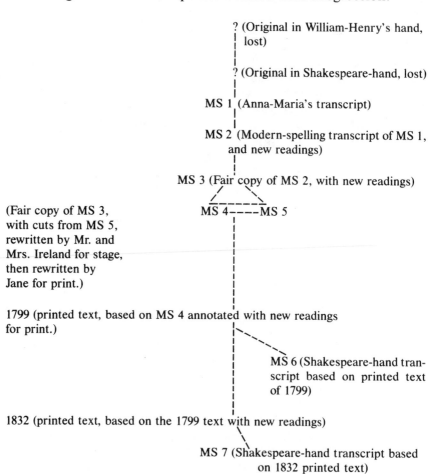

? (Original in William-Henry's hand, lost)

? (Original in Shakespeare-hand, lost)

MS 1 (Anna-Maria's transcript)

MS 2 (Modern-spelling transcript of MS 1, and new readings)

MS 3 (Fair copy of MS 2, with new readings)

MS 4-----MS 5

(Fair copy of MS 3, with cuts from MS 5, rewritten by Mr. and Mrs. Ireland for stage, then rewritten by Jane for print.)

1799 (printed text, based on MS 4 annotated with new readings for print.)

MS 6 (Shakespeare-hand transcript based on printed text of 1799)

1832 (printed text, based on the 1799 text with new readings)

MS 7 (Shakespeare-hand transcript based on 1832 printed text)

More Delays: The Fight for Scenery

As we have seen, even while these seemingly endless revisions were going on, Samuel had other worries: Sheridan's growing indifference and Kemble's growing hostility. These forces would combine to deny Samuel his request for new scenery. While this may not seem like a tragedy to the modern reader, Samuel saw it as nothing less than a catastrophe. His reasoning was understandable. He was only splitting profits above £350. That meant the play had to be a great, sustained success. If the poetry of the play couldn't pass, then the acting and visuals would have to carry the day. Samuel did not want a scholar's production; he wanted the equivalent of a West End musical, the 1790s version of *Miss Saigon*. He wanted a grand spectacle. He was not to get one. *Vortigern* was Samuel's number one priority. But by 9 October 1795, Ireland saw that Sheridan was not rating it as highly. He wrote to Sheridan that he called on:

> Greenwood [the set designer] . . . expecting to see some progress made in his design for Vortigern and then to my great Surprise I learnt that he had an order from some person about the Theatre to lay aside the Designs . . . [in favor of] a pantomime.[61]

Understandably, Samuel was not impressed. As time went on, he would be less impressed. He did, however, hold a trump card: the play. Samuel had kept possession of the script. As long as he kept the script he might be able to negotiate with Sheridan from a position of strength, while improving a play that apparently was to receive, at best, mediocre treatment.

While Samuel had been desirous that Sheridan look at the MS as much as possible, that tactic had changed sometime in early November. Since it was clear that Sheridan was not going to contribute to any revisions, Samuel, as we have seen, farmed the play out to family and friends. While the bulk of the rewrites were now complete, Samuel decided to hold back the play, gambling that Drury Lane would give in to his demands for new scenery, rather than lose the surefire success of staging a new Shakespeare. On 6 November 1795, Drury Lane called Samuel's bluff. Kemble, the man picked to play Vortigern, and a man Samuel knew to be only a "luke warm friend of the play," wrote to Samuel:[62]

> Sir,
> I am desired by the Proprietors of the Theatre Royal Drury Lane to request of you the Copy of Vortigern, as they are apprehensive that,

unless it is sent immediately, there will hardly be time to produce it according to your Agreement.

I am, Sir,

your most obedient Servant

J. Kemble.[63]

But Samuel was not caving in to pressure: no scenery; no play. On 10 November 1795, Samuel wrote a letter to Sheridan, again reminding him:

It is now more than 3 months since you gave order to Mr. Greenwood . . . to proceed on the Scenery for *Vortigern* and I am much Surprised after so long a time has elapsed I found no attention has been paid to that order or that it has given place to subsequent directions. I am the more surpris'd to have reciev'd a pressing letter from Mr. Kemble requesting that the Manuscript might be immediately forwarded to him. This urgency I do not apprehend can be necessary- unless it is intended to substitute old Scenery for the new ones which you have always promised should be prepared. . . .[64]

Samuel apparently thought that rehearsals could only take place on a finished set! As for the new scenery promised, Samuel should have read his contract. There is no mention of a new set. Paradoxically, Samuel evolved the contract to remind Sheridan of his verbal agreement. On 13 November 1795, Samuel wrote to Sheridan, reminding him that the play was to be performed before 15 December. But, according to Samuel, that "Nothing is yet done although the play is now ready. . . ."[65] The very same day he also wrote to Mr. Greenwood, the set designer, reminding him that *Vortigern* was to be staged in one month.[66]

On 18 November 1795, Samuel showed the Shakspeare Papers to the duke of Clarence. He told Clarence of his dispute with Drury Lane. According to Samuel, Clarence

highly approved of my withholding the Mss of Vortigern till I saw preparations of Scenery etc- making for the representation- and Said I should beware of the Manager who was one of the greatest Vagabonds on the face of the earth, and his Deputy the Greatest Jesuit.[67]

Buoyed by his meeting with the duke, the very next day Samuel wrote an aggressive letter to Sheridan:

I must refer myself to *you* to know *your decision* as to the *Scenery-* which certainly may be forwarded by Mr.Greenwood without the manuscript- which I repeated to you is quite ready. . . . I am strictly justified in keeping back the Manuscript. My Situation with respect to this piece is not that of a mere Author. I have a great Stake at risk and much will depend on your execution with regard to the Play. . . . I beg the favor of you to give me an immediate answer by letter that I may understand fully your intentions and that I may not have so much time, in attendance of appointments that seem made only for the purpose of breaking them.[68]

The letter was not as confident as it could have been. It vacillates between begging ("I have a great Stake at risk") and scornful pride ("not that of a mere author" and his closing swipe at Sheridan's "in attendance"). But it was all to no avail. Sheridan knew Samuel was desperate. Though he still publicly maintained that *Vortigern* should be performed no later than 15 December, privately Samuel had long ago admitted defeat. On 27 October 1795, he had written to Oliver Beckett that:

Vortigern I presume will be on the stage in the month of December or beginning of January. The middle of December is the time defined by agreement to bring it out but that I fear from the New Scenery . . . [such a schedule] will not be possible.[69]

Sheridan knew Samuel was running out of options. He did not budge in his stance. His answer came through Kemble, who wrote:

Sir,
    The Proprietors of the Theatre Royal Drury Lane have desired me to let you know, that, unless the Play Vortigern is sent to me, in order so its being copied for Rehearsal, in the Course of tomorrow at farthest, they must suppose that you consider your Agreement with them to be at an End, and shall expect you will immediately be so good as to return the money that has been advanced by them upon the Faith of that Agreement.[70]

If there was one thing that could force Samuel into reconciliation, it was money. He wrote to Sheridan again, the fire gone from his language. This time he came cap in hand. He was genuinely afraid that the play could not stand on its own, and that only a fantastic set could save the play: "If therefore the play is to be introduced with old or vamped Scenery, it can neither save the play nor my own interest. . . ."[71]

But Sheridan decided to placate the old man. The same day Greenwood sent Samuel a note, informing him that "there is no doubt every thing required will be ready in time."[72] The next day, 18 November 1795, Samuel met with Sheridan.[73] Later that same day Sheridan gave Greenwood the go-ahead for the new scenery to be made "without delay."[74]

But there were to be many more delays. Sheridan had apparently decided again to play the waiting game. By 7 December 1795, neither party had moved significantly. Greenwood had yet to start the scenery and Samuel had yet to deliver the manuscript.[75] Samuel threatened to pull the play from the Drury Lane and transfer it to Smock Alley in Dublin, where Talbot might ensure its success.[76] On 12 December 1795, an unspecified list, probably of open dates for Smock Alley, was forwarded to Samuel.[77]

But Samuel was only threatening. On the deadline of 15 December, the *Telegraph* reported that *Vortigern* would be staged after Christmas, but also that the play was "not yet in the hands of the Manager."[78] On 19 December Samuel threatened legal action over allegations that the principal people in the theater were unaware that the play was to be presented at all and the even more injurious report that Sheridan "had declared an opinion that it [*Vortigern*] was not written by Shakspeare."[79] But again, Samuel was only threatening.

By 30 December 1795, the play was in the hands of Kemble.[80] Nonetheless, things continued at a snail's pace. On 15 February 1796 the *Oracle* reported that Samuel continued to demand "entirely new-scenes" but Sheridan maintained his preference in adapting old ones.[81] Ideologically, they were not that far apart. For at the very same time that Samuel was arguing against the adapting of old scenery, he and his entire family were busy adapting the "old" play.

8

In Defense of the Realm: The Critics Strike Back

UNTIL now, I have been treating the William-Henry Ireland story as a tale containing very few characters; indeed, as a family business with a few unwanted interlopers. This isolation was effective in unraveling the intricate knots within the different confessions William-Henry published. Of course, in reality, the forgeries, though a family creation, were not isolated to the family. From almost the first forgery, the Irelands courted critical endorsement. Some experts lent their support to the papers, others determined to expose them.

The Irelands always failed to get the proper professionals to endorse the Shakspeare Papers.[1] If, for example, the matter called for a paleographer, they consulted a critical theorist. While it is true that established men of letters such as Parr, Warton, and Boswell supported the papers, not one was a paleographer.

Nor were the visitors given much opportunity to examine the papers. In fact, many of the Believers had not even seen all the papers! For instance, the reporter for the *Telegraph* was convinced the papers were genuine but admitted that he had not even inspected the *Lear* and *Vortigern* manuscripts.[2] One day after this report was issued, Boswell examined the papers. But even he made only a cursory inspection of the originals before turning to the transcripts.[3]

SAMUEL'S SO-CALLED "EXPERTS"

It is true that Samuel consulted the manuscript expert at Trinity College, Cambridge, but their correspondence ceased when Mr. Pardoes found *"no Book* or *Manuscript* whatever relative to the Play of *Vortigern. . . ."*[4] Pardoes never examined the Shakspeare Papers. On the other hand, Samuel did continue his correspondence with a Robert Relhan, of King's College, Cambridge, who was convinced the papers were genuine because they were damp around the edges, "a convincing proof of antiquity. . . ."[5] It was like calling in an painter to look at the plumbing. Moreover, to compare Relhan to a painter or plumber might be to overly qualify him. Cambridge does not list Relhan among its graduates or teachers. The exact position Mr. Relhan held is unclear, but it certainly was not prestigious, distinguished, or even recorded.[6]

When the Irelands did get someone trained in the proper field, he was never an expert, but an enthusiastic amateur. So, for example, to validate the Fraser Deed, one of the first forgeries, as authentic, Samuel did not go to Edmond Malone but to Sir Fredrick Eden, an economist Marx later compared to Adam Smith, but still not a paleographer.[7] Eden noted that the seal mark was a quintain or tilting post. The sign on the seal was interpreted as a clever analogue based on Shakespeare's family crest. William-Henry was very lucky. The forger later admitted he had never heard of a quintain.[8]

In the case of the Shylock portrait, another so-called expert was consulted: a Mr. Hewlett, a Biblical scholar and an expert on the Arundel marbles.[9] Studying the painting with a magnifying glass Hewlitt stated that he could detect the signature of John Hoskins, a painter in the reign of James I.[10] Why the painter would sign his name so minutely that the reader was forced to use a magnifying glass, was never explained.

An early supporter was Francis Webb, a miscellaneous writer and secretary at the College of Heralds.[11] Like Boswell, Parr, and others, Webb was not qualified to authenticate Elizabethan secretary-hand. He could only formulate an opinion from the text of the Shakspeare Papers. Apparently the papers satisfied his criteria:

> these papers bear not only the Signature of his [Shakespeare's] hand; but the Stamp of his Soul, and the traits of his Genius- his mind is as manifest, as his hand. . . . They [the papers] exhibit him full of Friendship, Benevolence, Pity, Gratitude, and Love. The milk of human kindness flows as readily from his Pen, as do his bold & sublime descriptions.-Here we see the Man, as well as the Poet. . . .[12]

Further, these documents were not to be regarded as merely rediscovered possessions of Shakespeare's, but a concrete testament to his living genius. Indeed, Webb stated that the documents in question carried such, "weight with me, that I am free to declare, that had not Shakspeare's name appeared upon these papers, I should not have hesitated to have ascribed them to him."[13]

The idea that these papers were the work of a forger was ridiculous to Webb, who stated unequivocally:

All great and eminent Geniuses have their characteristic peculiarities, and originality of character which not only *distinguish* them from *all others, but make them what they are*. . . . He [Shakespeare] was a peculiar Being- a unique- he stood alone. To imitate him, so as to pass deceit upon the World, were impossible. The Tragedy of Vortigern as well as his smaller pieces, lately discovered bear indubitable marks and proofs of his sublime genius, boundless imagination, pregnant wit, and intuitive sagacity into the workings of the human mind, and evolution of the passions. . . . It must be Shakespeare's, and Shakespeare's *only*. It either comes from his pen or from Heaven. . . .[14]

The papers themselves hardly sparkle with wit, sublimity, or genius. Webb was obviously very willing and ready to believe in the papers because they provided the image Webb had wanted. Webb, William-Henry might agree, suffered from a suspension of disbelief. Years later, when referring to Webb, William-Henry wrote:

his [Webb's] enthusiastic regard for every thing relating to our immortal Shakspeare (which for once overcame his better judgement) has led him to pour forth praises . . . much above my humble deserts. . . .[15]

Other supporters suspected the truth. Among them was Thomas Caldecott, a bencher at Middle Temple and bibliophile.[16] On 13 February 1795, Caldecott wrote to Samuel about the merits of the newly discovered poetry, judging:

their great inferiority, throughout and as a whole and intire [*sic*] piece, to anything of Shakespeares [*sic*]. . . . here is . . . irregular flight, no flash of imagination: the verses run in one beat, in one measure, in which they are neither smooth in numbers or easy in expression. . . . The verses must in each case have made every man pronounce the letter a Forgery. Fortunately you have other, and sufficient supports: but these verses, making all allowances for their simplicity, are *in themselves* . . . ordinary specimens; not equal to the muse of Shakespeare under any, and particularly such circumstances. . . .[17]

Suspicious or not, these amateur and professional men of letters signed a statement of endorsement drawn up by Wallis on 22 March 1795 that stated, "We the undersigned have inspected the [Shakspeare Papers and] . . . we declared our firm belief in . . . [their] authenticity."[18]

Samuel Ireland's friends signed: Francis Webb, Byng, Wyatt, John Hewlitt, and James Bindley, a book collector who worked in the Stamp Office; powerful people signed: the duke of Somerset, and Sir Isaac Heard, Garter Knight of Arms.[19] Two early supporters, Herbert Croft and John Pinkerton, should have known better. Croft had written *Love and Madness,* the novel that included histories of Chatterton and Macpherson. Pinkerton might have signed out of professional courtesy: he was a forger of ancient Scottish ballads.[20] If Pinkerton's name taints the quality of this list, he was in like company. Another supporter, Richard Valpy, was an adaptor of Shakespeare for the stage but also the headmaster of Reading and said to be the hardest flogger of his day.[21] But many of the major names were absent. Boswell and Parr did not sign, nor had Warton.

JAMES BOADEN DEFENDS THE PAPERS

While Boswell's absence from the list might have been telling, in fact, his apparent abandonment of the papers was not even commented upon. Indeed, the Irelands gained further support in the popular press, particluarly from James Boaden, who was an early, important friend. Charles Mathews called him a "celebrated dramatic critic"; an arbiter of "the fate and fame of many a Thespian hero."[22] Boaden was also a playwright of musicals, comedies, and melodramas. Even more importantly, he had a background in forgery detection. He had helped expose both Percy and Macpherson. Unlike the other Believers, Boaden had the bibliographic and paleographic background to assess accurately the authenticity of the papers. But he had been convinced by the testimonials of others. On 23 April 1795, on the anniversary of Shakespeare's birth and death, the *Oracle* printed Boaden's viewpoint of the controversy:

> The SHAKESPERIANA, which have been so luckily discovered, are now considered as genuine by all but those who illiberally refuse to be convinced by inspection.[23]

Indeed, he had gone so far as to say that on the whole "the conviction produced upon our mind, is such as to make scepticism ridiculous. . . ."[24]

Although Boaden was qualified to judge the papers in all their contentious aspects, he initially followed Boswell, Parr, and Warton in only superficially studying the paper and ink while concentrating on a study of the text. But unlike Webb, Boaden did not find Shakespeare the genius. He did, however, find Shakespeare the gentleman. In his coverage of the papers, Boaden had noted approvingly that Shakespeare's Profession of Faith is "rationally pious and grandly expressed," his love letter to Anne is "distinguished by the utmost delicacy of passion and poetical spirit"[25] and that:

In the title-page [of the manuscript of *King Lear*], the great Bard professes to have taken his story from HOLLINSHEAD; and has, in the true spirit of modesty, apologized for the liberty he took, in departing from the exact statements of the chronicle.[26]

As for the Pope-ish editorial changes, they met with Boaden's approval:

Our suspicions of the *licentious* Passages are confirmed by this the original - they are not SHAKSPEARE'S; but the foisted impurities of buffoons upon the Theatre, recorded in the prompt books.[27]

We might forgive Boaden and the others for their initial enthusiasm. The existence of the papers did not surprise them. Indeed, they had been expecting them to surface. As Boaden later reflected:

It was a subject of infinite surprise to the admirers of Shakspeare's genius, to observe from age to age, that while discoveries, very material to our knowledge of the period in which he lived, occasionally occupied the press, yet that with respect to himself little could be known; and all the effusions that friendship or business must have poured from his pen during a town life, and the reasonable produce of his retirement from a mind so essentially active, ALL, as if collected together in one mass destroyed BY AUTHORITY, had vanished away, and were entirely lost to posterity.[28]

For his own part, William-Henry was amazed he had fooled the world so easily. On the subject of the Deed of Gift, for instance, he noted, he was "absolutely astonished . . . that even credulity itself should have been duped by this flagrant document. . . ."[29]

But not all inspectors of the papers were so taken in. Indeed, the very fact that they drew up a certificate of belief may point to a growing opposition that the Irelands and their supporters felt they had to counter. Certainly there was opposition. Joseph Ritson, a critic who had been instrumental in exposing Percy's *Ancient Ballads,* saw the papers at Norfolk Street, asked a few quiet, purposeful questions and left without saying good-bye. William-Henry interpreted Ritson's actions. "In fine, I do as firmly believe that Mr. Ritson went away fully assured that the papers were spurious, as that I have existence at this moment."[30] William-Henry had shrewdly deduced Ritson's opinions. In a letter to a friend in Edinburgh, Ritson stated that the papers were "a parcel of forgeries, studiously & ably calculated to deceive the public. . . ."[31] He publicly said so. The *True Briton* reported on 14 January 1796, that Ritson was ready to attack the forgeries if no other critic stepped forward.[32] Perhaps he naturally felt that a Shakespeare scholar would expose the papers. Perhaps his long battles with Percy had made him weary of entering the lists for a similar encounter. Ritson remained silent, but he was not needed. A champion soon emerged, and from the most unlikely of places.

MALONE, STEEVENS, AND A LITERARY TURNCOAT

It was expected that a Shakespeare editor would be the first to attack the papers, and most of all, the *Lear* and *Hamlet* manuscripts. These manuscripts seemed to demonstrate that Shakespeare's plays had been cut, altered, mutilated, and debased by printers' errors and squabbles. If true, then all the Shakespeare editors would be forced to acknowledge that Shakespeare never wrote many of the passages they had poured so much "sweat, and ink . . . in explaining. . . ."[33]

The two most respected Shakespeare editors of their day were Steevens and Malone. And it was naturally expected that one or both would soon inspect the papers. Grebanier goes so far as to say that "Most people were suspending opinion [on the papers] until Malone should be heard. . . ."[34] Indeed, Malone's credentials were impressive.

After a successful law career, Malone had retired in 1777 to devote his life to literature. He had written a scholarly study of the chronology of the plays; he had exposed the brilliant forger Chatterton; he had edited the apocryphal plays, judging and accepting their categorization, with the exception of *Pericles;* he had written a detailed study of the English stage; he had studied the dispute concerning the authorship of the *Henry VI* cycle; he had restored *The Sonnets* to a legitimate part of a Shakespeare edition; he had combed laboriously through the legends surrounding

Shakespeare scholar Edmond Malone, portrait by Joshua Reynolds. Photo obtained from the Shakespeare Birthplace Trust.

Shakespeare's life in all its lurid aspects from deer poaching and hard drinking to sexual performance; and he had edited the plays. Indeed, his 1790 edition of Shakespeare is still thought of as a landmark in Shakespeare scholarship.[35] Moreover, he was well connected. Burke dedicated his *Reflections on the French Revolution* to him. Boswell dedicated his *Tour to the Hebrides* to him, and worked with him in writing *The Life of Samuel Johnson.*

Malone is often described as a sort of Shakespearean white knight; a champion of facts, chronology and collation. Yet Malone was far from perfect. Boswell describes Malone as "cordial and steady" but also "Tenacious . . . of his own opinions, which he had seldom hastily formed. . . ."[36] Walpole said that Malone had a habit of destroying his enemies with their "own artillery."[37] But he also had a habit of stealing his enemies' artillery. He had denigrated Capell's 1768 edition of Shakespeare and then stolen its best readings.[38] In 1783, he had squashed Ritson's attempts to edit Shakespeare and had again stolen his rival's best work.[39] Further, Malone's editorial principles were sometimes compromised by an ongoing struggle within the scholarly community over what authenticated authenticity. In 1773, he contributed introductory material to George Steevens's edition of Shakespeare—the very same George Steevens who had forged the Peele letter mentioning Shakespeare. One of his dearest friends was Bishop Percy, the forger. In 1793 he painted the funeral monument of Shakespeare "a good stone-colour," so as to make Shakespeare more classical in appearance.[40] The bust has since been restored, but Malone's damage to the monument tells us much about his personality. Malone wanted a classical author and he wasn't going to let a possible charge of public defacement of property get in his way. All in all, he was brilliant, obstinate, and ruthless.

Steevens's scholarly credentials were equally impressive and his personality equally self-willed. Steevens had been the first editor to fully understand the significance of the quarto editions of Shakespeare's plays and reprinted twenty quartos for general availability to the scholar. Samuel Johnson had given him his edition to improve and the Johnson, Steevens edition duly appeared in 1773, again in 1778, with additional notes by Isaac Reed in 1785 and 1793.

In character, Steevens, like Malone, was not a man one might wish as an adversary. As stated in my introduction, Steevens was an especially dangerous opponent to William-Henry, as Steevens was a forger in his own right. Grebanier described him as possessing "the most unfortunate inconsistencies of temperament."[41] Dr. Johnson said Steevens was "not malignant" but merely "mischievous"; Boswell called Steevens a man "of good principles but bad practice."[42] Others were less kind. Dr. Parr called him "one of the wisest, most learned, but spiteful of men."[43] Another called him a "*Compiler* of Scandal and defamation."[44]

Part of that inconsistency of temper led some to believe that Steevens had helped William-Henry Ireland forge the papers. Certainly the rumor hung over William-Henry during his lifetime. In the preface to his 1832 edition of *Vortigern,* he noted that "some persons have been led to imagine, and still conceive, that the late George Steevens was my secret abettor, and gave me assistance."[45] It does seem clear that Steevens helped substantiate the forgeries by forging an entrance of a play called *Vortiger* in Henslowe's diary.[46] However, I do not share Ganzel's view that Steevens might actually have forged the papers.[47] Steevens would certainly have done a better job. Moreover, Steevens obviously felt that Samuel Ireland was far beneath him in social standing. As he remarked snubbingly, "were He disposed to play such a trick it would not be in conjunction with Samuel Ireland."[48]

Certainly, in the public mind, Steevens, like Malone, was seen as an authority on Shakespeare documents, rather than a possible collaborator or mastermind of the forgeries. The *Gentleman's Magazine* published a letter from a K. S. who commented "The public would certainly have been gratified to know that these extraordinary Mss. have been deemed genuine by . . . Messr. Steevens or Malone."[49] The *True Briton* printed a letter by one William Homespun which read:

> I would wish to ask, and to have an answer, from one of the great critics and commentators of Shakespeare, all how and about them; or if this report be a humbug. . . .[50]

As it happened, neither scholar would personally inspect the papers but both would be instrumental in ruining the Ireland family. Less than one week after *Miscellaneous Papers* were published, Steevens was ready to attack the Shakspeare Papers. Farington noted that on 29 December 1795, George Steevens "came in. He brought in his pocket a manuscript play written by Middleton, to prove the difference of orthography when compared with Irelands [*sic*] imitations."[51] Malone was not far behind. Farington noted that on 20 January 1796, Malone had "completed his remarks of Irelands [*sic*] Manuscripts. . . ."[52] But Malone's book would not come out for another two months.

In the interim, instead of Steevens or Malone, the scholarly attack was launched by James Boaden, who had apparently been convinced by Steevens that the papers were fraudulent. Steevens himself never wrote about the papers but allowed his name to be used by Boaden. Others believe that it was Steevens who had used

Boaden. Mair, in his book *The Fourth Forger,* believes that the pamphlet entitled *A Letter to George Steevens, Esq* by James Boaden was actually a forgery of sorts. Mair believes that the bitterness and learning exhibited in the pamphlet points to Steevens being its author.[53]

Steevens was, by temperament, against staging forgotten plays. When a theater tried to revive Congreve's *Way of the World,* he called the manager a "resurrection-man" whose "business is with bodies that should lie in their graves."[54] Certainly, William-Henry believed that Steevens was connected to this first scholarly attack. He describes Steevens as the instigator behind the work: "he [George Steevens] did not boldly enter the lists; but, like a mole, worked in secret; and, when occasion served, stung with the subtlety of a viper."[55]

Boaden's *A Letter to George Steevens* was indeed stinging. The dedicatory poem demands the forger be punished with "deserv'd contempt" which "the vengeful muse shall pour / On that bold man, who durst thy [Shakespeare's] works profane, / And thy chaste page pollute with mongrel strain."[56] But it is also an honest account as to how visitors were so easily fooled by the Shakspeare Papers.

Boaden freely accepts that "credulity is no disgrace" and that he was "eager to believe" that the papers were genuine.[57] He "beheld the papers with the tremor of the purest delight- touched the invaluable relics with reverential respect, and deemed even existence dearer, as it gave me so refined a satisfaction." He had been "disarmed of caution by the character too of the gentleman [Samuel] who displayed them" and "the matter [that was so] diligently applauded." When examining the papers, Boaden was fooled by their technical details: "They bore the character of the poet's writing- the paper appeared of sufficient age- the watermarks were earnestly displayed. . . ."[58]

But once the papers were published, Boaden could study them in private and at his leisure. The more he thought about them, the more they filled him with doubts:

> [Examining] those facts [presented in the papers] scrupulously by the light of history; and applying to things the rule of chronology, and to persons the record of biography. I found myself . . . at war with known events. . . . all of the facts I had relied on as true, was of necessity to be sacrificed to the new creed of recent discoveries.[59]

Boaden does not bother himself about the mysterious Mr. H., since the papers would then in part be judged by a character reference.[60] His judgment has come from "*internal* evidence alone"—though he does note that it is very suspicious that the man we are to believe saved Shakespeare's life two centuries before, had the same name as the discoverer of the papers.[61]

BOADEN'S NEW ARGUMENT

His criticisms are logical and irrefutable. As to the note from Elizabeth to Shakespeare, which mentions Leicester, Boaden simply says that Leicester died in 1588, far before Shakespeare had proven himself a successful actor, much less a skilled poet and a prized dramatist.[62] The love letter to Anne Hathaway has "nothing of the character of our prose in that period of our literature. . . ." Shakespeare's letter to Southampton is addressed to "Hys Grace"—which is an improper way to address a lord.[63] The Deed of Gift states that *King John, Henry IV* and *Henry V* are not in print. Yet the letter is dated October 1604, by which time all these works had been printed in quarto. Even more startling, *King Lear* is also mentioned, but by October 1604, this play has yet to be written.[64] As to the *Hamblette* fragment, Boaden notes that the changes,

> dilute [the] . . . sense with unmeaning expletives and impede the fluency of his [Shakespeare's] versification. The orthography in the monosyllables is remarkably absurd;- but compared with LEAR, Hamblet is purity.[65]

It is in his examination of the *King Lear* manuscript that Boaden is most effective. He points out that the manuscript does not follow either folio or quarto but a curious mix of quarto and second folio. The aim was not a full text, as many quarto passages are missing.[66] He also notes many small passages that either appear or disappear, depending on which copy text the forger was using. Boaden's conclusion is that the quarto was used "with so determined a preference . . . that . . . [it] preserves its readings to the absolute injury of the sense of the passages."[67]

He examines the spelling, noting that it is at "defiance [with] the spelling of all periods, and bring[s] to the recollection the only typographic parallel in the forgeries of Chatterton. . . ."[68] He shows eleven instances where the manuscript does not correspond to the spelling in either the folio or quarto texts of *King Lear*. But rather than this showing the uniqueness of Shakespeare's own hand, the bizarre, neo-ancient spellings, which Boaden refers to as "vicious and fantastic orthography,"[69] can only cast suspicion on their authenticity:

Ireland Manuscript Spelling	Quarto-Folio Spelling
Innefyrmytyes	Infirmities
Unnefreynnedidde	Unfriended
adoppetedde	adopted
dyshonnorredde	dishonoured
unnepryzedde	unpriz'd
Burregannedye	Burgundy
scannetedde	scanted
slennederrelye	slenderly
dymennesyonnes	dimensions
perrepennedycularelye	perpendicularly
helas	alas.[70]

Boaden also makes a study of the forger's versification. His results are not flattering: "His [the forger's] *Lear* contains no three consecutive lines, that possess any metrical exactness. . . ."[71] Sometimes meter is ignored completely and the passage is rewritten in prose. Summing up his study of the spelling and grammar in this bogus manuscript of *King Lear,* Boaden writes, "it is impossible that either Shakspeare should write this, or any human being comprehend it. . . ."[72]

However, the main problem for Boaden is the forger's propensity to augment his selection of readings with both shortened and expanded versions, which was a "source of astonishment and laughter."[73] For instance, where Shakespeare has written "We make guilty of our disasters *the sun, / The moon, the stars,* as if we were villains / On necessity," the manuscript reads "Wee make guiltye of oure dysasterres / Vyllaynes bye niscessytye fooles bye compulsyonne. . . ."[74] Another paraphrase occurs on Edgar's lines "Poor Turlygood, poor Tom! / That's something yet- Edgar I nothing am." The manuscript has "Poore Tom, poore Edgarre. / Thatte innedeede is somethynge. I amme nothynge."[75]

Boaden also notes several contractions, that lead to "almost impossible errors": one of which occurs when Edgar says "Keep Thy word justly; swear not; commit not with man's sworne spouse." The forger has written, "Keepe thye worde ande whore with man's sworne spouse."[76] Another contraction which he cites is the folio and quarto reading:

> Such smiling rogues
> Like rats, oft bite the holy cords in twain
> Which are too intrinse t'unloose: smooth every passion
> That in the natures of their lords rebels . . .

which he compares with the manuscript reading of "Like ratts nibble those cordes inne twaine, / Which are toe intrenche ande loosen everye smooth passyon."[77]

I have already quoted William-Henry's new, expanded ending when discussing his official story. Boaden is quick to point out another addition. Whereas Shakespeare has written, "What is't thou say'st-Her voice was ever soft, / Gentle and low; an excellent thing in woman," William-Henry rewrites and extends the passage to read:

> Whatte ist thou sayst herre Voyce was everre softe
> And lowe *sweete musyck oere the ryplynge streame*
> Qualytye rare ande excellente inne womanne
> *O Yesse bye heavennes twas I kyll'd the slave*
> *Thatte dydde rounde thye softe necke the murderous*
> *Ande damnede Corde entwine.*[78]

Other changes and additions seem rather pointless. William-Henry's version, as Boaden points out, makes reference to Goneril beating her dog.[79] Lear has not a hundred but four hundred knights. Yet other changes are puritan, cleaning up all salacious references. Where Shakespeare wrote, "leave thy drink and thy whore," William-Henry writes, "leave thy drinke and thy hope."[80] Edgar does not have "presented nakedness" but "*A-dam-like* nakedness."[81] Still other passages are purely nonsensical. In one passage, we are asked to believe Shakespeare wrote, "Whenne wee are borne we crye that wee are comme / To thys sayde stage thys sayde *shyppe o fooles.*"[82]

Of course Samuel's explanation is that all these manuscript readings are correct, and that all the folio and quarto readings are the interpolations of actors. Boaden argues that this statement is "miserably fallacious" as:

It at once converted the PLAYERS into the most elaborate and polished masters of versification, and SHAKSPEARE into a writer without the necessary ear for rhythm- a man . . . not being able to number ten syllables upon his fingers.[83]

Besides, writes Boaden, what could even the most skilful actor do with lines that were unintelligible "to the shrewdest philologist[?]"[84]

Boaden's sarcasm is palpable as he rails against the long-supposed poor printings of Shakespeare's plays:

> Let us hear no more of the carelessness of HEMINGE and CONDELL!- They were compared with the poet himself, the correctest writers, the most judicious critics, the most elegant of poets. For one absurdity in their copy he has left an hundred in his MSS. and if we regard versification as a merit, it must be severed from this spontaneous writer.[85]

ATTACKING BOADEN AND DEFENDING THE PAPERS

Boaden's book was an impressive, highly disseminated attack that went through two editions.[86] George Steevens told Boaden— on what might have been his own work—"Sir, you have very fairly gibbeted the culprit, and Mr. Malone will take him down and dissect him."[87] But the Believers were not waiting for Malone, nor had they seen Boaden's criticism as scholarship. Rather, they saw it as a challenge. The gauntlet had been thrown down. It was soon to be picked up. James Boaden's pamphlet was answered in a matter of days by Francis Webb, who, writing under the pen name Philalethes, issued *Shakespere's Manuscripts Examined*. Webb's argument was the same as Boaden's original position, the papers were real because they looked too good to be anything else.

Despite the fact that Webb had no background in forgery nor in paleography to answer any of Boaden's clear, logical judgments, he stated:

> I am as fully satisfied and believe, that no human wisdom, cunning, art or deceit, if they could be united, are equal to the task of such an imposture.[88]

Webb was soon assisted by another Believer, John Wyatt, who attacked Boaden, not as an intellectual, but as a traitor and turncoat. His *A Comparative Review of the Opinions of Mr. James Boaden (Editor of the Oracle) in February, March and April, 1795*, written under the pen name "*By a Friend to Consistency*" was devastatingly simple. Wyatt merely quoted from Boaden the Believer and turned his own words on Boaden the Doubter. Apparently, Wyatt did not allow for the possibility that a man could change his mind.[89]

Wyatt was defending the papers by taking the offensive, by discrediting the opposition. It was an indication of how weak the Believers' critical position really was. When Wyatt turned from attacking Boaden to defending the papers themselves, his arguments were, at best, threadbare. The thrust of his defense was that the forgeries were so outrageous they had to be real:

Would a forger incumber himself with unnecessary letters after the *fatal model* of Chatterton?- Would he not rather have studiously avoided the rock on which that youth split? Would he not follow the *orthography* as carefully as he must have done the *character* of the MSS. of that age?[90]

Wyatt's pamphlet hardly proved that the papers were by Shakespeare. Perhaps the intended effect was to silence Boaden. If anything, Wyatt's attack had the opposite effect. There is no doubt that the sheer malevolence of Wyatt's attack contributed in large measure to what William-Henry described as Boaden's "implacable hatred, and unremitting vindictiveness."[91]

Boaden's further attacks would come through a different medium. In the interim, other critics rushed to the attack. Boaden (or possibly Steevens) had done his best to expose the weaknesses of the papers. Now word came that the great Malone was about to issue his own report on the matter.

Malone realized that his judgment would weigh heavily with the public and was aware that the Irelands might try to manipulate his visit for their own ends. He would not just glance at the papers and give his opinion, as Boswell had done. If he did not at once give sufficient evidence that the papers were a forgery, the Irelands might well claim his silence to be a tacit endorsement:

I very early resolved . . . not to inspect them [the papers] at the house of the possessor [Samuel Ireland's], and I was glad to find that my friends Dr.Farmer, and Mr. Stevens [*sic*] had made the same determination; from an apprehension that the names of persons, who might be supposed more than ordinarily conversant with the subject of these MSS might give a countenance to them, to which from the secrecy that was observed relative to their discovery, they were not intitled [*sic*].[92]

Therefore, he first tried to see the papers on neutral ground and in secret. He contacted Thomas Caldecott. Through a Mr. Humphrey, Malone asked if it could be arranged for him to inspect the papers at Caldecott's house. Caldecott refused.[93] Three days later, Malone then tried John Byng, another supporter. He told Byng that the inspection would be a brief one. Malone owned a signature of Southampton's. Matching up his signature with the newly discovered paper would soon settle matters. Byng passed along the message. Samuel refused.[94] But on 24 December 1795, Samuel published *Miscellaneous Papers*. Of course in the judgment of paper and ink, a reprint of the forgeries was of no use. But it did give Malone his first opportunity to study the handwriting, spelling, word selection, and historical accuracy of the papers. Malone set to work.

Samuel was not waiting for Malone's scholarly bombs to drop on him. He tried a preemptive strike by enlisting the early supporter, Dr. Parr. Parr refused. The problem of defending the papers, the full manuscript of *King Lear,* the fragment of *Hamlet* and, most controversial of all, the newly discovered play, *Vortigern,* next fell to Wally Chamberlain Oulton, a dramatist and theatrical historian.[95] His contribution was *Vortigern Under Consideration*. His defense was facile in the extreme:

> I think it . . . impossible that any man, however ingenious and accustomed to art, could ever have completed so laborious an undertaking; for the uniformity of the hand-writing is throughout so apparent, that the autography must evidently have been the work of *one person only.*[96]

This statement does not make sense. The very fact that all the papers had a tendency toward uniformity in the handwriting is in itself proof that all the papers were done over a short span of time, not over a matter of years, as everyone's handwriting changes with age.

GUTTER JOURNALISM: DIRTY TRICKS TO UNDERMINE THE SHAKSPEARE PAPERS

Pamphlet wars are limited in scope. They are read only by those specialized enough to be aware of the controversy. A general reader may not have the inclination to read about such scholarly matters. In other words, despite the often offensive remarks found within these pamphlets, as a medium it caters to a select, informed readership. However, the controversy surrounding the Shakspeare Papers had not been confined to the pamphlets. There had been newspaper coverage as well. James Boaden, who had started the pamphlet war, also opened a new front when, in the January issue of *Monthly Mirror* (1796), he wrote, "THE WHOLE IS A GROSS AND IMPUDENT IMPOSITION, AN INSULT TO THE CHARACTER OF OUR IMMORTAL BARD, AND A LIBEL ON THE TASTE AND UNDERSTANDING OF THE NATION."[97] The 17 January issue of the *Telegraph* went even further, suggesting the case ought to be turned over to the "Society for the protection of the public against swindlers and sharpers."[98] But as the controversy dragged on, it was the Irelands who needed protection, as the newspapers struck low blow after low blow. Gutter journalism had entered the scholarly debate. The controversy quickly turned from fight to farce.

In this too, James Boaden was part of the offensive, with a parody of the forgeries, claiming on 24 December 1795 to have received a letter from the spirit of Shakespeare to be delivered to Samuel Ireland. It read:

(3) CUNUNDRUMS! LOVE LETTERS! PROFESSIONS *de foi!*
And Straggling INDENTURES in form de *la Loi;*
A copy corrected of Britain's old LEAR,
(4) (Where with pleasure I see nothing ribald appear).
Add to these many sports of the sons of the STAGE,
And the favorite works in retirement of AGE,
On which my weak brain you affirm set more (5) store
Than all it had ever engendered before.[99]

Such sarcastic attacks were not new. On 21 July 1795, the *Morning Herald* commented on the Deed of Gift, wherein it was reported that Shakespeare had been saved from drowning. It remarked dryly:

The *swimming* reasons given in a paper yesterday in favor of the authenticity of certain *musty manuscripts,* shew to what Dangers we may expose ourselves, by wading too far in pursuit of an *object.*[100]

The newspaper then descended further from sarcasm to outright parody. It published a letter by an "S. England"—an obvious variation on S. Ireland—to the effect that Mr. S. England had a friend that had recently discovered a lost work by Sophocles in an old trunk. However, when the piece was translated, it turned out to be the English nursery rhyme "Three Children Sliding on the

Ice."[101] On 14 January 1796, the *Telegraph* printed newly discovered documents of its own, parodying the orthography and faulty dating of the Shakspeare Papers:

> Tooo Missterree Beenjaammiinnee Joohnnssonn
> DEEREE SIRREE,
> Wille youe doee meee theee favvourree too dinnee wythee meee onn Friddaye nexte, attt twoo off theee clockee, too eatee sommee muttonne choppes andd somme poottaattoooeesse
> I amm, deerree Sirree,
Yourre goodde friendde,
WILLIAMME SHAEKSPERE.
> Gloobbe, Blackke Friarres,
>   Jannuarrie 27, 1658.[102]

Note the date of the letter: Shakespeare died in 1616. One month later *Gentleman's Magazine* printed a letter from Anne Hathaway, imploring "Edmonne [Malone's] . . . worrethyerre defcerrenyenges inne thys matterre."[103]

Samuel later tried to limit these defamatory attacks by claiming that the "infinite variety of the papers" made the suspicion of forgery impossible.[104] Samuel's defense was as shaky as Webb's and Wyatt's: the fact that a massive forgery was being perpetuated is only proof of what Mason later called the forger's "four fold impudence," not the papers' authenticity. Indeed, the "infinite variety" of the Shakspeare Papers was in itself a target for derision. In the 17 February 1795 issue of the *Morning Herald,* the paper's editor, Henry Bate Dudley, wrote:

> The SHAKSPEARE *discoveries,* said to have been made by the son of MR. IRELAND of Norfolk-street, are the Tragedy of LEAR, and another entitled VORTIGERN and ROWENA, now first brought to light, both in the bard's own hand-writing: -in the same chest are said to have been also found, an antique MELANGE *of love-letters!-professions of faith!-billets-doux!- locks of hair!-and family receipts!-* The only danger, respecting *faith in the discovery,* seems to be from the indiscretion of *finding too much!*[105]

By 19 February the *Morning Herald* was no longer waiting for the Irelands to tell them what was in the trunk. The staff began inventing assortments of their own! The most outrageous of their announcements concerned Shakespeare's cookbook, with its much used recipe for a "GOODLIE PLUMBE PUDINGE."[106]

WRITERS FORGE THE SHAKESPEARE FORGERY!

Dudley apparently found that he had whet the public's appetite for insidious attack. Had he been a gentleman, he might have let the qualified scholars settle the matter. Instead, he pandered lies and slanders against the papers and in particular, against *Vortigern.* In 1795 he began a serial appearing in the *Morning Herald,* called "The Mock Trial of *Vortigern and Rowena.*" It was a devastating attack on a play he had not even read. And like the play itself, it suffered delays. The first entry, on 23 March 1795, apologized for the delay in "opening the Literary Court of Inquest, to try whether this DRAMA is or is not written by SHAKESPEARE," due to an unpleasant accident; "*Signor* DELPINI that man of *mighty mouth,* who was to have walked as *Champion* to a PRODIGIOUS COURT-IER, unfortunately dislocated his *jaw-bone* in practising an *Aristocratic Grin. . . .*"[107] To counteract this deficiency, Dudley simply invented his own passages from the play and then scorned them as unentertaining. Paradoxically, these slanders were so popular among his readers that Dudley eventually expanded his attacks into a book that went through several editions.

Dudley was not alone in faking passages from *Vortigern.* As with the pamphlets and the satiric journalism, here too James Boaden entered the fray. Boaden was a dramatist in his own right. He had written a play called *Fountainville.* Now he would turn his attack from the scholarly to the literary. He would show the public that any trained writer could write a passable Shakespearean play. His passages were, therefore, written not for egotistical reasons, but to demonstrate, attempts to

imitate the inimitable, because, if the play of VORTIGERN, announced for representation, should, in a trifling degree resemble the great Poet, such partial resemblance may be here shewn not to be decisive of the question of ORIGINALITY.[108]

However, he did not say that his play bore no resemblance to the Irelands' *Vortigern.* Instead, he stated that no printed extracts from the Irelands' *Vortigern* yet existed and that these extracts were "transmitted us by a learned friend." His ambiguity worked to his advantage. Boaden at once referred to the Mr. H. controversy, by saying that the papers came from some unknown source. He also inferred that these extracts corresponded to the real *Vortigern;* that this was somehow a bad quarto, a memorial reconstruction of the actual text. This was believable enough. Boaden, as a former supporter, had seen and doubtless read bits of the play.

Vortigern had not been printed in *Miscellaneous Papers* because it was being fitted for representation. If a patron had bought a copy of Samuel's book and disliked *Vortigern,* then he might not spend even more money on a theater ticket to see the play. Samuel needed a drawing card. He wanted to maintain an element of mystery to ensure *Vortigern*'s box-office success. Boaden's extracts changed all that by giving the public what it thought were bits of the play. Indeed, when Samuel complained that Boaden was not reprinting the real *Vortigern,* Boaden challenged any but the commentators' right to authenticate a text:

> Ours is the sole copy which will have the Commentaries [of] Messrs. STEEVENS, MALONE, and RITSON-consequently the only Edition of any *authority*.[109]

But to give Boaden his due, he wrote the outline and finished passages of a very good play. Indeed, his passages prove that had he been tempted to the forgeries, he might have made a better play than William-Henry's. In Boaden's version, *Vortigern*'s opening speech contains echoes of *Macbeth:*

> It cannot faile- I left them flush'd with wine;
> My well-feign'd wronges, and bounteous largesses,
> Have work'd me to their heartes, and not a PICT
> But thirsts to plunge a dagger in his bloode.
> Yet, should they chill their purpose and reveal me,
> Such is my summe of influence and wealthe,
> I well might brave avowel. CONSTANS sleeps.
> SECURITY seems guardian of his pillow,
> But DANGER hides his poinarde in the downe.
> What means this tremoure?- O, thou murderous thoughte,
> Hast thou more mightye influence than thy acte?
> The deed's not done. . . .[110]

Boaden's attack was joined by the anonymous *Precious Relics; or the Tragedy of Vortigern Rehearsed,* which spoofed both the play and its supporters.[111] At one rehearsal "Sir Mark" and "Dupe" listen and then comment as an actor playing the part of "Vortimer" recite the following lines:

> Out—out—vain folly!
> Love is an idle fancy—a mere toy,

To win and please an hour before the marriage,
And then to charm no more! A theme fit for a novel,
Full of darts and Cupids, swelling out the volume!
Sir Mark. Egad, that is Shakespear's style.
Dupe. No one can doubt it.[112]

Francis Waldron's *Free Reflections on Miscellaneous Papers* contributed another false play, and G. M. Woodward's *Familiar Verses from the Ghost of Willy Shakespeare to Sammy Ireland* added yet another account of the rehearsals. Waldron, who was a Massinger scholar, had written a sequel to *The Tempest* but could not find a company that would stage it.[113] Now, under the guise of attacking the forgeries, Waldron released his own play, not only exhibiting that it was easy to write like Shakespeare, but that he was better at it than the Irelands! G. M. Woodward's *Familiar Verses from the Ghost of Willy Shakespeare to Sammy Ireland* was less self-serving and far more interesting. Through Woodward's muse, Shakespeare himself was allowed to attack Ireland for the forgery and Kemble for agreeing to play in it.[114] Obviously, Woodward had no idea of Kemble's own machinations. However, Shakespeare's ghost also attacks Kemble for the adapted versions of his plays, which he refers to as cut, "press'd down, and . . . puff'd to air; / That I make oath, and swear it on the spot,/ I know not what is mine, nor what is not."[115] Samuel was attacked in a number of ways: by pamphlets, newspapers, letters; and in various places: at the negotiation table, behind the stage, even from beyond the grave. But the night of the play would prove to be the unkindest cut of all.

9

Prologue to Tragedy

THERE was a very good reason Samuel wanted *Vortigern* performed on or before 15 December 1795: *Miscellaneous Papers* came out the same month on the twenty-fourth. The play was supposed to be judged before the papers by the public at large. James Boaden was aware of the initial strategy. Had *Vortigern* and *Henry II* been presented before Samuel issued *Miscellaneous Papers*

> discovery would have been averted or delayed. The plays, under the notion of curtailment (always necessary to Shakspeare it seems), might have been purified sufficiently for success; our enthusiasm would soon have heightened to the *wonderful* any tolerable passages they might contain; and, at the PRESENT HOUR, some people might have thought it possible for Shakspeare to have written Vortigern![1]

Who knows? Judged as a whole, William-Henry's *Vortigern* might have succeeded. Had the documents been published soon after or coincident with the representation of *Vortigern,* doubtless the reaction would have been similar: some would have believed, some would have not. But it might take weeks, even months, for any of the sceptics to publish their material. In the interim their very silence might be used as proof of the papers' validity. *Vortigern* might have been produced without a major scholar publicly denying its authenticity. In 1795, only Boaden's *A Letter to George Steevens* could be evidenced against the papers. But Boaden was hardly a Shakespeare scholar, and Steevens had not publicly replied.

But by 2 April 1796, *Miscellaneous Papers* had been out for months. Critics examined them and found flaws. Judged independently, the papers could only throw suspicion onto the play and it was well known that Malone was working on a book denouncing all the papers as forgeries.

Vortigern was supposed to be the icing on the cake. It was not, but the reason was not entirely due to the scholarship of Malone.

166

The public had tired of experts supporting, experts promising to denounce. Shakespeare was the public's author. He belonged to the playhouses, playhouses that relied on their audiences. In the end, the final verdict remained with them. As the *Telegraph* noted:

> *Vortigern*, a play is announced for performance; and it is to be left to the audience to determine the species- whether *tragedy, comedy,* or a *mere farce!*[2]

The supporter Oulton agreed:

> Let Vortigern be tried by a JURY of *Boxes, Pitt,* and *Galleries;* the verdict of "Genuine" or "Not Genuine" belongs to THEM only; and it is impossible to judge of a Play before representation. . . . JOHN BULL is no *Calf* to be led by every *Ass.* He had rather . . . that VORTIGERN and the Play succeeding may be the genuine Works of SHAKSPEARE; that the Stage, too long disgraced with pantomimes in prose and metre, may resume its wonted dignity. . . .[3]

The evening was to be many things, dignified was not one of them. For the audience did not come to praise *Vortigern*, but to bury it. As one commentator later put it, the play was "announced for general condemnation."[4]

BELIEVERS AND UNBELIEVERS RECRUIT SUPPORTERS

Samuel knew he had enemies. The night before the premiere, he received a note informing him that "a Party intends being present at the performance of Vortigern . . . for the express purpose of interrupting the representation."[5] This information could hardly have surprised Samuel. Years later, he recalled that as the production date loomed, "Every undue stratagem, and every mean and petty artifice, was resorted to within doors and without, to prejudice the public mind. . . ."[6] Samuel feared disaster and enlisted mighty men whom he regarded as supporters to "vindicate" what he called "this great literary treasure."[7] Months before, Samuel had shown the papers to the prince of Wales. He had been a lukewarm supporter of Samuel's claims, but still Samuel begged his assistance. He had shown the papers to the prince of Wales on 28 December 1795. On 22 March 1796, Samuel wrote to the prince informing him that he had:

> reason to believe a very great Combination is formed with a view to damn the play of Vortigern unheard. Thus injuriously treated, Mr Ire-

land feels it a duty he owes to the great literary treasure in his possession, to obtain such a degree of patronage as may counteract the plot
of his Enemies.[8]

The prince declined.[9] But the duke of Clarence, who had also
seen the papers, attended on the insistence of his mistress, Mrs.
Jordan, who was taking part in the play.[10] Of course, royalty made
no difference. The public had a long tradition of damning new
plays. Unless it could be proven as Shakespeare's, the play was
fair game. The two authorities who could validate its legitimacy,
Malone and Steevens, had not done so. The very silence that
might have worked for *Vortigern* in December 1795, now worked
against it.

MALONE PREPARES TO STRIKE

But Malone had been making noises that his silence was about to
end. As long ago as 1 April 1795, Malone had called the Shakspeare
Papers a "very thin Forgery."[11] In February 1796, Malone had
stated that his *Inquiry* was now in press and would be ready by or
about the eighth or tenth of March.[12] The public was told to prepare
for a critical "sledge hammer."[13] But March passed without the
book's release, though Malone had begun speaking publicly about
its content:

> For some weeks previous to the performance of the play of Vortigern,
> Mr. Malone had daily given intimation that his *Inquiry* into the validity
> of the Papers attributed to Shakspeare was on the eve of publication.[14]

According to Mair at least, Malone's study "swelled into a
lengthy book with an ever receding date of publication."[15] If so, it
must be counted as sheer coincidence that Malone's *Inquiry* was
finally released only one day before the play's opening night. I find
such a coincidence hard to believe.

It seems clear to me that Malone was awaiting the performance
date of *Vortigern*.[16] His strategy seems to have been to release his
book just before *Vortigern*'s representation, to damn the play by
damning the papers it was built upon. Indeed, Malone's book was
not seen as an attack on the papers but a "treatise on the play of
Vortigern."[17] There is even evidence that he had been ready to
publish for months. He had told his friend Joseph Farington that
he was ready on 20 January 1796, two and a half months before

he finally released his study. But the play was delayed, and so too, apparently, was Malone's study. It seems very likely that Malone's delay was connected with *Vortigern*'s. His study, though not of the play, was written to put a stop to the forgeries, of which *Vortigern* was the crowning achievement. Now, on the eve of the play, all his work would go for naught.

For Malone had not been confident in his scholarship, or, at least, in its effect. He obviously feared that an academic work alone might not convince the layman that the papers were forgeries. If the papers were to be judged by the play, then it was vital that the play should fail. Sometime before 2 April 1796, Edmund Malone, scholar and lawyer, began his plans to wreck *Vortigern*.

KEMBLE IN LEAGUE WITH MALONE

Like most well-organized conspiracies, it was an inside job. Malone was in league with Kemble and others in the cast. And it was Kemble, as William-Henry noted, who was able "to strike a more deadly blow, as regarded the success of my play. . . ."[18]

By reputation and occupation, Kemble's power to endorse or destroy *Vortigern* was enormous. He was the leading Shakespeare actor of his day, and had been since his first appearance at Drury Lane in his much admired portrayal of Hamlet in 1783. Thirteen years later his reputation as Shakespeare's principal male star was undiminished. His sister was Sarah Siddons, reputedly the finest Shakespeare actress of her day. Both had agreed to take part in the play. In addition, Kemble was acting manager of Drury Lane and in "that capacity, [he] was of course empowered to direct his whole influence against the piece, of which he did not fail to take advantage. . . ."[19] For Kemble, "made up his mind early that all good tragedies which could be written had been written; and he resented any new attempt."[20] As one commentator later noted, "nothing short of downright MURDER would satiate Mr. Kemble's thirst of vengeance" on the play.[21]

Malone wrote neat books, full of facts. He was a scholar and stated his case logically and systematically. In the case of the Irelands, Malone could justly claim to have worn white gloves throughout the encounter. But that was only because he left the dirty work to others. Kemble acted as Malone's backstage henchman, threatening others to make them obey him. One of the first he threatened was Henry James Pye, poet laureate.

John Philip Kemble, as Hamlet. Photo obtained from the Shakespeare Birthplace Trust.

Sarah Siddons, as Lady Macbeth. Photo obtained from the Shakespeare Birthplace Trust.

Pye had read the play at Samuel's house on 28 December 1795 and had been impressed. He "thought it a very excellent play, and wished he could put his name to it as the author."[22] Pye was not an overly impressive playwright. Certainly he was not a great poet. Southey denigrated Pye's verses as dogged and dull. Walter Scott merited the man, but not his poetry. Pye, he wrote, "was eminently respectable in everything but his poetry."[23] To this unimpressive resume we may also note that he was a lousy scholar. Pye declared that:

> there were so many-passages in his [Shakespeare's] style and so much excellence that he could not think it the production of any other person- at the same time he declared that he had shed many tears and had been more affected than at the reading of any play for a long time.[24]

Samuel was delighted with Pye's response. As far back as 27 October 1795, Samuel had been wondering about an introductory address for the play.[25] Samuel asked the poet laureate to write the play's prologue. Pye was delighted, asked for cash, and agreed. The prologue was to declare the play Shakespeare's. And so it would have had not Kemble intervened. Kemble spoke to Pye and Pye listened. Later he would confess that he feared Kemble's displeasure. Pye was writing a play about Henry II and wanted it performed at Drury Lane. If Pye went against Kemble now, he could count on Kemble destroying his play as well. Pye was not so selfless as to put the concerns of Shakespeare before those of his own. If a play was to be damned, let it be Shakespeare's. Besides, many did believe that *Vortigern* was a fake.

On 23 January 1796, Pye delivered a prologue but one that had fallen from ringing endorsement to sceptical judgment.[26] Samuel was not pleased. Pye rewrote it but Samuel still found it unacceptable.[27] Pye, the poet laureate, was fired. To William-Henry, it must have come as a doubly bitter blow. Not only had the poet laureate written a poor prologue to his play, he had also stolen the subject matter of his newly announced play, *Henry II*![28]

REPLACING THE POET LAUREATE

The search for a new prologue went on. Samuel approached his friend Francis Webb. Webb was hardly a poet laureate but he was a supporter of the papers. Webb delivered his prologue on 29 January 1796.[29] However, parts of his prologue also questioned the play's authenticity:

> What Counterfeit dare make rash Essay,
> To imitate this Gem of matchless ray?
> Vain were th' attempt to rival Shakespeare's fame:
> Impious the fraud to arrogate his name.[30]

Webb's prologue was similarly rejected. No doubts were to be presented.[31]

Next, Samuel turned to Sir James Bland Burgess. Burgess, an amateur poet, was at the time working on a eighteen-book, Spenserian-verse poem concerning Richard I.[32] Burgess set aside his masterwork and began work on *Vortigern*'s prologue. Samuel accepted Burgess's prologue but cut six lines that called on the audience to judge the play:

> If no effulgent spark of heavenly fire,
> No ray divine the languid scene inspire;
> If no internal proofs denote its worth,
> And trace from Avon's banks its happier birth,
> With just disdain the dull attempt discard,
> And vindicate the glory of your Bard.[33]

Samuel was not seeking judgment but veneration. Equally, Kemble was not seeking judgment but the play's damnation.[34] Pye had been taken care of, but Kemble was not stopping at that. There was more mischief to be done. He was, after all, in charge of the play's rehearsals.

MISCASTING *VORTIGERN*

It is true that even the most successful plays in Kemble's repertoire had been staged with little rehearsal. The popular *Wheel of Fortune* had been staged after just nine, one hour rehearsals. Kemble's *Measure for Measure* had only two rehearsals.[35] Still, no matter how little rehearsal time Kemble's cast generally needed, rehearsals for *Vortigern* were not constructive, rather they were destructive. Kemble did not work alone. Many of his cast were willing to comply. As long ago as 24 September 1795, the *True Briton* had noted that "the *Players* speak unfavourably of the New Play . . . [though] not one of the Players has yet seen a line of *Vortigern and Rowena*.[36]

Like the negotiations, the rehearsals were to be plagued with disagreements and delays. They began well enough. On 4 January 1796, a scribe began copying out the various parts.[37] Meanwhile,

Kemble actually allowed Samuel to cast the play himself. His selections were as follows:

Constantius	—Mr. Bensley or Mr. Aiehin
Vortigern	—Mr. Kemble
Aurelius	—Mr. Palmer
Uter	—Mr. Caulfield
Wortimer	—[left to Kemble's discretion]
Catagrinus	—[left to Kemble's discretion]
Pascentius	—Mr. C. Kemble
Hengist	—Mr. Barrymore
Horsus	—[left to Kemble's discretion]
Fool	—Mr. King or Mr. Bannister Junior
Edmunda	—Sarah Siddons
Flavis	—Mrs. Jordan
Rowena	—Mrs. Miller.[38]

On 11 January at twelve P.M., Samuel was allowed to share in the first read through. In fact, he was allowed to do the reading.[39] Less than a month later, the play was in daily rehearsal with a premiere planned for March.[40]

Things were going along well. Things would change. The first thing to change was the cast selection. Phillimore was selected by Kemble to play Horsus because he was totally unsuitable. Palmer had been given the role of Aurelius, but had apparently wounded his leg in rehearsal.[41] Palmer was replaced by Barrymore, which was fine, except that Hengist was now to be played by Benson, a stooge and relation of Kemble's. Dignum, another Kemble stooge, was brought in as one of the minor barons. Kemble was equally careful when selecting the two parts Samuel had left to his discretion. Kemble selected Whitfield, "a tolerable second-rate actor" to play Wortimer and Trueman, "a useful and respectable actor" to play Catagrinus.[42] But both acted incompetently.

Samuel Ireland's friend Byng attended one rehearsal and wrote of his disapproval of the casting. He suggested, "At all Events-Remove King from the Part of the Fool; Change Aiehin for Bensley. . . ."[43] No changes were made.

With Kemble firmly in charge, rehearsals were not going well. Actors began openly sneering at several passages of the play.[44] By 9 February there had been no technical rehearsals.[45] Sometime in mid-February rehearsals ground to a halt. Though the prompter,

Powell, assured Samuel on 20 February 1796, that the play was "intended to [be] performed immediately" the truth was that nothing had yet been done.[46] By 12 March 1796, Samuel was sarcastically questioning whether the play would ever be properly rehearsed:

> Sir
>   I requested the favour of you a few days since to inform me when there is a *probability of Vortigern* being represented and what is the Cause of the delay- I presume there has been no rehearsal or I should have been acquainted therewith- the favour of an answer is required-
> I am
>   Yours truly S.I.[47]

There was little Samuel could do. Three key members of his cast, including Kemble's sister, the great Sarah Siddons, had been mysteriously struck down. Their illness was so sudden and so severe, that the three actors actually had to be confined to their beds.[48] There they lay, crafty sick, the play on hold. Samuel would have to wait. He needed Siddons. She had been cast in the vital role of Edmunda. Her reputation alone added support to the play.

It is for this very reason that Kemble probably thought it best that she not perform. There was no doubt she was ready. She had been studying her lines for weeks.[49] But by 21 March 1796, Sarah Siddons had been replaced by Mrs. Powell. Samuel was not even consulted. He read about the casting change in a newspaper.[50]

The loss of Sarah Siddons was a perilous gash, a very limb lopp'd off. But in all probability, she had done Samuel a favor. Like her brother, Sarah Siddons was hardly a supporter of the play. In a letter to a confidant, Siddons noted that:

> All sensible persons are convinced that 'Vortigern' is a most audacious impostor [*sic*]. If he be not, I can only say that Shakspeare's writings are more unequal than those of any other man.[51]

Four days before the play's representation, Sarah Siddons finally sent Samuel official conformation:

> Mrs. Siddons complements Mr. Ireland. She finds that Vortigern is intended to be perform'd next Saturday, and begs to assure him that she is very Sorry the weak State of her health after almost Six weeks of Severe indisposition renders her incapable of even going to the necessary Rehearsals of the Play, much less to act.[52]

The text had to be altered to accommodate her departure. Her place was filled by Mrs. Powell. A song had been written especially for Siddons's part but Powell was not a great singer. Changes were made. The "verse was sung by Miss Leake (who performed the part of an attendant), at the request of her royal mistress."[53]

At least one Believer saw her abandonment of the play as an indication of the "*Conspiracy*." We have every reason to suppose him right. Indeed, hostility from some of the cast toward Samuel was so severe that he was warned not to "venture alone" to the rehearsals.[54]

Still Kemble was not content. As acting manager, he had a say in the scheduling of the play. He selected the date 1 April, commonly referred to as April Fool's Day. William-Henry notes that in this alone Kemble was "overruled, by the decided opposition of my father; although he found it necessary to interpose the authority of Mr. Sheridan for that purpose."[55] Is it significant that Samuel had to go to Sheridan for assistance? Does this imply that Sheridan was ignorant of Kemble's scheduling or that Sheridan was quite happy to have the play performed on 1 April? Certainly Sheridan himself was not perceived as a friend of the play. On 21 January 1796, the *Oracle* listed his name alongside Steevens, Malone, and others as sceptical of the play's legitimacy.[56] On 8 February 1796, Samuel wrote to Sheridan, concerned about this very rumor.[57] If Sheridan responded, it is unrecorded.

Kemble had still more malicious tricks up his sleeve. If he failed to organize the worst possible performance date for the play, he could at least affix a piece that might discolor *Vortigern*. Originally, *Vortigern* was to be accompanied by a "splendid new Pantomime" by Richard Cumberland.[58] However, the piece was soon discarded, probably once Samuel discovered that Cumberland was not among his supporters.[59] Still, Kemble knew of one entertainment that "might carry a sting in its tail. Mr. Kemble announced *My Grand-mother* for the farce, intending that all the bearings of that production should be applied by the audience to the subject of the Shaksperian papers."[60] The farce concerns a gullible art collector.

SUPPORT FOR THE SHAKSPEARE PAPERS BEGINS TO WANE

On 27 March 1796, Richard Valpy wrote to Samuel, informing him that he would not attend the performance, though he had secured "many promises of support" for the premiere. Continuing, he wrote, "I do not believe you will be ruined, yet I fear you may be strongly opposed. . . ."[61] Others were more realistic. Things were out of hand. As 2 April approached, even a supporter such as Francis Webb begged Samuel to call off the play. On 27 March he wrote to his old friend:

> Were I in your situation I would at once have an Interview with Sheridan talk freely, and suspend, or wholly withdraw the Play. . . .
>
> How is your *hidden* friend [Mr. H.] affected by all this[?] Will aught prevail on him to come forward in some shape or other to frustrate these bold and infamous designs? Here's the stop-here we hitch, and here we shall hang. Depend upon it. *Vortigern* will not go down.[62]

Samuel either did not listen or could no longer withdraw. Within days, the poster for *Vortigern* was released. Even in this Samuel was thwarted. The poster merely advertised a "play called *Vortigern*." Samuel had begged that they call it *Vortigern from an ancient Mss in the possession of Mr. Ireland signed and supposed to be written by William Shakspeare.*[63] But Kemble threatened to ruin the play if Shakespeare's name was associated with it.[64] Samuel complied. In the end, even Shakespeare's name deserted the play, from William-Henry's night to Edmond Malone's day.

10

Opening Night: The Play's the Thing. . . .

On the eve of the performance, the final attack began. Handbills were distributed at the several avenues leading to Drury Lane theater, which was to

> contain an affirmation, that Mr. Malone, in his work, would prove the whole to be a rank forgery; and that, consequently, he had issued the said paper in order to caution persons against the fraud, and leave them to judge of the play in its proper light.[1]

Malone was aware how effective a printed statement could be to an ignorant public. Four years before, a pamphlet attacking his 1790 edition had been released, and had done damage to his reputation, despite it being error-filled and falsely argued.[2] But the handbills carried by these theatergoers could not have been more deadly had they been plucked from the trees of Birnam Wood. New plays were regularly catcalled off stage. Indeed, as I explained previously, it was common to organize parties for just this purpose. To judge *Vortigern* in its proper light was to judge it as a new play, which was often not to judge it at all but to condemn it to death.

CROWDS AND RIOTS OUTSIDE AND IN THE THEATER

Samuel had prepared for such an eventuality and issued his own handbill as the crowd entered the theater:

> VORTIGERN.
>
> A *malevolent* and *impotent* attack on the SHAKSPEARE MSS. having appeared, on the *Eve* of representation of the Play of *Vortigern*, evidently intended to injure the interest of the Proprietor of the MSS., Mr. Ireland feels it impossible, within the short space of time that intervenes between the publishing and the representation, to produce an answer to the most illiberal and unfounded assertions in Mr. Ma-

VORGIGERN.

A *Malevolent* and *impotent* attack on the SHAKSPEARE MSS., having appeared, on the *Eve* of reprefentation of the Play of *Vortigern*, evidently intended to injure the intereft of the Proprietor of the MSS., Mr. Ireland feels it impoffible, within the fhort fpace of time that intervenes between the publifhing and the reprefentation, to produce an anfwer to the moft illiberal and unfounded affertions in Mr. Malone's enquiry. He is therefore induced to requeft that the Play of *Vortigern* may be heard with that *Candour* that has ever diftinguifhed a *Britifh Audience.*

*** *The Play is now at the Prefs, and will in a very few days be laid before the Public.*

Samuel Ireland's leaflet, distributed on *Vortigern*'s opening night. Reprinted with permission of The Folger Shakespeare Library.

lone's enquiry. He therefore is induced to request that the play of *Vortigern* may be heard with the *candour* that has ever distinguished a *British audience.*

It was exactly the wrong move. True, Malone could hardly damn a play he had yet to see or read. And, true, most of the theatergoers probably had not inspected the papers personally. And, true, most of theatergoers had not read Malone's book, which had only issued the day before. Still, the only effect Samuel's handbill had was to widen the distribution of Malone's message. Those who had not received a handbill outside were informed that the world's leading Shakespeare scholar was damning the play as a forgery. But then again, most of the audience did not care. They had not come to see a performance. They themselves were the performance. Again, as with any new play of the period, both sides had persuaded their friends to show up and voice their support. They were nothing if not enthusiastic.

The Times reported that:

In the annals of the Theatre, there never was such a crowd. . . . There were people enough who flocked for admission, to have filled the house twice over. Many persons were waiting at the doors, so early as three o'clock in the afternoon.[3]

The crowds were so intense that the doors had to be barricaded. When the theater was finally opened, the public found that the pit was already filled with supporters of both factions.[4] The *Telegraph* reported that the "house was the fullest ever known."[5] William-Henry reported that people "dropped down from the lower tier of boxes into the pit, in order to procure seats."[6] When Samuel appeared in his box, located in the center of the house, he was saluted by gentlemen in the pit. When the curtain went up, "a warm burst of applause broke from every part of the House. . . ."[7] Supporters were in evidence. Some were friends Samuel had invited months ago to "serve the Cause."[8] Others had begged Samuel for invitations as late as the night before.[9]

Samuel had prepared well. One supporter later noted that the "whole of the Boxes and Pitt were in favour of the Play."[10] But Samuel did have enemies. Perhaps Malone's faction had yet to arrive. Or if it had arrived, it was remaining silent.

By this time, William-Henry was afraid to be seen. He says:

> the box being so very conspicuous, I soon retired from observation behind the scenes; where I continued the greater part of the time of representation, engaged in conversation with Mrs. Jordan.[11]

Jordan was the duke of Clarence's mistress, and mother to ten of his children. She was also a fine actress, "singly capable of supporting the interests of a theatre."[12] She could not have spent all night talking to William-Henry. She was playing the part of Flavia in the play. She could, however, report to William-Henry between her scenes, inform him how the play was proceeding, or more importantly, how the audience was responding.

Conspiracy Among the Cast to Discredit the Play

William-Henry was not the only nervous one. The actors themselves felt as though they were being thrown to the lions. The play began at 6:35 P.M.[13] Whitfield stepped onto the stage:

No common cause your verdict now demands:
Before the court immortal Shakspeare stands;
That mighty master of the Human Soul,
Who rules the passions, and with strong control

Mrs. Jordan

From an Original Picture in the possession
of the Duke of Clarence.
In the Character of Euphrosyne in Comus.

Mrs. Jordan, played Flavia. Photo obtained from the Shakespeare Birthplace Trust.

> Through every turning of the changeful heart
> Directs his course sublime and leads his powerful art.[14]

However, he was filled with such trepidation that he could not get through the first six lines of the prologue without the assistance of the prompter.

> The Audience called upon him to read the Prologue, and upon his assuring them that his hesitation proceeded not from being imperfect, but from the flurry of his feelings in consequence of his reception, he was allowed to read it through. . . .

Yet even reading the lines, Whitfield's performance was described as "indifferently executed."[15] Another paper wrote, more candidly, that the prologue was "ill *read*."[16]

Despite this less than auspicious start, all apparently went well for the first two acts. William-Henry informs us that:

> at the commencement of the third act (at which period not a dissenting voice had been heard) [Mrs. Jordan] congratulated me on the success of the piece, and gave it as her opinion that it would succeed.

Nonetheless, William-Henry seems to have been filled with a dreadful foreboding. He replied to Mrs. Jordan, "notwithstanding appearances [which] were auspicious to the success of the play, I felt a full conviction that it would not be a second time represented."[17] He was right. This was to be *Vortigern*'s first and last performance. And, as he doubtless later found out, the first two acts had hardly been successful, not because of the text but because of the actors.

The entire cast cannot be charged with this crime. Certainly Mrs. Jordan did her best, as did Mrs. Powell and Miss Leake, to whom William-Henry extended his thanks in his *Confessions*.[18] Mrs Powell had tried especially hard. Her part had been extended with the loss of Sarah Siddons. It was the best and certainly the biggest part she ever had. Had *Vortigern* succeeded, it might have made her a star. He also thanked many of the male cast members who had done their best: Bensley, Barrymore, Caulfield and King.[19]

So the uprising in the cast was not a popular one. But limited as it was to only four members, the havoc they wrecked was overwhelming. As one reporter noted, "the gravity of one or two actors, while the rest were laughing round them, only added to the farce of the scene."[20] Phillimore, who played the minor part of Horsus,

the Saxon general, and Benson, Hengist, lurched across the stage
with the "lubberly auwkwardness" of "walking automatons."[21]

Charles Stuart, an MP and a staunch supporter of the play, arrived drunk.[22] As the performance progressed, he became so upset
by Phillimore's conduct that he made several attempts from his
box "to seize him [Phillimore] by the robe."[23] At other points in
the performance, he shouted out "Give the thing a fair trial."[24]
Stuart's heart was in the right place but it hardly helped matters.
Later, Phillimore literally helped to bring the curtain down on
Vortigern:

> on receiving . . . [his] deathly wound [in the play] . . . either from prior
> tuition or chance . . . so placed his unfortunate carcass that on the
> falling of the drop-curtain he was literally divided between the audience
> and his brethren of the sock and buskin; his legs, &c., being towards
> the spectators, and his head, &c., inside the curtain, which concealed
> them from observation. This, however, was not the only calamity: for
> as the wooden roller at the bottom of the curtain was rather ponderous,
> Mr. Phillimore groaned beneath the unwelcomed burden; and finding
> his brethren somewhat dilatory to extricating him, he adopted the more
> natural expedient of extricating himself; which, for a *dead man,* was
> something in the style of Mr. Bannister, jun., in the Critic, who tells
> Mr. Puff "that he cannot stay there *'dying'* all day."[25]

Clearly, Phillimore and Benson were treating *Vortigern* as if it
were a farce. They were joined by Mr. Dignum, whose acting was
defined by one reporter as "execrable" throughout.[26] Apparently
Dignum, who played the second baron, spoke throughout with a
"nasal and tin-kettle twang."[27] The house broke into laughter when
he cried out in his best alto, "let them bellow on!"[28] Even the
loyal "performers could not refrain from joining in. . . ."[29] It was
enough, remembers Boaden, to have "damaged Shakespeare
himself."[30]

KEMBLE'S PURPOSEFULLY POOR PERFORMANCE

But above all, William-Henry blamed Kemble for this theatrical
coup d'état. He was not alone. One audience member later recalled,
"I have scarcely ever observed a more glaring instance of clumsy
misrepresentation."[31] Certainly Kemble had some powerful, if
fairly unmetrical, lines to work with. One of his best speeches
comes in the very first scene. The king and his attendants have
left the stage. Vortigern ponders on the crown and murder:

> But soft! Now conscience, how is't with thee?
> Oh, wherefore, why, why dost thou pinch me thus?
> Did I but lend attention to thee
> Then must my work crumble and come to naught.
> Come then thou soft, thou double-faced deceit!
> Come direst flattery, come dire murder!
> You now must be the sole inhabitants
> Of this soft, and pelican-like bosom.
> Attend me quick, and prompt me to my work!
> What! Jointly wear the crown? No, I will all!
> And that my purpose may soon find its end,
> This, my good King, must I unmannerly
> Push from his seat and fill it mine own self.
> Welcome then glittering mark of royalty!
> And with thy ponderous and pleasing weight
> Bind fast this firm, this determined brow.
>
> (1.1.44–59)[32]

Another of the play's best moments is when Vortigern falls in love with Rowena. His sons threaten rebellion and Vortigern rages defiantly:

> Dare you then my power to account!
> Must I, a king, sit here to be unkinged
> And stoop the neck to bear my children's yoke?
> Begone I say, lest that my present wrath,
> Make me forget the place by blood I hold,
> And break the tie 'twixt father and his child.
>
> (4.6.39–46)

Unfortunately, the verse could hardly be heard over the commotion in the pit. An anti-*Vortigern* faction—later referred to as the "Malonites"—had been shouting "*Henry the Sixth!*"[33] Nor had they limited themselves to this activity. When someone in the boxes applauded the play, he was immediately pelted with oranges.[34] One would assume that Samuel's box must have looked like a fruit market.

But in a rare display of good sense, Samuel remained subdued. Early on in the evening, he had "occasionally clapped, but towards the end of the 4th. act He came into the front row, and for a little time leant his head on his arm, and then went out of the Box and behind the scenes."[35]

CONSPIRACY AMONG THE AUDIENCE TO DISCREDIT THE PLAY

But the Malonites did not need to hit Samuel Ireland to hurt, indeed kill, his play.

Apparently Kemble and Malone had set up a watchword with their large faction in the theater. For aside from shouting and pelting, the Malonites were also listening very carefully for their cue. They need not have. The *Observer* recorded that:

> Towards the end of the fourth act, Kemble addressed the audience, reminding them, that the Piece had very credible claims to authenticity, and that in order to judge, it was necessary they should hear.[36]

THE SIGNAL SET UP BY MALONE AND KEMBLE

But as fair-minded as this sounds, it seems that Kemble was simply stopping the play to make sure his faction was prepared. It was. It happened during the fifth act. Vortigern's kingdom is in tatters. The rebels are closing in and Vortigern, in despair, contemplates suicide:

> Time was, alas, I needed not this spur,
> But here's a goading, and a stinging thorn,
> That doth unstring my nerves. Oh, conscience, conscience!
> When thou didst cry I then did stop thy mouth
> And thrust upon thee dire ambition.
> Oh, I did then think myself indeed a god!
> But I was sore deceived, for as I passed
> And traversed in proud triumph the base court
> There I saw death clad in most hideous colours,
> A sight it was that did appal my soul,
> Yea, curdled thick this mass of blood within me.
> Full fifty breathless bodies struck my sight,
> And some with gaping mouths did seem to mock me
> Whilst others smiling in cold death itself,
> Scoffingly bad me look on that, which soon
> Would wrench from off my brow this sacred crown
> And make me too a subject like themselves.
> And to whom? To thee
> Who hast for thy domain this world immense.
> Church yards and charnel houses are thy haunts,

And hospitals thy sumptuous palaces,
And when thou wouldst be merry thou dost choose
The gaudy chamber of a dying king.
Oh, then thou dost ope wide thy bony jaws
And with rude laughter and fantastic tricks,
Thou clapst thy rattling fingers to thy sides. . . .

(5.2.35–61)

On Kemble's enunciation of "rattling fingers" some members of the audience began laughing "loud and long." This was a false start. The key phrase was the following line. William-Henry reported that with "the most sepulchral tone of voice possible" Kemble enunciated the line that destroyed *Vortigern,* "When this solemn mock'ry is ended" (5.2.62).[37]

This line set off a "discordant howl" which "echoed from the pit" and lasted ten minutes. When the audience finally calmed down, Kemble simply redelivered the very line, with an "even more solemn grimace. . . ." The play continued on to its conclusion, but never recovered. The supporters voiced their applause, Malone's group voiced their disapproval. The result of their conflicting uproar was that "not one syllable more of the play was rendered intelligible."[38]

The epilogue was "exquisitely delivered" by Mrs. Jordan.[39] She had taken it upon herself to cut any references in the epilogue to Shakespeare, and questions of authorship, but her speech did not meet with success.[40] Another actor, Barrymore, came forward to announce the play would again be performed on Monday.[41] The play had ended at ten o'clock but this announcement set off a "violent contest" that lasted a further "quarter of an hour."[42] Finally, Kemble came forward to announce a Monday night performance of Sheridan's *School for Scandal.* For his pains he was pelted with apple peelings.

SHERIDAN'S REACTION

Whether Sheridan was a supporter of the play or not, Kemble's actions must have upset him. It was common that such outbreaks led to riots wherein great damage might be caused to the theater. Aside from physical damage, there was the reputation of Drury Lane to consider. His theater was now a laughingstock. Shakespeare had been disgraced, either through the staging of a forgery ascribed to him or in the poor reactions of his actors and his audience. On top of it all, Sheridan had lost a potential box-office hit. Publicly at least, Sheridan showed his displeasure at Kemble's actions by issuing the following disclaimer:

> he [Sheridan] . . . had nothing to do with the private piques and animosities of Mr. Kemble, or whether he approved of the manuscripts or not: that he regarded that gentleman merely as a servant of the theatre; and that it was consequently his duty to have exerted himself to the utmost for the benefit of his employers.[43]

To this Kemble did not utter one word in reply.[44] Kemble did not care. He had done his job. This had not been the first time Kemble had ruined a show. Just weeks before, he had exhibited a similar malice toward Colman's *Iron Chest*. He coughed and plodded the production into purposeful ruin. Colman blamed Kemble and moved the play to The Haymarket Theatre where it became a stock piece.[45]

Kemble might have saved Shakespeare, but he paid a heavy price. His reputation within the theater, and with his audience, suffered. With the exception of Kemble, no actor partaking in the coup suffered reprimand. Despite being at the height of his powers, a mere four years later, Kemble left Drury Lane. His performance in *Vortigern* may not have been the cause, but it certainly had not enhanced his position. As for his fellow collaborators, life and the theater continued, though in the case of Benson, not for very much longer. On 20 May 1796, at about three A.M., he threw himself out of a garret window and dashed out his brains.[46]

For all their work and promise of riches, the Irelands derived little from their first and only royalty payment. The day after the play, father and son returned to Drury Lane for their money. After expenses, the theater had earned £205.6.6. As per their agreement, this sum was cut between the theater and the Irelands. Samuel was given £102.13.3.[47] Of this sum, he gave William-Henry £30.[48] Had the play been successful, they might have earned thousands.[49]

11

Aftermath: Confession and Disgrace

MALONE did not just hire his friends to hiss *Vortigern* into oblivion. He also wrote a book attacking the published Shakspeare Papers. James Boaden justly recognized that Malone's scholarly exposure of the Shakspeare Papers was "A TASK PERFORMED BY HIM WITH AN ANATOMICAL MINUTENESS, WHICH LEFT NOT THE SMALLEST NERVE OF THAT BODY OF FRAUD UNEXPOSED TO THE PUBLIC EYE."[1] There is no doubt that Malone's book, *An Inquiry into the Authenticity of Certain Miscellaneous Papers and Legal Instruments,* is an impressive and scholarly work, delivered with the vengence of the Furies.

Appropriately, the Irelands had no one to blame but themselves. Had they not published *Miscellaneous Papers*, Malone would have had no access to the text of the papers without visiting the house personally—something he refused to do. Now everyone could look at the papers for as long as they liked. The mystery was over. As one bookseller noted after the publication of *Miscellaneous Papers,* "what Ireland has published will cut off all hopes of his succeeding in the imposition."[2]

Vortigern was supposed to appear before the publication of the papers. Through the delays in rehearsal, this schedule was reversed. According to the contract with Samuel, the play was to have appeared on or before 15 December 1795, with the publication of the papers following three weeks later. But the play was delayed. It premiered on 2 April 1796, thirteen weeks after the publication of *Miscellaneous Papers.*

The publication of the papers and the play's delay gave the critics time to attack the papers and then use the discredited papers as ammunition against the play. Malone's study also used this technique, for it had originally been scheduled to come out before the play and it is for this reason that it makes no full attack on *Vortigern* itself. As Malone wrote, "any disquisition on this subject is, I conceive, wholly unnecessary; the outworks being all demolished, the fort must surrender of course."[3]

MALONE'S LITERARY ATTACK

Malone's demolition of the papers was achieved through an examination of five separate categories: forgeries derived from authentic documents, orthography, phraseology, dates given or deduced by inference, and dissimilitude of handwriting. I will not list any criticisms made previously by Boaden. Nor will a complete list be necessary to indicate how exhaustive Malone had been. As Malone himself admitted, "The badges of fiction [in the forgeries] are so numerous, that the only apprehension I entertain is, that you may be fatigued before I have done. . . ."[4]

In terms of the papers being derived from authentic documents, Malone noted that a passage in the Profession of Faith came from *The Merchant of Venice*,[5] and the rest was based on a similar document pertaining to John Shakespeare.[6] The letter from Elizabeth to Shakespeare seemed based on Congreve's reference to a lost letter from James I to Shakespeare.[7] The letter to Southampton anachronistically echoed a passage of Milton.[8] The self-portrait included in the letter to Cowley is clearly based on Droeshout's engraving, made seven years after Shakespeare's death.[9]

In terms of orthography, Malone notes that William-Henry uses spellings that had never existed in Elizabethan times, such as his spelling of Hampton as "Hamptowne," Leicester as "Leysterre," "Masterre" for the Elizabethan "maister," "Chamberlayne" for "Chamberlain," "youre" for "your," "goode" for "good," "off" for "of," "doe" for "do" and so on.[10] The forger has also misspelled the name of one of Shakespeare's closest associates, John Heminges, forgetting the "s." He has even misspelled his hometown, Stratford, spelling it "Statford."[11] "Themmselves" should be spelt as two words, not one,[12] the same argument is employed against the forger's use of the word "hymsselfe."[13]

In terms of phraseology and usage, Malone attacks a reference to Hampton Court and "Hamptowne," a "termination entirely repugnant to the genius and analogy of the English language,"[14] the misuse of "prettye,"[15] "Complemente"[16] and "amuse."[17] The money notes from Leicester use modern numeration. They should be in Roman numerals,[18] besides the actors shared the profits, as opposed to drawing a salary[19] and in the Deed of Trust, the money distributed should be for round amounts, not with odd change added.[20] John Lowin's name is misspelled "Lowine."[21] "William" is misspelled "Willam" twice in these papers.[22] The forger refers to "Dear" and "dearest" Anna, not the more common "sweet."[23]

He calls the crown a "gyldedde bawble." Malone doubts that bauble would have been used and besides, the crown was not gilded.[24] Manuscripts of this period use both sides of the page, the *King Lear* manuscript only uses one side.[25] It is odd, that Shakespeare, who never mentions his sources, on the title page to his "Lier" manuscript, mentions using Holinshed and asks forgiveness for occasionally diverting from the source. The new verses in the *Lear* "are not better than any school-boy who had ever composed a line of poetry could write. . . ."[26] On the subject of *King Lear,* Malone concludes that "Life is not long enough to be wasted in the examination of such trash. . . ."[27]

In terms of dates, he notes that Elizabeth's letter to Shakespeare "at the Globe by Thames" is dated September 1588, long before that building existed.[28] The name of Shakespeare's wife, Anne, is therein referred to as "Anna," a form sometimes found in poems but never in prose during this period.[29] The letter to Anne makes reference to a tall "Cedarre," a tree that did not yet exist in England.[30] It is odd that Shakespeare cannot remember the date when his friend William-Henry saved his life.[31] In this same document, written in October 1604, Shakespeare states that the previous month was August![32] The Deed of Gift is not signed by a scrivener, unheard of in a legal deed of this period.[33] In Shakspeare's letter to Cowley, the Bard gives his friend printing rights to *The Tempest, Macbeth,* and *Henry VIII,* should they "bee everre agayne impryntedd." But these plays were not printed until 1623.[34] The drawing of Shakespeare's house, included in the Cowley letter, shows an old-fashioned house with modern windows.[35]

In terms of dissimilitude of handwriting, Malone notes six errors in the forged hand of Queen Elizabeth: (1) the size of her signature, which seems to have grown larger as she aged; (2) the autograph inclines, the queen's was usually "bolt-upright"; (3) the queen has a flourish under her name that completes the bottom of the first "E" in her name, the forger leaves it incomplete; (4) the same is true of the "b"; (5) the letter "a" is too high; and (6) this same letter is too disjointed, appearing more like an "I."[36] Altogether, he sees the forgery of the queen's hand as a "miserable and imperfect" attempt,[37] a "manifest and bungling forgery."[38] In some other papers the forger is also faulted for his use of the Chancery hand "r" with secretary-hand.[39] Heminges's hand is so unsteady and irregular that Malone says that it is either the hand of "a drunkard or a madman."[40] As for Shakespeare being saved by William-Henry Ireland, it was unusual, even exceptional, for a man to have two Christian names.[41]

As for *Vortigern,* Malone would not condescend to consider its
merit. Mocking the Chattertonian spelling, Malone merely remarked that any disquisition on "KYNG VORRTYGERNE, and
all the KKINGES and all the QQUEENES which have been announced from the same quarter . . . is, I conceive, wholly
unnecessary. . . ."[42]

But the same might be said of Malone's study. Though the book
came out 1 April 1796, few must have had a chance to buy, or
having bought, read such a massive book. Nor was it likely to have
changed many hardened minds. One supporter wrote to Samuel
the night before the play, informing him that although he was only
"nearly half through" Malone's book, he thought it a "weak, futile
. . . illiberal Performance written by the Pen of an inferior Special Pleader."[43]

William-Henry thought the book came out after the play.[44] This
was not merely a mistake on William-Henry's part but an indication
of the book's relevance to the destruction of the play. *Vortigern*
failed because of the venomous conspiracy of Kemble and Malone.
Malone's book had only a minor effect. The failure of *Vortigern*
was a triumph of slander rather than scholarship. When Malone's
book came out, the day before the failure of the play, it was largely
irrelevant. By the time the public had read it, the play was dead,
and with it, the dream that the Shakspeare Papers might have
been real.

Samuel Ireland noted the irrelevance of a "volume long before
promised, and long since forgotten."[45] If the forgeries were to be
authenticated in part by their very bulk, then Malone's book was
to do the same by its thoroughness. As Samuel noted:

> They, who take up the book, not indeed from its bulk, but from the
> amplitude of its materials, are disposed to feel a prepossession in its
> favour; for where much labour has been obviously bestowed, some
> learning is necessarily inferred. Thus the greater part of its readers are
> stupified into assent, and are perplexed into acquiescence. . . .[46]

It must be allowed that the book has a sense of overkill. As William-
Henry pointed out, the book consists

> of upwards of 400 pages, written expressly to prove that a forgery
> which the author [Malone] asserts was so palpable a one as to be
> discoverable at the first glance. . . .[47]

Malone was exacting, even punishing in his commentary, and in
the end he was cruel. At the close of his *Inquiry,* he relates a dream

in which the guilty forger stands trial before the God of Melody. In attendance are Spenser and John Suckling. Ben Jonson, we are told, would have attended but due to his "great corpulency and unwieldiness of his frame he was unable to join."[48] Defending Shakespeare, who is discovered playing bowls, is, naturally, Malone. We are not told who defends the forger. The judgment is that all the copies of *Miscellaneous Papers* are to be burned by himself, Dr. Farmer, Mr. Tyrwhitt, and George Steevens.[49] Most of the Believers are let off lightly but warned never to talk about things of which they are ignorant. But the key supporters and the forger are to be lampooned in satires by the ghostly pens of Dryden, Swift, Pope, and Butler until they are "Sacred to ridicule."[50]

PROTECTING SAMUEL AND THE BELIEVERS

After *Vortigern*'s failure, a committee of Believers made William-Henry sign a carefully worded statement that hinted at Samuel's innocence and William-Henry's crimes:

> It is stated that the present committee is appointed to investigate Mr. Samuel Ireland's concern in the business, and ease him of the calumnies which are heaped upon his head; I therefore will make oath that he received the papers from me as Shakspeare's, and knows nothing whatsoever concerning their origin, or the source from whence they came.[51]

No one paid much attention. Futilely, they pressed on. On 24 May 1796, Albany Wallis printed in many newspapers, including the *Morning Herald* and *True Briton*, the following message from William-Henry Ireland. It had a familiar and hollow tone:

SHAKESPERE MSS.

In justice to my father, and to remove the Reproach under which he has Innocently-fallen respecting the papers publish'd by him as the MSS. of Shakspeare, I do hereby solemnly declare that they were given to him by me as the genuine productions of Shakspere, and that he was and is at this Moment totally unacquainted with the source from whence they came or with any Circumstance concerning them save what he was told by myself and which he has declared in the preface to his Publication. With this firm belief and Conviction of their Authenticity, founded on the Credit he gave to me and my Assurances they were laid before the World. This will be further confirm'd when at some future period it may be judged expedient to disclose the means by which they were obtained   S.W.H. Ireland, Esq

Witness Albany Wallis; Thomas Trowsdale, clerk to
Messrs. Wallis & Troward
Norfolk Street
May 24, 1796.[52]

THE FEEBLE COUNTERATTACKS

But admitting they had been fooled by a nineteen-year-old boy
only reinforced Malone's verdict that the Believers should be held
"Sacred to ridicule." The Believers did their best to avoid their
fate. After all, nothing had been proved. Other plays had failed
without being forgeries. There were mitigating circumstances to
Vortigern's failure. Malone's book, though huge, was inaccurate in
parts. He had not even seen the papers in person. Many believed,
as Samuel had before the production of *Vortigern*, that there had
been a conspiracy against the papers. From as far away as
America, Believers in the authenticity of the papers rallied. In May
1796, the *Massachusetts Magazine* deplored attempts "made, with
equal illiberality and malignity, to excite doubts in the public mind"
about the Shakspeare Papers.[53] The following year, an attempt was
made to hold a forum on the papers. The speakers were to include
Samuel, William-Henry, Parr, and Kemble.[54] The meeting never
took place.

However, later in 1796, Samuel issued his own rejoinder to Malone's work, *Mr. Ireland's Vindication of his Conduct, Respecting
the Publication of the Supposed Shakspeare MSS. Being A Preface
or Introduction to A Reply to the Critical Labors of Mr. Malone,
in His "Enquiry into the Authenticity of Certain Papers, &c. &c.*
and then in the following year, launched an attack on Malone himself entitled, *An Investigation Into Mr. Malone's Claim to the Character of a Scholar or Critic, Being an Examination of his Inquiry
into the Authenticity of the Shakspeare Manuscripts, &c.*[55] It attacked Malone on niggling points of accuracy, while maintaining
that the papers were authentic. But no one was really listening. By
this time, even the Believers who had always supported Samuel
had deserted him. In 1799, George Chalmers issued the very curious *A Supplemental Apology for the Believers in the Shakespere
papers*—654 pages!—and a year later followed that work with his
An Appendix to the Supplemental Apology—a mere 147 pages!
These two deservedly uncelebrated books tried to mitigate the
Believers' gullibility by showing that Malone had overstated

the case. Yes, the papers were frauds, Chalmers argued, but damn fine ones!

WERE ONLY THE FOOLISH FOOLED?

Chalmers was not just satisfying his own ego, but also diverting stinging and lasting criticism, for history was to prove Malone a prophet. The corporeal ghosts of the great satirists did not literally rise up against the Irelands, but the spirit of their satire was felt. *The British Critic* whitewashed recent history by implying that only subintellects were fooled by the papers:

> Suspicion, from the very beginning, has hung on every part of the transaction. The original story was improbable, and it has strangely varied, without becoming probable. The papers themselves and the printed book offer in every part of their contents innumerable topics for objection, and little but objection; and the miraculous box or trunk, which, after having produced letters, drawings, printed books, Ms plays, still teems with discoveries. . . . Would you imagine, dear reader, that in a year and a half, or two years, the contents of one trunk could not be ascertained? . . . . [If it is the work of Shakespeare, then Shakespeare is] a down right blockhead.[56]

Later that year, on 29 October 1796, a satire of Samuel Ireland, entitled *Fortune's Fool,* was produced at Covent Garden. Samuel was lampooned as Sir Bamber Blackletter and, unlike *Vortigern, Fortune's Fool* was staged with entirely new scenes and dress.[57]

Caricaturists such as Gillray, Harding, and Nixon contributed: Gillray depicted Samuel holding a volume of his forgeries, Harding depicted Shakespeare rising from the dead, and Nixon drew a picture of the whole family participating in forging the papers.[58] Nor would Chalmers and the rest of the Believers be forgotten. One year later, George Steevens described those who had been fooled by the forgeries as a "Nest of Ninnies" consisting of "the Sapient Antiquaries and Heralds, Messieurs Noodle, Doodle, Foodle and Co."[59] By 1834, the die was permanently cast. Thomas Campbell reviewed the case, noting:

> The most respectable of the believers was Dr. Parr, who, with all his learning, was in many respects a simpleton: another was John Pinkerton, who, with a little learning, was a great charlatan: and a third was George Chalmers, who, with no learning at all, was equally destitute of taste.[60]

Example of the caricaturists' attacks on the Ireland family. Shakespeare rises from the dead to stop the forgeries. Photo obtained from the Shakespeare Birthplace Trust.

Not one friend came to Samuel's defense publicly. Privately, Thomas Caldecott, a former supporter, maintained that Samuel was a blameless fool "not at all capable of judging upon the subject" of the forgeries.[61] Samuel was probably glad that this defense remained closeted.

WILLIAM-HENRY TRIES TO TAKE THE CREDIT AND THE BLAME

With a significant portion of the scholarly community and the general public convinced that Samuel was to blame for the whole fiasco, William-Henry was telling anyone and everyone that he had forged the papers. Pathetically, few believed him. At best, the scholarly world allowed that William-Henry might have been a copyist, but who, asked one reporter, "composed the play he Copied[?]"[62] Even fifty years later, the notion persisted that William-Henry was only a cog in a forgery machine. C. M. Ingleby, who exposed the forger Collier, wrote with assurance in *The Shakspeare Fabrications* (1859) that it was Samuel who had masterminded the forgeries: the eldest daughter had written the text, assisted by the youngest daughter, while William-Henry copied the text in Shakespeare's hand.[63] Ingleby also suspected some sort of collusion between the Irelands and the Stratford forger John Jordan.[64]

In 1796, desperate to make his rightful claim, and to save his father's neck, William-Henry wrote his first confession, *Authentic Account*.[65] But much of the world, including his own father, did not believe him. He wrote of his father:

> he still believed the papers genuine; that no set of men could have produced the mass of evidence then in his possession; and that . . . he was as fully convinced as that he then had existence I never could have produced them.[66]

Samuel insisted that Mr. H. was real, that the papers were real, and that William-Henry would continue to deliver them. "I likewise insist," wrote Samuel, "on having the remainder of the papers, so often promised me."[67]

WAS SAMUEL PROTECTING HIS SON?

In May 1796, William-Henry confessed to his family. They told Samuel. Samuel insisted that William-Henry was lying.[68] Samuel wrote to Talbot, demanding the identity of Mr. H.; Talbot remained silent.[69] Wallis showed Samuel the rest of the papers, samples, inks, seals, and fragments that William-Henry had given him after his confession, with no effect.[70] Also in that month, Samuel noted that "my Son had been prevailing on Mr. Wallis to believe that he was Author of the papers (a Circumstance that he had several times had the arrogance and vanity to declare to all the family but was never bold enough to say as much to me. . . ."[71]

Still, William-Henry labored on. By now father and son were not communicating face-to-face. William-Henry had moved out of the house. He approached Samuel's friend, and former supporter of the papers, John Byng. William-Henry forged a new set of Shakspeare Papers in front of him. Byng then took the papers to Samuel and told him what he had seen. Still, Samuel refused to believe.[72] Samuel granted "no more than the possibility that his son had *copied out* the documents; that the boy had been their *author* he would continue stoutly to deny."[73]

William-Henry's reply to Samuel's concession was not hope but indignation:

Can you for a Moment think so meanly of me as be the *Tool* of some person of Genius no Sir I wou'd scorn the thought, and were it not that I am *Author* as well as Writer I would have died rather than confess'd it.[74]

Time would not modify his father's public opinion. Over a year later, William-Henry told Samuel of his plans to write a confession for "want of Money, and must publish it, to get Money." Samuel commented that if William-Henry was "the *Author* and no one was called in to correct it, that it would be so ill written" no one would believe it came from the pen of the man who wrote like Shakespeare.[75]

Who knows, perhaps William-Henry's interpretation of the events was the correct one: perhaps his father really did think him merely a mole obscuring the face of a genius. What is certain is that these affidavits and letters, like the Samuel Ireland-Mr. H. correspondences dealt with earlier, cannot be taken as unshakeable evidence of Samuel's innocence. It must be remembered that one or both of these men are liars and forgers. They might easily have written these letters to each other in an attempt to cover up a far more calculated fraud. At least George Steevens thought so. On 26 December 1796, Steevens wrote to Bishop Percy and referred to Samuel Ireland's literary defense and supposed innocence as "fresh indications of forgery."[76]

One letter from Samuel to William-Henry may justify Steevens's accusation of fraud. Samuel wrote to his son:

> I forget to hint to you, the dangerous predicament you stand in, if you are, as you say the writer etc. of these deeds. Your Character if you insist on this will be so blasted, that no person will admit you into their house, nor can you any where be trusted-therefore do not suffer yourself from Vanity or any other motive to adhere to any such Confession.[77]

Samuel's letter is compassionate and insightful. He knew the future awaiting William-Henry should the boy confess. Perhaps it was solely for this reason that from here onward, despite his son's many confessions, Samuel denied his son's story. Perhaps Samuel realized that it was the only chance his son had of escaping literary and perhaps even legal persecution.

From here on to his death, Samuel never admitted publicly that his son was a forger. It was a wretched situation. It may well have been that William-Henry perpetrated the papers entirely to win his father's love. Now, when he needed it most, his father denied him credit. The papers, he maintained, were the work of a genius, not his son. And yet it is clear from the above-quoted letter that Samuel had to discredit his son in order to save him. Samuel's act of rejection may have been the most loving act a father could give.

His mother's letters give us no clearer indications of the truth. In fact, Mair says that she regarded her son "with a mixture of spiteful jealousy and honest contempt. . . ."[78] According to Mrs. Freeman, her son had never shown "the least trait of *Literary Genius* in his character. . . ."[79] Mrs. Freeman thought Talbot forged the papers and that William-Henry was his stooge. After the premiere of *Vortigern,* Mrs. Freeman wrote to Talbot asking him to confess that William-Henry was merely his partner in crime:

> After such a Declaration can I then suppose that *Sam* [William-Henry], who is equally involved with yourself, had ever any intention of mentioning the *real truth* either to Mr. Wallis, or any other person?[80]

And yet there are signs within this very same letter that Mrs. Freeman, possibly like Samuel, was covering up the truth. For although her son apparently had shown no talent, she admitted that "of late he has been inspired with all the Furor of a Divine Poet" and that he now openly proclaims himself as a genius.[81] Like Samuel's letters and public declarations, Mrs. Freeman's statements may well be part of an orchestrated attempt to save her son.

Samuel Continued to Deceive Himself or Pretended to Do So

Publicly, Samuel aggressively maintained his innocence. But even his innocence was of such a duplicitious nature that we are forced to question it. For Samuel simultaneously declared that he had been cheated and that the papers were genuine. On the one hand, Samuel was insisting that the documents were authentic and that his son was forced into a false confession. On the other hand, he insisted that he, like many others, had simply been fooled.

Who knows, maybe Samuel actually believed it himself. If he did, he was probably the only one. Worse yet, when he wasn't being accused of being a fool, he was being accused of forging the Shakspeare Papers himself. Even one year after *Vortigern,* the press was still having its fun:

> Four forgers in one prolific age
> Much critical acumen did engage
> The first was soon by doughty Douglas scar'd
> Tho' Johnson would have screened him had he dared
> The next had all the cunning of a Scot
> The third, inventions, genius,-nay, what not?
> Fraud, now exhausted, only could dispense
> To her fourth son, their threefold impudence.[82]

Samuel was this fourth forger, following in the footsteps of Lauder, Macpherson and Chatterton; famous footsteps William-Henry would have been proud to call his own. But Samuel only felt bitterness toward a world that thought him either a fraud or a fool. For a time, Samuel consulted lawyers on suing the newspapers and the critics for their malicious slander. The lawyers told him to ignore the defamatory attacks.[83] Samuel refused. One year after Malone had exposed the Shakspeare Papers and William-Henry's own confession, Samuel was still maintaining his innocence.

But things weren't all bad. He did find yet more ways of making money from the forgeries. Aside from his attack on Malone, Samuel tried to sell the other play in his possession, *Henry II.* There were no offers. He then tried to hire Arthur Murphy, a popular dramatist of the period, to rewrite the play. The choice of Murphy was an appropriate one. Steevens had called him a "Compiler of Plays"; one who borrows "Plot and Outlines of his Characters. . . ."[84] Like Shakespeare and William-Henry, Murphy had begun his career in "borrowed feathers." One critic noted that he borrowed so much from dead authors that should they "call out for their own . . . you would soon perceive him in a state of poetical nakedness."[85]

Negotiations ensued. Samuel offered half the profits of the play, estimating them to be £1,400, an insane figure, considering the debacle of *Vortigern*. Murphy countered with a proposal of a flat fee of £150. Samuel turned him down.[86] Evidently, Samuel did not believe the play would be successful either. Both *Vortigern* and *Henry II* were published in 1799. *Henry II* was never staged.

William-Henry stated that it was Charles Marsh "a Barrister and subsequently Judge in India and on his return MP. [*sic*] who undertook to render my Vortigern . . . for Theatrical Representation."[87] But he is lying or mistaken. Charles Marsh did help recopy MS 3, but his role was limited to scrivener, simply recopying the finished version of MS 2 into a fair copy. Marsh, according to his own letter, did rewrite *Henry II* in 1797. The manuscript is in Jane Ireland's hand. Perhaps Marsh did rewrite the play. Perhaps Jane Ireland only acted as Marsh's secretary/scribe. However, since his only previous contact with the Irelands seems to be in the capacity of an amanuensis, it seems unlikely he'd have another copyist. If he did indeed collaborate, like Samuel's other supposed allies, Marsh became a Brutus to Samuel's Caesar. Years later, Marsh wrote a book, *The Clubs of London* (1828), in which he damned the play while omitting any reference to his own support and collaboration on *Henry II*.[88] Samuel probably underpaid him.[89]

Samuel still had not exhausted his potential sources of income. He was so unshamed in his tactics that one newspaper accused him of keeping the controversy alive merely "to put more money in the family purse."[90] In 1799, he published *Vortigern* and *Henry II*. The original manuscripts of *Vortigern* and *Hamblette* were sold to a Dr. Dent for £300. In 1828, William-Henry sold what he purported to be the original manuscript of *Henry II* for a mere £4.4.0.[91] In July 1800, Samuel Ireland died. "The shock of the whole business [being caught!] very probably hastened the elder Ireland's death. . . ."[92] Out brief candle. . . .

REFORGING THE SUPPORTERS' HISTORIES

While William-Henry pleaded with the world to forgive and forget his wrongs, many of those involved deliberately tried to reforge their own histories in the Ireland case. Dr. Parr, one of the earliest Believers, the critic who had judged the Profession of Faith finer than many litanies, denied ever having been fooled. After his death, his library was sold off. An annotated bibliography was issued as a sales catalog. It was entitled *Bibliotheca Parriana*. Parr's library contained a copy of Samuel's *Miscellaneous Papers*. In the marginalia of this book he had written the following:

> I almost ashamed to insert this worthless and infamously trickish book. It is said to include the tragedy of *King Lear,* and a fragment of *Hamlet.* [William-Henry] Ireland told a LIE, when he imputed to *me* the words which Joseph Warton used. . . . In my subsequent conversation, I told him my change of opinion. But I thought it not worth while to dispute in print with a detected impostor.[93]

For his part, Joseph Warton denied that he ever went to the Irelands' house, or inspected the Shakspeare Papers.[94] And we may deduce that after *Vortigern*'s failure, even Mrs. Jordan denied ever having supported the play, as years later Boaden noted that he "used to think [she was] a true *believer.*"[95] But strangest of all is Kemble's revisionist history of *Vortigern*. According to Kemble, it was Phillimore, not himself, who played the lead role of *Vortigern!*[96] True, the account was published in 1828, thirty-two years after the show, but the very fact that he is telling the story yet again, after so many years, is indicative of how important he felt it was in his long and glorious career.

In this account, Kemble is capable of recalling the controversy over the play and papers, the temperament of the audience, and of quoting nearly perfect from the play. Surely Kemble could not have forgotten that he was the star! The only answer is that Kemble did not wish to revive memories of his bad performance. He had damned the show as manager, not as an actor. Marsh, who recorded the account, never corrected Kemble's falsified story.

AND WHAT BECAME OF WILLIAM-HENRY?

It was not just the Believers and doubters who retreated from actual fact into fantasy. Immediately after *Vortigern*'s failure, William-Henry cloaked himself in a security blanket of lies. He ran away from home maintaining that he was going to live with the mysterious Mr. H. on his estate.[97] On another occasion, he told Samuel that Mr. H. had promised him an estate of £300 a year, with an old house four or five miles from the sea. He reported that the house had a cellar full of good, old port and that Mr. H. had even provided a stable full of horses.[98] He even showed them the horses, and paraded around town with them. When Wallis found out about the horses, he made the boy stop his nonsense.[99] There were other purchases of this sort. But when Samuel inquired into these matters, he found that his son had bought them on credit or in exchange for some rare books.[100]

Mair's opinion is that William-Henry might have gone temporarily insane. Perhaps he is right. Certainly there was an enormous amount of pressure on him. Jaggard quotes a letter by William-Henry written soon after *Vortigern*'s failure. The forger writes, "Pray excuse this scrawl, but I have had another night without a moment's sleep, and am more like a man drunk than in his senses."[101]

The lies continued. He told his father that Mr. H. "had sent Mr. J. Palmer ten pounds for three Tickets which he meant as a gratuity for the service he would have rendered" had he performed. He also intended to send Mrs. Powell a "handsome present" for her performance as Edmunda.[102] Of course, neither performer received any money.

The next fantasy involved Mr. Harris and Covent Garden. William-Henry told his family that Harris had bought *Henry II* and offered him £700 for two plays a year. Harris, it is true, had once been interested in the play, but was no longer. Samuel was surprised by this turnabout in interest and asked Harris if this was true. Harris replied that William-Henry's "brain was affected."[103]

By 16 April 1796, Samuel uncovered yet another of his son's bizarre fantasies. William-Henry had told him that Mr. Mitchell, the banker through whom William-Henry had said he had met the mysterious Mr. H., was willing to employ him to copy out all of Shakespeare's plays. Once copied, they were to be bound in "Crimson Velvet and with his arms embroidered on one side and Shakspeare's on the other side." Samuel asked Mitchell if he had placed such an order. Mitchell did not even know who William-Henry was.[104] On 24 May 1796, William-Henry was telling his family that he was making immediate arrangements to leave Great Britain.[105] He never left.

His next fantasy involved marriage. He told his father that he was marrying a Miss Shaw, a seventeen-year-old beauty with an income of £4000 a year, who "could not live without him." Samuel began to plan the wedding, the number of servants required, if £300 in plate was enough, the quality of the linen, etc.[106] In reality, there was no Miss Shaw. Instead, on 4 June 1796, he married one Alice

Crudge, whose social background was as unattractive as her name.[107]

William-Henry might well have been mad, but like *Hamlet,* he might well have been mad in craft. If the letters to and from Mr. H. are part of a larger, family fraud, then surely this too must be included. If William-Henry was telling the truth that he alone produced the forgeries, then these actions must have thrown his family into despair. But if the whole family was party to the fraud, as the manuscripts of *Vortigern* suggest—albeit do not prove— then William-Henry's actions are perfectly understandable. If the forgeries were to be exposed, and William-Henry was to take the entire blame, then it must seem that he was partially irrational. The family had to suggest that the boy's penchant for forgery was only one of a number of odd behavioral traits he had exhibited of late.

Despite William-Henry's obvious crimes, one feels for his personal tragedy. Two years before the failure of *Vortigern* he had been on "a course of studies to enable him to enter as a practitioner at the Chancery Bar."[108] He proved that he could write in the style of a great dramatist. Now he was blacklisted. No theater was interested in offering a contract to "Shakespeare Ireland," as he was commonly dubbed.[109] He left the bar, left his home, relied on the charity of others.[110] He wrote to Samuel requesting, among other things, that he send him his writing desk and book case, as they were to be sold in an attempt to stave off "immediate Want." With this, or perhaps other finances, he visited Bristol and spoke with Chatterton's sister. William-Henry became a hack writer, working, as his idol Chatterton had done, on Grub Street.[111]

But Chatterton died and was made a hero, whereas William-Henry lived and was branded a criminal. On 9 June 1796, *The Public Adviser* summed up the difference between William-Henry and his more successful forebearers:

> The forgeries of ROWLEY and OSSIAN were evidently the efforts of powerful genius. They will be admired as works of fancy, as long as English is a living language. The late impostors have only struggled for the disgrace of *unmitigated fraud.*[112]

There were brief moments when it seemed the forgeries might have actually enhanced William-Henry's career opportunities. On 20 December 1796, the *Morning Herald* announced that William-Henry would appear as *Richard III* at Covent Garden. Whether or not the story had any basis, William-Henry never appeared. On 15

August 1799, the *Oracle* began a long, serialized poem entitled "Shakespearean Hunt." Much of the poem was sympathetically devoted to William-Henry. It might have been an initial process of apotheosis similar to the one undergone by Chatterton.

Indeed, in "Shakespearean Hunt" William-Henry is not faulted for his crime but painted as a Greek hero, whose only crime is that "like APOLLO's Son, he aim'd too high."[113] The forgeries did bring him notoriety, if not fortune, and he was able to earn a modest living as a writer. As late as 1832 he was the key speaker at a fund-raising event for the Bookbinders' Pension Society. The poster advertising the event proclaimed that the address was to be "Spoken by the Author, W.H. Ireland (of Shakespeare celebrity.)"[114] His name extended beyond his life, reaching something like fame. In 1885, James Payn wrote a two-volume novel based on the Ireland family, *The Talk of the Town*.

But, more often than not, William-Henry was merely a bull's-eye for darting retribution, which would follow him to his death. As William-Henry noted:

> . . . the shafts of persecution have been so relentlessly levelled against me for upwards of thirty years. . . . every inimical feeling, which now remains, is but the foul lees of rancour, malice, and uncharitableness.[115]

William-Henry confessed to the forgeries in 1796. He wrote a letter of apology to the main Believers, but most of them never forgave him.[116] Some became his enemies, openly referring to him as an "ignoramus"; one "deficient in grammar" and "unable to write a correct sentence."[117] Even the sympathetic Caldecott noted that William-Henry was "to my certain knowledge . . . [neither] capable of writing a sentence of English correctly, or know even the common parts of Speech."[118] In 1805, William-Henry published a fuller confession. In 1832, he published a new, short confession as part of his edition of *Vortigern*. In all three published accounts he doggedly maintained that he alone created the forgeries and that money was never an issue. I maintain he is lying but there is something heartfelt about his last published denial:

> . . . suffering thirty-six years incessant persecution and obloquy, for the commission of an act intended only to please a parent, and which, in reality, has injured no one but its author. . . .[119]

There is no doubt that he was serious and truthful about the shafts of persecution. Years later, feeling that "upwards of a quar-

ter of a century must have cancelled all recollections of the past"
he offered to help James Boaden write a book about forged
paintings of Shakespeare. Boaden refused his help.[120] Indeed, he
referred to William-Henry's own drawings as "impudent and un-
skillful."[121] When asked why he still held a grudge after all these
years, Boaden replied:

> You must be aware, sir, of the enormous crime you committed against
> the divinity of Shakspeare. Why, the act, sir, was nothing short of
> sacrilege; it was precisely the same thing as taking the holy chalice
> from the altar, and ****** therein!!!![122]

Of course, William-Henry cannot really be blamed for making
the best of a bad situation; for capitalizing on his failure, but the
plain truth is that, despite confessing, he was never really repent-
ant. Indeed, he maintained that he had done what many could only
dream of:

> Invariably, when descanting with persons on the subject of the pa-
> pers, they have applauded the cheat, expressed a wish of having been
> capable of deceiving the world in a similar manner. . . .[123]

Hastings noted that he was "proud of his success in fooling the
learned," abnormal in his candor, and "quite untouched by
shame. . . ."[124]
Indeed, if the forgeries were a kind of madness, it was a madness
that would grip him until the day he died. The best reason for not
accepting William-Henry's excuse that he was too young to know
what he was doing, is that he never stopped forging Shakspeare
Papers, even after he was exposed! After failing to sell any of his
new plays, William-Henry opened a modest lending library. But
whenever William-Henry was short of money, he would recopy the
1799 printed version of *Vortigern* into his Shakespeare-hand and
sell it as the original forgery. This man was such a fake he even
forged his own forgeries! He also sold endless copies of his supposedly original rough drafts. The first major sale seems to be what
we now refer to as the *Shakespeare Ireland First Folio,* sold in
March 1797 to a bookseller and eventually became the possession
of George Steevens. I have mentioned the contents of this collection in my chapter, The Shakspeare Papers: The Master Plan. If
we are to believe Steevens, the forgeries found therein were the
rough drafts to the finished pieces shown to the public. But more
than just a collection of a few rough drafts, the book also contains

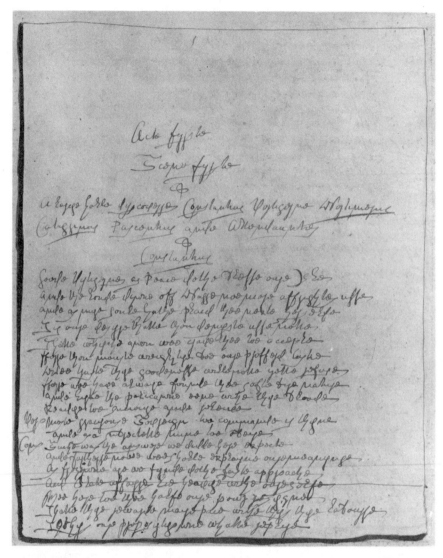

William-Henry forges his own forgeries. MS 6, text derived from the 1799 quarto. Reprinted with permission of The Folger Shakespeare Library.

some new works, not meant to fool the public but done merely to demonstrate William-Henry's facility for forgery. The first verso page includes some lines written in Ireland's archaic spelling, including a version of Hamlet's famous speech, "Too bee orre note too bee thatte is the questyonne." It also includes signatures by

Elizabeth, Southampton, and Heminges. The paper is scorched on three sides to give the appearance of antiquity to both paper and ink.[125]

Ireland had obviously bought more ink and paper. He had set up shop again, but with an important difference. Ireland was not aiming at historical accuracy. The verso containing "Too bee orre note too bee" is dated 18 April 1617.[126] Shakespeare had died in 1616.

But it really did not matter. The forgeries had been exposed. They were no longer saleable as authentic treasures, but there was a market for them as literary oddities. Unable to rewrite history, William-Henry rewrote his own forgeries. He was no longer a discoverer of important papers, but a cheap artist, able to knock off signatures of Shakespeare as easily as a tattoo artist draws an anchor. Nor were these the first Shakspeare Papers he sold. The original papers remained in his father's possession and were sold among his valuables at his death. But authenticity was hardly a major concern of William-Henry Ireland. Throughout his life he forged and reforged the papers that had made him famous for a time and infamous for eternity.[127]

Similarly, when William-Henry edited the play in 1832, he again created a forgery. He claimed that his 1832 version of the play had "As few alterations as possible . . . and those with a view to restore the original text."[128] Time had not altered William-Henry. Once more, he was lying. The "corrections" William-Henry made to the play were based either on his own aesthetics, or a memorial reconstruction of his own text or the texts of his mother and sister that he had inspected eight years before. The 1832 text bears no reference to any manuscripts of the play he had written over thirty-five years before.

Instead, he simply tampered with the text his father had printed in 1799. The changes that he did make are for the most part minor and in most cases do not correspond with the original Shakespeare-hand MS or the acting version presented to Drury Lane. After he published the play, he recopied the 1832 text into his Shakespeare-hand and sold it as yet another long-lost original.[129]

Nor were future forgeries to be confined to the recycling of his Shakspeare Papers. In 1805 William-Henry published *Effusions of Love From Chatelar to Mary, Queen of Scotland. Translated from a Gallic Manuscript, in the Scotch College, at Paris. Interspersed with Songs, Sonnets, and Notes Explanatory, by the Translator.* William-Henry was at it again.

In 1812, writing under the name Cervantes, William-Henry wrote a poem about the death of Napoleon. There was little chance of him passing it off as the work of the Spaniard commonly associated with windmills, but in this case William-Henry's aims were more insidious and long-term. In 1821, William-Henry published what he claimed was Napoleon's will. In 1822–23, he published *The Napoleon Anecdotes,* a collection of spurious tales at least partly his own work. In 1828, he published a life of Napoleon, under the name Baron Karlo Excellmans. In 1829, he assumed the name of the late French leader, actually publishing a book under the name Louis Bonaparte. The book was entitled *King of Holland,* and William-Henry said he had only translated it. His other forgeries include *Memoirs of a Young Greek Lady; or, Madame Pauline Adelaide Alexandre Panam, Versus His Most Serene Highness the Reigning Prince of Saxe-Cobourg* (1823), *Memoirs of Henry the Great, and the Court of France During His Reign* (1824), *Memoirs of Jeanne d'Arc, Surnamed La Pucelle d'Orleans; With the History of Her Times* (1824).[130]

In 1836, a Dr. Lee sent his lawyer, Mr. Till, to acquire some of the remaining Shakespeare forgeries. A list of the remaining papers, which might be purchased separately or as a lot, were drawn up. They included four or five leaves of his version of *King Lear,* an annotated edition of his *Confessions,* a drawing by Samuel Ireland, with an autograph letter of his and a few poems, an unpublished opera called "Robin Hood" and a manuscript note stating that the *Flitch of Bacon,* by Henry Bate was actually pirated from Samuel's opera, "The Matrimonial Relish." But they also included a few forgeries no one had yet seen, including:

    a. another set of the Holmes-Shakspeare correspondence
    b. a memorandum by Shakespeare noting that Southampton ordered him to restage *Richard II,* another attempt to link Shakespeare with the gunpowder plot
    c. several letters to Heminges, including one asking him to patch things up between Ben Jonson and Shakespeare
    d. a complaint of the worsening of his "olde syckness"
    e. a newly discovered will.[131]

The list also included a piece describing as "Byronns' sucundas, or Don Juan the second Canto 1st being all he wrote unpublished with Notes in his hand writing." The sale price was £2.[132] Apparently William-Henry's death came as a surprise. He was obviously planning new forgeries, this time "discovering" works by Byron, who had died in 1824.

William-Henry, still forging at age forty-four.

William Henry, literary hack, age fifty. Photo obtained from the Shakespeare Birth-place Trust.

It seems that everything William-Henry wrote was sprinkled with fool's gold. Pathetically, this trait extended even to his own correspondences, and this is yet another reason to believe that the letters between himself and Talbot, as well as those between Samuel and Mr. H., are all forgeries. For, in the end, William-Henry even forged letters to himself! Among William-Henry's papers preserved in the British Library are two letters in the same female hand addressed to Ireland. The first letter, signed merely "Incognita," begs William-Henry to meet her "alone in the Parish . . . as a clue to my person I have very long Flaxen Hair." This light lady begs Ireland's help, calling him a "Man of *Honor*" and hints at her undying love for him. The letter is dated Thursday night, 13 October 1796, four months after he had married Alice Crudge.

Apparently Incognita did not keep her own meeting. In a second letter, dated 27 October 1796, she apologizes for breaking the appointment. She was sick. On top of that, she now says that she has been forced into an engagement with a man she does not love. If only William-Henry can save her! This time she signs off as "Seraphina." She also mentions that these letters are not to be shown to Samuel, as he knows her guardian. Apparently she does not mind if Alice reads them or not.

Seraphina also has a flare for poetry, for as a preamble to her letter to William-Henry she writes:

> Dull languor sad and irksome care
>   The frequent sigh, the falling tear
> Intrusive guest- my hours employ
> And rob them of their wanted joy:
> Ah Lifes [*sic*] gay prospects all are tain
> The gilded pleasures end in pain.[133]

This drivel can only have come from William-Henry. Like his *King Lear* manuscript, his poetry lacks almost all punctuation. The sentiment is Romantic, a style he much admired. The contents of the letters are, to say the least, unbelievable. Only months after being exposed as a forger and married to the unfortunately named Alice Crudge, William-Henry Ireland receives two letters from the beautifully named Seraphina, begging him as a "Man of *Honor*" to rescue her from a life of misery. This intrigue is truly the stuff bad romantic novels are made on. Not surprisingly, William-Henry had many romances published. They were *The Abbess, a Romance* (1799), *Rimualdo; or, The Castle of Badajos* (1800), *The Woman of*

Feeling (1804), *Gondez, the Monk. A Romance of the Thirteenth Century* (1805), *The Catholic, an Historical Romance* (1807).[134]

Perhaps these two letters tell us more about William-Henry than all his "truthful" confessions. He was a dreamer, and his dreams, though mediocre, were more exciting than his reality. He died 17 April 1835, age 59.[135] He was buried at St. George-the-Martyr, Southwark, on 24 April one day after Shakespeare's birthday.[136]

12

The Legacy of *Vortigern*

In James Boaden's biography of John Philip Kemble, he notes that "Ireland's fancy or his fears had converted that mild gentleman, Mr. Malone, into a furious Saracen, fighting with poisoned weapons against Vortigern. . . ."[1] His victory was complete. And for that we must be forever grateful. Had Malone lost, the Shakespeare studied by ensuing generations might not have simply been distorted, but completely rewritten. For as Boaden noted, had the forger but kept "to history, the manners, the diction and the metre of his presumed original, it would be, perhaps impossible to detect him completely."[2] While it is impossible to judge how long people might have remained duped, 1796 was nearly contemporaneous to the rise of the Romantic poets, who looked upon Shakespeare as a poetic god. Without Malone's "poisoned weapons," William-Henry's plays and documents might have changed how Coleridge, Wordsworth, and even modern generations of writers, actors, readers, and theatergoers viewed Shakespeare.

Yes, Malone saved the day, but even he could not have fully understood the influence Shakespeare was to have on future generations. The reasons for his defense of the Bard must be found elsewhere. Indeed, rereading *Vortigern* two hundred years later, it is initially difficult to understand Malone's extreme hostility and obvious anxiety. *Vortigern* is hardly a great play. Indeed, it is a rather dull drama, its limited excitement caused by the vibration or reverberation of its Shakespearean background. William-Henry was not counting on the spectacle of a newly discovered play, but the recognition of bits of well-known speeches.

But while some speeches and devices are recognizable—a young woman disguised as a man, the murder of a king, a caustic fool, disenfranchisement and reincorporation of the family unit—these quilt workings of Shakespearean plotlines and phrases are not entirely concerned with fidelity to Shakespeare, just to marketing. William-Henry correctly labored under the assumption that Shakespeare's name and Shakespearean characters and situations were indispensable in a successful, new tragedy. At the same time, the papers solved sphinxlike riddles as to Shakespeare's personality, business dealings, marriage, and writing habits.

But while William-Henry offered imaginative solutions to both Shakespeare scholars and contemporary playwrights, as a craftsman he could not match the boldness of his ideas. Instead, Shakespeare's reputation was used to make excuses for the silliness of the newly discovered works. Shakespeare's imaginative fairy dust obscured William-Henry's banality and lack of originality.

But it was this seeming obscurity that paradoxically made William-Henry such a target. Malone did not expose the papers because they were so good. Rather, it was because they were so average. Unlike Chatterton and Macpherson, or any of the other great eighteenth-century poets, playwrights, or novelists, William-Henry lacked any vital poetic essence of his own or anyone else's. At best, he could only water down the reputation of an established master and the accepted knowledge of a given age. Ironically, it is Samuel Ireland who has left history with a definition of its greatest threat. For he said that forgeries and fakes "rob the age of the testimony it gives of itself, they pollute the source from which only the scholar can draw his materials to deduce the history of his native tongue. . . ."[3] For Samuel Ireland, a forgery not only deceived the scholar, it attacked a society's cultural heritage. He was not alone in this belief.

SHAKESPEARE'S POLITICAL ROLE IN THE 1790S

In the mid-1790s, it was essential that Shakespeare's cultural power was not polluted. Shakespeare had long been at the core of English culture, a body of literature the English were "acquainted with without knowing how."[4] Editions of Shakespeare served as a buffer against the French Revolution, a "bastion against the forces of 'astonishing' change at home and abroad that threatened to undermine political and cultural stability."[5]

Thus it was not only Malone who felt threatened by *Vortigern* but also political thinkers like Edmund Burke, because William-Henry's role model was not just a literary figure, but a national institution. And, as Derrida has noted, what the "institution" cannot tolerate is

for anyone to tamper with language, meaning both the *national* language and, paradoxically, an ideal of translatability that neutralizes this national language. . . . It can bear more readily the most apparently revolutionary ideological sorts of 'content', if only that content does not touch the borders of language and of all the juridico-political contracts that it guarantees.[6]

William-Henry's appropriation of Shakespeare was considered revolutionary in a time when the establishment considered it vital that Shakespeare remain an "anti-Revolutionary."[7] Any debasement of Shakespeare's cultural coinage was a political threat, a weakening of the national, cultural identity.[8] Without intending to do so, William-Henry turned Shakespeare into a double agent, a turncoat suddenly threatening to render the existing power structure alien, arbitrary, powerless to avoid outside influence and cultural corruption.

It may seem a little strong to compare *Vortigern* with the French Revolution, or to insinuate that it posed as great a threat to Britain as the armies of France. Indeed, that other dubious eighteenth-century Shakespeare play, *The Double Falsehood*, might be marshaled in opposition to this argument. *The Double Falsehood*, though never incorporated in an edition of Shakespeare, enjoyed a long and successful life in print and on stage. The third edition of the play was published in 1767. It was staged respectably often: twenty-three times over sixty-four years.[9] Even after the French Revolution of 1789, the play hardly caused a stir. Indeed, its last eighteenth-century production was 6 June 1791 at Covent Garden. And unlike *Vortigern,* it hardly caused a riot. In fact, it barely filled half the house. The receipts tallied just £188.15s.[10]

But there is no denying that the 1790s was a politically charged period and that *Vortigern* was judged in both literary and political circles. Indeed, if many believed that Kemble was in collusion with Malone, others believed that Malone was in collusion with Burke. On 21 February 1796, Thomas Caldecott wrote to Samuel Ireland, informing him that "Edmund Burke is, I know, at the head of the combination against you and Malone is his instrument. Politically against you the first, and every way as against the other."[11]

If the newspapers of the period are of any use as a guide, Burke's objections to the play were manifold: On 8 September 1795, the *Times* reported that:

The *pros* and *cons* between *Vortigern* and *Shakspeare* rest their arguments chiefly on the character of the Fool, which is strongly *Democratic*. One party contends that it cannot be *Shakspeare's*, as all his writings are peculiarly Loyal and Aristocratic; the other, that he always stuck close to nature, and that nothing can be more natural to a fool, than *Democracy*.[12]

On 18 February 1796, the *Oracle* reported:

We understand from good authority, that the Lord Chamberlain has refused to license the play of the new Shakspeare, upon three distinct grounds of objection- that it is *immoral, indecent,* and *Jacobinical*.[13]

Vortigern was a threat to Burke and Malone because it dealt with democracy, regicide, and incest. Three days after *Vortigern* had been destroyed, Burke wrote to Malone, favorably comparing his love of Shakespeare with "a perfect abhorrence of the French Revolution. . . ."[14] The pro-*Vortigern* party also adopted politically charged phrases, describing those who had shouted down the plays as "Democrats."[15] Another complained that the doubters were "Infidels" who had "extended from Religion and Politics unto the Authenticity" of the Shakspeare Papers.[16]

If William-Henry had unintentionally rallied the British to protect one of its institutions, he also helped the British recognize just what it was protecting. It must be remembered that in 1796, for all his cultural power, it was very rare to see untampered Shakespeare upon the stage. And it was this fact, according to Bernard Shaw, that was the key to William-Henry's initial success:

his [Shakespeare's] plays were so abominably murdered and mutilated until Granville-Barker, twenty years my junior, restored them to the stage, that it was shamefully evident that the clergymen who knelt and kissed Ireland's forgeries and the critics who made him ridiculous by their senseless idolatries had never read a line of his works and never intended to.[17]

Shaw has his facts slightly skewed. It was Boswell, not a group of clergymen, who knelt before the papers. And no one would claim that Boswell had never read the plays! Still, it is a valid point that most of the audience for *Vortigern* did not approach the plays with a solid textual and performance base. Dr. Johnson, who had edited Shakespeare in 1756, declared:

the best Play of SHAKSPEARE, though abounding in passages of unrivalled excellence, would not be endured, if brought forward, for the first time, in these days.[18]

The intervening forty years had not changed theatrical tastes. Only the year before, Kemble had staged a highly successful production of *King Lear*: not Shakespeare's *King Lear* but Tate's; *sans* Lear's and Cordelia's deaths, *sans* the fool, *sans* sad ending.

Reading *Vortigern*, there is no doubt that it is heavily derivative of *King Lear*. But it is derivative of Shakespeare's *King Lear*, not Tate's. The fool was missing in Kemble's *King Lear* but he was present in William-Henry's *Vortigern*. In this way, *Vortigern*'s Shakespeareanness actually helped direct theatrical tastes back toward unaltered Shakespeare. For in asserting itself against the plagiarisms of *Vortigern*, British theatrical society was forced to accept *Lear*'s fool as part of what constituted Shakespeare. Just as people may become ecologically aware after an oil spill, *Vortigern* was a significant consciousness-raising experience. It reminded the public how important Shakespeare's untampered plays were, and, more vitally, how rarely seen.

Vortigern and the Modern Stage

On the other hand, all the benefits of William-Henry's forgeries are not necessarily the result of great disasters narrowly averted. For instance, although *Vortigern* is hardly a great piece of drama, its very lack of originality is in itself an explicit theme. Thus by limiting his creativity to an enclosed canon, William-Henry opened the plays up to new potentialities with which we are only now coming to terms. Indeed, Charles Marowitz has recently defined this kind of intertextual splicing as "the future of Shakespearian production. . . ."[19]

But one need not look to the future to see the shadow of *Vortigern* on our stages. Witness the 1989 Royal Shakespeare Company production of *A Midsummer Night's Dream* in which Puck intermittently imitated Olivier's *Richard III*, Bob Carlton's recent West End musical *Return to Forbidden Planet*, in which Prospero and Miranda of *The Tempest* were cast into an outer space fantasy with such new characters as "Cookie." His 1992 successor, *From a Jack to a King*, came closer still to *Vortigern*. It was billed as "the first rock'n'roll musical from the pen of Mr. Bill Shakespeare to be unearthed by Bob Carlton." Other examples of borrowing Shakespeare's feathers are the Reduced Shakespeare Company, a trio who perform bits of all of Shakespeare's plays, forward and backward, within two hours, or, on a more intellectual note, the Greenaway film, *Prospero's Books*, a *Tempest* adaptation that repeats key speeches for emphasis, reassigns almost all the dialogue to Prospero, interchanges three actors for Ariel and adds a fictional index of study material. The recent Baz Luhrmann film, *William Shake-speare's Romeo and Juliet,* included oblique references to other Shakespeare plays: Romeo's men chant lines from *Macbeth,* Mecutio and Tybilt brawl on a beach that includes bistro-bars called "Jack Cade's" and "Rosencrantzy's" and billboards for "Bolingboke Beer" and "Prospero" brand cigarettes.

Other companies have gone even further. The Custard Factory's acclaimed recent productions of *Hamlet, As You Like It,* and *Measure for Measure* have all cut the text, reassigned speeches, cut characters, altered plot, added modern songs, dance and masque elements. In the words of Custard Factory director Clayton Buffoni:

> We turn Shakespeare inside-out. Each play has a series of plays within it. And what we do is select one, bring it from the text and allow it to create its own story and set of circumstances. We turn subtext into text and then use modern songs to fine tune the phrasing and emotions.[20]

What Edmond Malone would make of the Custard Factory's *As You Like It* adaptation, *Wicked Bastard of Venus,* with songs by 1950s hero Jacques Brel, 1980s psycho-punk-rocker Nick Cave, its sadomasochistic manipulation and lesbian erotica, must remain a matter of speculation. But what is clear is that Malone's 1790 edition and his exposure of the Ireland forgeries have brought the world no closer to creating a universal standard for judging and accepting authenticity.

COULD WE BE FOOLED AGAIN?

As a literary forger, William-Henry worked under almost ideal conditions. The study of English had yet to be incorporated into the educational system, many books and manuscripts of significance were in private collections, hoarded rather than shared. Books and papers were traded like stamps and discussions regarding their significance took place not in classrooms but in smoking rooms, parlors, and clubs. Access to these discussions, like the materials involved, was limited to a select few, and the selection process need not necessarily have been based on knowledge of the subject. Malone had not shared his bust with Ireland and Steevens held Ireland in low regard. No wonder that when the shoe was on the other foot, Samuel kept his precious Shakspeare Papers away from the so-called experts. Samuel Ireland found more than just

Shakespeare documents, he had found a way to snub those who had snubbed him, and created the basis for starting a rival study group/gentlemen's club, with himself as president.

Even if this had not been the case, even if Samuel had long been a member of Malone's inner circle, the public at large was all but ignorant of Elizabethan handwriting, vocabulary, printing techniques, etc. In other words, although interest in the subject of Shakespeare was high, actual access to important materials was limited. And even if the materials were available, forensic analysis of papers and inks was primitive at best. One need only remember the "expert" Robert Relhan's argument that the Shakspeare Papers were genuine because they were damp around the edges to realize how primitive was their scientific apparatus.[21]

In the intervening two hundred years many changes have taken place that would certainly make William-Henry's task more difficult. English is studied at all educational levels, primary materials have been published and dispersed into libraries all over the world. Information is shared, new ideas are published and openly debated. The British Library, and other institutions of its kind, ensure that knowledge is, at least theoretically, accessible to everyone. The gentlemen's clubs are gone. In their place institutions and departments have arisen, filled with qualified personnel: some expert in chemical analysis, others in watermarks, still others in Elizabethan language. Scholars now debate the authenticity of pieces such as the supposed Shakespeare plays *Edmund Ironside* or *Edward III* by writing articles in learned journals, not by staging popularity contests at Drury Lane. An impressive array of new detection equipment that utilize transmitted and ultraviolet light, infrared radiation make the contemporary forger's job far more difficult.[22]

THE 1990S: THE NEW GOLDEN AGE OF FORGERY

Of course the point is not to congratulate ourselves while comically surveying our often fumbling predecessors. In fact, the idea that technology and academe can now easily detect forgers is illusory. Forgery expert Antony Grafton believes that institutions of learning and instruments of detection have made forgers more skilled, not necessarily less successful.[23] Indeed, each age has seen its own version of the Shakspeare Papers. Whether it be the Cunningham or Collier Shakespeare forgeries, the "priceless" Chinese manuscripts of Edmund Blackhouse, the Charles Dawson's Piltdown man skull, the first editions of Thomas Wise, the paintings of Van Meegereen and de Hory and Otto Wacker, the Collingley fairies of Frances Griffiths and Elsie Wright, each age has been equally gullible. Indeed, the 1990s may prove to be the forgers' most successful decade ever. The fake designer clothes and jewelry problem is growing at the rate of one hundred percent a year and sales account for over £1 billion a year in Britain alone.[24]

More to the point of this book, sale of collectibles and published memoirs worldwide still carry no guarantee of authenticity. The 1990 Montreal Festival of Elvisabilia marketed tiny fabric swaddles snipped from the King's costume for $200 a square inch. I attended this festival. It was evident that even a rotund Elvis could not possibly have worn that many studs. The same year also saw the publication of *Black Plume, the Suppressed Memoirs of Edgar Allan Poe*. Though a work of fiction by David Madsen, the book presents itself as an authentic memoir with Madsen acting as editor. Andrew Field has written a similar memoir of Edward Devere (1990) and Graham Clark has recently "discovered" and published the comical *Shakespeare's Nottebooke* (1992).

London's *Sunday Sport* has recently printed a story entitled "Lesbian Witches Plot to Bring Back Hitler."[25] But in 1990, the pranks of the *Sunday Sport* witches were not needed. The serious German news publication, *Stern,* and the American magazine, *Newsweek,* among others, published excerpts of the *Hitler Diaries*. And in one last case of Hitler mania, *Punch* magazine resubmitted works by various authors to different publishing houses. A "thinly-disguised" retyping of *Mein Kampf* was accepted by Adelphi Press, while Samuel Beckett's *Stirrings Still* was rejected by even the vanity presses.[26] As William-Henry knew all too well, a rose by any other name does not sell as well.

In 1990, the British Library exhibited fakes (that they are aware of) from their own collection.[27] In 1991, Britain's *Guardian* newspaper published an article on Rembrandt in which art experts declared that one-third of Rembrandt's paintings and two-thirds of his drawings had been falsely attributed to him. However, rather than informing the public, the facts have been consciously played down. As Pieter Van Thiel, director of paintings at the Rijks Museum said, "It would only be disturbing if we confronted the public with these facts."[28]

A front-page headline in London's *The Times* recently declared that "Fakes are the genuine art of the recession."[29] Some fakes are of such quality that they have duped Sotheby's, Christie's, and Philips'. One disreputable art dealer, John Fairchild, fooled the experts by including bogus signatures by famous artists and letters of authentication from legitimate Parisian galleries.[30] And Eric Hebborn, the undoubted master of art forgery, has sold millions of pounds worth of his fakes in the styles of Michelangelo, Rembrandt, Rubens, Gainsborough, and Reynolds. His pictures hang in many of the most famous art collections in the world. In 1991, he published his memoirs, *Master Faker*. It became a best-seller. In 1992, Britain's *The Independent Magazine* actually invited its readers to write an extract from an undiscovered poem or novel. Submissions included unknown "first drafts" from Wordsworth, Eliot, and Camus.[31] In 1993, experts at New Scotland Yard's Black Museum said they had discovered the diary of Jack the Ripper. They were fooled, though precisely who faked the manuscript remains a mystery.[32] In 1996, a prominent Canadian gallery was accused of selling fake Russian avant-garde paintings.[33] In 1997, *The Art Newspaper* declared that over one hundred Van Goghs, including one of the Dutch master's famous sunflowers series, are probably fakes.[34] Recently, a lost Mozart aria was discovered and authenticated by experts. The aria joins a host of other recently discovered treasures which include three letters by Defoe, three hundred poems apparently by Samuel Coleridge, four long-lost notebooks by Whitman, one hundred and forty-three letters and two unpublished poems by T. S. Eliot, as well the war notes of Jean-Paul Satre.[35] Only time will tell whether these works are authentic. Meanwhile, an innumerable amount of newspapers, magazines, and books continue to report Jim Morrison, and Elvis Presley sightings, and crop circles.[36] Somewhere in forger heaven, William-Henry must be smiling.

VORTIGERN AND THE SHAKESPEARE CANON

Anyone who follows Shakespeare scholarship is aware that lost or overlooked Shakespeare works are, once more, beginning to appear. In fact, so many "lost" Shakespeare's have been turning up that one recent *Times Literary Supplement* reviewer referred to the discoveries as a "growth industry."[37] The recent Oxford edition of Shakespeare, *The Complete Works,* included many unfamiliar pieces, including the sonnet "Shall I fly" and even the quatrain on Shakespeare's tombstone.[38] The Cambridge Shakespeare series promises to include the play *Edward III*. Recent editions arguing that Shakespeare was at least partial author of two other plays, *Edmund Ironside* and *The Birth of Merlin*, have also appeared.[39] Charles Hamilton says he has found the lost Shakespeare play, *Cardinio,* and Donald W. Foster says he has found a lost Shakespeare elegy.[40] While none of the aforementioned scholars has been accused of forgery, their research is testament to the fact that we are living through the most radical reinterpretation of Shakespeare since Ireland tried to reforge Shakespeare in his own image. Shakespeare may have proven himself to be timeless, but even Edmond Malone would have to agree that *Vortigern* has proved itself topical.

Postscript

UNIVERSITY of California at Riverside, 1997: I have worked on this book for years, carefully reconstructing the historical evidence, rediscovering the lost manuscripts of *Vortigern,* uncovering William-Henry's elaborate and systematic schemes and lies. Despite these triumphs, I never thought I would see the entire play enacted.

Happily, I was proved wrong. In 1992, I gave a copy of the play to West End director Joe Harmston, who immediately saw its box-office potential. Although swamped with projects, he promised that, one day, he would restage the play.

A year passed and I gave up hope of ever seeing *Vortigern* on the boards. But then in 1993, Joe and I did stage parts of the play at the Theatre Museum in Covent Garden. I do confess it. The audience laughed in all the wrong parts.

The following year, Jonathan Bate, who had written a few articles on the forgeries, contacted me and asked me to contribute to the BBC documentary, "The Irresistible Rise of William Shakespeare." In conjunction with my appearance, the Beeb staged one scene from the play. This time, the excerpt worked surprisingly well. And even more importantly, the media, particularly the major newspapers, showed great interest.[1]

From time to time, I'd see Joe and he'd promise he'd get around to it, but there were delays and other projects, and reschedulings and further commitments, etc. etc. I too had been occupied, teaching in France, Hong Kong, Canada, and America.

Then quite unexpectedly, things began to progress apace. Somehow we convinced the celebrated playwright Alan Ayckbourn, and eminent Shakespeare actor Kenneth Branagh to support the project. Our company, Tour de Force, had a fundraiser at the Fortune Theatre, right across the street from Drury Lane. With patrons and funds secured, we began casting the parts and were delighted with some of the star actors who approached us for the plum roles: James Simmons, a West End actor who had recently finished a long and successful run as the male lead in *The Woman in Black,* was cast as Vortigern; Pippa Haywood, well-known to British television viewers as Helen Brittas in the BBC comedy, *The Brittas Empire,* was cast as Edmunda.

We staged the play at the Bridewell, a well-known and well-respected theater. While economics played a hand in our selection process, there were other factors as well. The Bridewell is in Chancery Lane, the very place William-Henry worked as a law clerk. We were staging the play only blocks away from where the forger had hastily composed it over 200 years before. Chancery is only a stone's throw from Fleet Street, where, in later life, the forger worked as a hack. Between the promise of his youth and the disappointment of age, in many ways a more appropriate theater could not have been selected.

The play opened on 22 October 1997 and ran through 19 November. On opening night, the house was packed. Theater critics from *The Times, TLS, Guardian, The Telegraph* and the BBC were in attendance. Joe and I nervously paced. We need not have. Malone's ghost was not in attendance. In terms of audience reception, the play was a tremendous success.

Later, in the pub, I asked the actors what they honestly thought of the play and their parts. Simmons found playing Vortigern "a monster." As he put it, "the part is extremely long and difficult to memorize. But it's a great role and a challenge. Within one scene, you are Richard, Macbeth, and Brutus." Haywood revelled in her role. As she told me, "It's not often a woman gets to play King Lear!"

After the pub closed, I walked the streets of Chancery. The crowds filed to bus stops and tube stations, to late-night restaurants and nearby nightclubs. Turning up Chancery Lane, I lost myself in the now deserted Inns of Court.

I was here for sentimental reasons. My footsteps had led me to the very place the forger had worked. Two hundred years ago, he walked these very streets, two hundred years ago a boy very nearly fooled the world—and was punished for it. I found myself before an old gate of gray stone and black iron. He had worked here, passed this gate hundreds of times. I put my hand to the masonry. Rest perturb'd spirit.

In the morning, on my way to Heathrow, I checked the reviews. They were all negative.[2]

Notes

CHAPTER 1. BACKGROUND: *VORTIGERN* AND THE CRIMINAL QUILL

1. Peter Martin, *Edmond Malone Shakespearean Scholar: A literary biography*, 195.

2. Hans Tietze, *Genuine and False*, 55.

3. For literature, see Ian Haywood, *The Making of History*, 11; Laurence Lipking, *The Ordering of the Arts in Eighteenth-Century England*, 143. For Shakespeare's dominance in the theater, see *Index to The London Stage, 1600–1800: The London Stage, 1600–1800*; C.B. Hogan, *Shakespeare in the Theatre 1701–1800: A Record of Performances in London 1751–1800*.

4. Gary Taylor, *Reinventing Shakespeare*, 58.

5. *The London Stage*, Part 4, 1:CLXII,CLXIV.

6. Michael Dobson, *The Making of the National Poet: Shakespeare, Adaption and Authorship, 1660–1769*, especially his chapters, "Romance and Revision," 17–61, and "Nationalizing the Corpus," 186–98.

7. Brian Vickers, *Introduction to Shakespeare: 1693–1733*, 2:13. For more information as to how the plays were changed, I have also consulted the individual entries for each play in Wells's *Shakespeare: An Illustrated Dictionary*.

8. Numbers calculated from *Index to The London Stage*.

9. Epilogue to Aaron Hill's *Alzira*, 5:84.

10. See Harold Bloom, *The Anxiety of Influence*, passim. On the weakness of eighteenth-century drama, see Gary Taylor, *Reinventing Shakespeare*, 58.

11. Approximation based on numbers found in Hogan, *Shakespeare in the Theatre 1701–1800*, 2:715.

12. Nicoll, *A History of English Drama*, 2: 55.

13. Ibid., 2:56–58.

14. *The London Stage*, Part 4.1: CLXII.

15. Ibid., 4.1:CLXIV.

16. Ibid., 4.1:CLXIV-CLXVI.

17. The only pieces to rank before Shakespeare's tragedies were two Sheridan comedies (*School for Scandal* and *The Duenna*), one John Gay comedy (*The Beggar's Opera*), a comedy by Isaac Bickerstaff (*Love in a Villiage*) and two operas, one by Colman the Elder (*The Spanish Barber*), the other by Colman the Younger (*Inkle and Yarico*). See *The London Stage*, Part 5. 1:CLXXII.

18. Number calculated from Hogan, *Shakespeare and the Theatre: 1701–1899*, 2:716–19. *Richard III* was performed 523 times.

19. Gary Taylor, *Reinventing Shakespeare*, 58.

20. Quoted in *The London Stage*, Part 2.1:XX–XXI.

21. Judgement recorded in 1780, quoted in *The London Stage*, Part 3. 1:CXXXVIII.

22. Quoted in Nicoll, *A History of English Drama*, 2:62.

23. Letter "To the Right Honourable CHARLES LORD HALIFAX," prefacing Rowe's *The Royal Convert,* in *Bell's British Theatre,* 27: I.

24. Richard Cumberland, *The West Indian,* in *Bell's British Theatre,* 18: III.

25. Ibid., 18:IV.

26. Charles Johnson, *The Country Lasses or The Custom of the Manor,* 1:VIII.

27. Samuel Johnson, "Prologue" on the reopening of Drury Lane, 1747, *Eighteenth Century Plays,* 1.

28. Richard Cumberland, *The Brothers,* 30: V.

29. Prologue to Arthur Murphy's *All in the Wrong,* 7: III.

30. Preface to *The Rivals* (1775), in *The Dramatic Works of R.B. Sheridan,* 1:70.

31. *The London Stage,* Part 3. 1:CLXXIII.

32. Ben Jonson, title to the second epilogue to *The New Inn,* in *Ben Jonson Plays,* 2: 496.

33. Quoted in *The London Stage,* Part 2. 1:CLXV.

34. Quoted in Ibid., Part 2. 1:CLXVII.

35. Quoted in Ibid., Part 2. 1:CLXVI.

36. Quoted in Nicoll, *A History of English Drama,* 2:13.

37. Quoted in *The London Stage,* Part 3. 1:CLXXV.

38. Ibid., Part 4. 1:CLXXXIV.

39. Quoted in Ibid., Part 4. 1: CLXXXIX.

40. Garrick's epilogue, to Garrick and Colman's *The Clandestine Marriage,* in *Eighteenth Century Plays,* 335–36.

41. Quoted in Nicoll, *A History of English Drama,* 2:17.

42. Nicoll, *A History of English Drama,* 2:18.

43. Quoted in Nicoll, *A History of English Drama,* 2:19. Schneider lists this play under the title *The Covent Garden Tragedy or The Humours of Covent Garden* (*Index to the London Stage*).

44. *The London Stage,* Part 2. 1:CLXIV.

45. See his Introduction to *Great Writers of the English Language: Restoration and Eighteenth-Century Drama,* Gen. ed. James Vinson, assoc. ed. D.L. Kirkpatrick, 7. Scouten further notes that although new tragedies were written during this era, audiences preferred adapted versions of Shakespeare (12–13).

46. Essayists from the period did the same. See Gary Taylor, *Reinventing Shakespeare,* 62–63.

47. This trend can be seen in literature as well. In 1759, Samuel Johnson pointed out that "the first writers took possession of the most striking objects for description, and the most probable occurrences for fiction, and left nothing to those that followed them, but transcription of the same events, and new combinations of the same images." See Samuel Johnson, *Rasselas,* 40.

48. Nicholas Rowe, *The Tragedy of Jane Shore,* 60.

49. According to Bonamy Dobrée, *Restoration Tragedy: 1600–1720,* 151.

50. Rowe, *The Tragedy of Jane Shore,* 104.

51. William Harvard's *Charles the First,* 21: 46.

52. Prologue to Shirley's *Edward the Black Prince,* 4:IX.

53. William Shakespeare, *Henry V,* in *William Shakespeare: The Complete Works,* 2.4.50–64. All Shakespeare quotations derived from this edition unless stated otherwise.

54. M'Namara Morgan's dedicatory poem to Henry Jones's *The Earl of Essex,* 8:X.

55. Henry Jones's *The Earl of Essex*, 8:17.

56. *Index to The London Stage* spells the author's name "Francklin". My spelling is derived from the title page of the edition consulted.

57. Boaden, in Gray, *Theatrical Criticism in London to 1795*, 289–90.

58. Samuel Johnson, "Prologue" on the reopening of Theatre Royal Drury Lane, 1.

59. Quoted in *The London Stage*, Part 4.1:CLXXXV.

60. Henry Fielding, Preface to *Tom Thumb*, 166.

61. There may well have been psychoanalytic reasons behind the forgeries as well. See my chapter, Lies and More Lies: The Truth About The Ireland Family.

62. Haywood, *The Making of History*, 11.

63. Lawrence Lipking, *The Ordering of the Arts in Eighteenth Century England*, 143.

64. Zoltán Haraszeti, *The Shakespeare Forgeries of William-Henry Ireland*, 6.

65. Boaden, *A Letter to George Steevens*, 10.

66. Whitehead, *This Solemn Mockery*, 37–41.

67. Piozzi, *Anecdotes of the Late Samuel Johnson*, 174.

68. For overview of controversy, see Haywood, *The Making of History*, 63.

69. Fielding, Preface to *Jonathan Wild*, 29.

70. Quoted in McKillop, *The Early Masters of English Fiction*, 9. Ironically, after his death, Defoe himself was a target for forgery. Between 1790 and 1971, the list of his alleged works expanded from 101 to 570. See Griffiths, "Novel twist to Defoe's spying," 8.

71. Whitehead, *This Solemn Mockery*, 54–58. These relics were still being published as genuine discoveries more that one hundred years later—with no less an authority than the Shakespearean Fredrick James Furnivall as editor. See Thomas Percy's *Bishop Percy's Folio Manuscript* (1867).

72. For a fuller treatment of forgery in the eighteenth century see Ian Haywood, *The Making of History;* Mark Jones, Paul Craddock, Nicholas Barker, *Fake? The Art of Deception.*

73. As I will later detail, Boswell was fooled by the Shakspeare Papers. See my chapter, More Forgeries: The Authentication of *Vortigern* Continues.

74. Samples of his forgeries are reproduced in Sally Brown, "'The marvellous boy': Chatterton manuscripts in the British Museum," 83–92.

75. See, for example, Malone's *Cursory Observations* (1792). For works dealing specifically with Macpherson and/or Chatterton, see Ian Haywood, *Faking it: A Study of the Literary Forgeries of James Macpherson and Thomas Chatterton* and "Chatterton's Plans for the Publication of the Forgery," *The Review of English Studies* 36.141 (February 1985): 58–68; Linda Kelly, *The Marvellous Boy: The Life and Myth of Thomas Chatterton;* E. H. W. Meyerstein, *A Life of Thomas Chatterton;* Fiona J. Stafford, *The Sublime Savage: A Study of James Macpherson and the Poems of Ossian;* Donald S. Taylor, *Thomas Chatterton's Art: Experiments in Imagined History.*

76. Malone, *Cursory Observations*, 50.

77. Preface to Shakespeare's *The Double Falsehood*, 1. In terms of citation, I have listed the play as by Shakespeare, although with some hesitation.

78. See contract giving Theobald sole copyright of the play for fourteen years, added as a appendix to the text.

79. See Jaggard, *Shaksperian Frauds*, 2.

80. See Freehafer, "Cardinio, By Shakespeare and Fletcher," 501–13.

81. See Shakespeare, *The Complete Works*, 1191.

82. See Jonathan Hope, *The Authorship of Shakespeare's Plays,* 89–100; Charles Hamilton, *Shakespeare With John Fletcher: Cardinio or The Second Maid's Tragedy,* 223–36.

83. Dedication to Shakespeare's *Double Falsehood,* 2–3.

84. *The Grub Street Journal,* No. 98, 18 November 1731, quoted in Shakespeare, *Double Falsehood.* Edited by Walter Graham. Western Reserve Studies 1.6:33.

85. Peter Martin, *Edmond Malone,* 188–89.

86. Quoted in Jaggard, *Shaksperian Frauds,* 3–4.

87. Grebanier, *The Great Shakespeare Forgery,* 139.

88. Mair, *The Fourth Forger,* 72. See also Grebanier, *The Great Shakespeare Forgery,* 139.

89. Quoted in Ireland, *Confessions,* 34.

90. Malone did have his doubts about its authenticity. See Marder, *His Exits and His Entrances,* 217.

91. Ibid., 25–26. Jordan's letter to Malone, dated 17 March 1790, detailing the discovery of the document, is housed in the Folger Shakespeare Library, MS W.B. 17.

92. Haywood, *The Making of History,* 35.

93. DeGrazia, *Shakespeare Verbatim,* 4.

94. Ibid., 50.

95. *Dictionary of National Biography,* 35:436.

96. Ray, *Story and History,* 270.

97. Home, *Elements of Criticism,* 1:100–101.

98. Warton, *An Enquiry into the Authenticity of the Poems Attributed to Thomas Rowley,* 124. Though it should be noted that Warton still correctly judged the *Rowley* poems to be forgeries.

99. DeGrazia, *Shakespeare Verbatim,* 71.

Chapter 2. The Shakspeare Papers: The Master Plan

1. See William-Henry Ireland, *Authentic Account* (1796), *Confessions* (1805), and Preface to *Vortigern* (1832).

2. Ireland, *Confessions,* 300.

3. Quoted in Mair, *The Fourth Forger,* 211.

4. Quoted in *Confessions,* 269.

5. William-Henry's age derived from the family Bible. See Schoenbaum, *Shakespeare's Lives,* cf.132.

6. William-Henry Ireland, *Confessions,* 6.

7. Ibid., 8–9.

8. Ibid., 10.

9. Ibid., 9.

10. Ibid., 11.

11. Ibid., 12.

12. Ibid., 11.

13. Ireland, *Authentic Account,* 3.

14. Ibid., 4.

15. Ibid., 3. Actually, William-Henry says he used an earlier Steevens edition, but it lacks the facsimile. Schoenbaum identified the 1790 Malone edition as the forger's most likely source. See Schoenbaum, *Shakespeare's Lives,* 138.

16. William-Henry Ireland, *Authentic Acount,* 4.

17. Ireland, *Confessions,* 42.

18. Ibid., 43.

19. Ibid., 44.

20. Ibid., 45.

21. Ibid., 46.

22. Farington, *The Diary of Joseph Farington,* 1 January 1796, 2:464.

23. Ireland, *Confessions,* 19.

24. Ibid., 20–21.

25. Ibid., 20.

26. Ibid., 25–26.

27. Ibid., 27. There were major fires in Stratford in 1594, 1595, 1614, 1641. There was also a smaller fire in 1731 but only a few houses were destroyed (Morris, letter, 12 December 1992).

28. Ireland, *Confessions,* 30.

29. Ireland, *Authentic Account,* 5.

30. Ibid., 6.

31. On Williams, see Vol. XX of the Halliwell[-Phillipps] scrapbooks in the Folger Shakespeare Library, MS W.B. 223. William-Henry's analysis is found in a manuscript note in a British Library copy of his *Authentic Account* (shelf-mark 642.d.29). On these points, I am endebted to Schoenbaum's *Shakespeare's Lives,* 134, 579 n.73.

32. Ireland, *Authentic Account,* 7.

33. Ireland, *Confessions,* 45.

34. Samuel Ireland's diary, 22 November 1794, found in BL MS 30346, 6r. "Mr. M." has been identified as Mr. Mitchell, a banker. See Schoenbaum, *Shakespeare's Lives,* 138.

35. Ireland, *Authentic Account,* 11–12.

36. Ibid., 12. Date supplied from Samuel's diary, 2 December 1794, found in BL MS 30346, 7r.

37. Ireland, *Authentic Account,* 12–13.

38. Samuel Ireland's diary, BL MS 30346, 9r. The British Library bibliographical entry lists this work among William-Henry's. I have followed suit.

39. Samuel Ireland's diary, 18 December 1794, found in BL MS 30346, 13v. For Eden's bibliographical details, see Grebanier, *The Great Shakespeare Forgery,* 79–80.

40. Ireland, *Authentic Account,* 9.

41. Ireland, *Confessions,* 55.

42. Samuel Ireland's diary, 26 December 1794, found in BL MS 30346, 23r.

43. Samuel Ireland's diary, 17 December 1794, found in BL MS 30346, 15r.

44. All quoted Shakspeare Papers, unless otherwise stated, are from Samuel Ireland's *Miscellaneous Papers and Legal Instruments.* Some letters are reproduced as prose, others, like the note by Hemynge, have verse-like line breaks. In the latter cases only, I have retained the original line breaks.

45. Samuel Ireland's diary, 24 December 1794, found in BL MS 30346, 19r.

46. Ireland, *Authentic Account,* 10.

47. Ibid., 7.

48. Ireland, *Confessions,* 58.

49. Ibid., 60.

50. Quoted in Hastings, *Shakespeare Ireland's First Folio,* cf.6.

51. Ireland, *Confessions,* 99.

52. The title is not underlined in diary entry. See Samuel Ireland's diary, 26 December 1794, found in BL MS 30346, 23r.

53. See Samuel Ireland's diary, BL MS 30346, 24r.

54. Samuel Ireland's diary, 3 January 1795, BL MS 30346, 29r, date supplied on 28r.

55. Copy of letter from Webb to Rev. Dr. Jackson, 30 July 1795, BL MS 30346, 98r. Also reported in a copy of an article by the *Sun*, 2 October 1795, BL MS 30349, 22v.

56. The Holmes-Shakspeare correspondence is housed in the Folger Library, MS D.b. 44.

57. Samuel Ireland's diary, 26 December 1794, found in BL MS 30346, 24r.

58. Samuel Ireland's diary, BL MS 30346, 34r-35v.

59. Samuel Ireland's diary, 19 January 1795, found in BL MS 30346, 44r.

60. Ireland, *Authentic Account*, 15.

61. Joseph Warton is not to be confused with his older brother Thomas Warton, the critic who helped expose Chatterton. There is a further possible confusion in the spelling of his name. William-Henry spells his name "Wharton". Dr. Parr, writing on the forgeries years later, referred to his companion as "Warton". See his *Bibliotheca Parriana*, 522. I have corrected the forger except in cases of direct quotation. On Malone's assessment of Joseph Warton, see Martin, *Edmond Malone*, 56.

62. Grebanier, *The Great Shakespeare Forgery*, 92–93 and Martin, *Edmond Malone*, 64.

63. *Dictionary of National Biography*, 43:356–363.

64. Letter from Richard Valpy to Samuel Ireland, 27 March 1796, found in BL MS 30348, 221r.

65. Ireland, *Authentic Account*, 16.

66. Quoted in Ireland, *Confessions*, 67.

67. Ibid., 67.

68. Ibid., 69.

69. Samuel Ireland's diary, 10 February 1795, BL MS 30346, 40.

70. Curiously, Samuel's transcription of the latter mistakes "Kysses" for "Eysses."

71. Ireland, *Confessions*, 116.

72. Ibid., 115.

73. Ireland, *Authentic Account*, 19.

Chapter 3. Why *Vortigern*?

1. William-Henry Ireland, *Confessions*, 133.

2. Ibid., 135–36.

3. Grebanier, *The Great Shakespeare Forgery*, 142–43.

4. *Morning Post*, 12 February 1795, article found in BL MS 30349, 4r.

5. William-Henry Ireland, *Confessions*, 133.

6. Ibid., 133.

7. Ibid., 133.

8. She is also given the alternative names Ronix or Ronowen.

9. *A Catalogue of the Books, Paintings, Miniatures, Drawings, Prints, and Various Curiosities, the Property of the Late Samuel Ireland, Esq. of Norfolk*

Street, Strand; Author of the Tour to Holland; Views of the Rivers Thames, Avon, Wye, Medway, Inns of Courts, &c (London, 1801), 17–34.

10. Gilbert Benthall, "Draft Introduction to an Exhibition of Paintings, Drawings, and Etchings by John Hamilton Mortimer A.R.A. (1740–1779)." (London: Manuscript Collection, National Art Library, Victoria and Albert Museum Library, Special Collection LL 2261–1961 86.W.50–53, 1959), 2.

11. Ibid., 2 and 70.

12. Idem, "The Life and Works of John Mortimer." (Manuscript Collection, National Art Library, Victoria and Albert Museum Library, Special Collection LL 2261–1961 86.W.50–53), prefatory page.

13. Ibid., 108.

14. Ibid., opening page of chapter 4, numbered wrongly as 70, actual page 73.

15. Ibid., 74.

16. Idem, "Draft," 74, see also 123.

17. Ibid., 108–9.

18. See *A Catalogue of the Books*, 12–20.

19. This manuscript of *Vortigern* is a transcription of the 1799 edition. It is available on microfilm S795 at the Shakespeare Institute, Stratford-upon-Avon, England.

20. *The Meeting of Vortigern and Rowena* is listed as "LOCATION:unknown," in John Sunderland, *John Hamilton Mortimer His Life and Works*. The Walpole Society. Vol. 52 (London: The Walpole Society, 1986), 193.

21. Pat Rogers, "Introduction to Reynolds." in Joshua Reynolds, *Discourses*, 8.

22. See volume 1 of Tobias Smollett, *A Complete History of England*. 4 vols. 2nd edition (London, 1758). The prints were optional and their insertion unsystematic. If the print is in a volume of Smollett, it may not appear uniformly opposite the same page. I discuss this point in further detail in note 23 below.

23. Rapin reference found on print's subtitle. According to the subtitle, the picture was included for an edition of Rapin de Thoyras, *The History of England. Written in French Done into English, With Additional Notes Marked With an **, *by N. Tindal, M.A. Rector of Great Waltham in Essex*. 15 vols. (London, 1725). The book went through a vast number of editions. I have consulted all of the editions by Rapin in the British Library, without success.

This is not surprising. The reason why the picture has the subtitle is that the eighteenth-century book buyer often had an option as to which prints he/she wished to include in his/her edition. The more prints included, the more expensive the volume. We find the modern equivalent in optional features on motor vehicles. In any event, were I to find a copy with the added print, it is unlikely that the edition would tell me more than the print itself, since the title pages to Rapin's editions do not list the artists and engravers involved.

24. Rapin, *The History of England*. 1:95.

25. Edward Edwards, *Anecdotes of Painters Who Have Resided or Been Born in England; With Critical Remarks on Their Productions; Intended as a Continuation to the Anecdotes of Painting by the Late Horace Earl Orford* (1808), 4.

26. Quoted in Brian Allen, "Francis Hayman and the Rococo." Diss. 2 vols (London: Melon Institute, 1984), 1: 335.

27. Quoted in Ibid., 1:337.

28. An unfinished print of Angelica Kauffman's *Vortigern and Rowena* was listed as among William-Henry Ireland's possessions at the time of his death. For a listing of his possessions, see *Catalogue of an Extremely Curious, Highly*

Interesting and Valuable Library, Comprising Very Numerous, Rare, and Important Books, Many of Which Are of Early Date, The Works of the Best Modern Authors, Fine Books of Prints, Illuminated Missals and Borae (Including One Used By Mary Queen of Scots in Her Last Moments) Shakesperiana Including the Rare Folio Editions of 1623 (First) and 1632 (the Second), Also Numerous Other Editions By All the Celebrated Commentators; Lucrece, 1624; Early Editions of the Separate Plays; Very Many Historical and Critical Works and Other Books Illustrative of Shakespeare and Dramatic Literature Generally; W.H. Ireland's Own Collections, Relative to the Shakespeare Forgeries, Including the "Confessions" in his own handwriting; Numerous Old English Plays, From the Age of Shakspeare to That of Dryden; etc, etc. (London, May 14–17, 1866).

29. The picture is inserted in David Hume, *The History of England From the Invasion of Julius Caesar to the Revolution in 1668. To Which is Prefixed, A Short Account of His Life, Written By Himself* (1793), opposite p. 36. The print in the edition I consulted bears the date 1794. Obviously the prints were added later.

30. For a discussion of the contribution of all of these artists in relation to eighteenth-century Shakespeare editions, see T. Boase, "Illustrations of Shakespeare's Plays in the Seventeenth and Eighteenth Centuries." *The Journal of the Warburg and Courtauld Institutes* 10 (1947):83–108.

Chapter 4. More Forgeries: The Authentication of *Vortigern* Continues

1. Boswell died on 19 June, 1795, probably due to complications arising from gonorrhea. See William B. Ober, *Boswell's Clap and Other Essays: Medical Analyses of Literary Men's Afflictions,* 1–42.

2. William-Henry Ireland, *Confessions,* 95.

3. Ibid., 96.

4. Samuel Ireland's diary, BL MS 30346, 83r.

5. Ireland, *Confessions,* 96.

6. Samuel Ireland's diary, 20 February 1795, found in BL MS 30346, 77r.

7. Ireland, *Confessions,* 194.

8. Samuel Ireland's diary, 3 March 1795, found in BL MS 30346, 81r.

9. I am aware of the inconsistency in capitalization. I have followed Samuel Ireland's diary entry, 22 March 1795.

10. Samuel Ireland's diary, BL MS 30346, 81r.

11. This according to a copy of an article found in BL MS 30349, 39r.

12. Ireland, *Confessions,* 205.

13. Ibid., 119.

14. Ibid., 100.

15. Ibid., 110–11.

16. Advertisement found in BL MS 30347, 33r.

17. Farington, *The Diary of Joseph Farington,* 19 January 1796, 2:476; Caldecott tells a similar tale and suspected that William-Henry did not work alone. I agree. See Thomas Caldecott's letter to John Mander, 30 November 1797, in Schoenbaum, *Shakespeare and Others,* 150–53. The tireless Schoenbaum has also unearthed evidence that Samuel knew that the date on the Leicester document was torn off. See Schoenbaum, *Shakespeare's Lives,* 145.

18. Ireland, *Confessions,* 183.

19. Ibid., 184.

20. Jaggard, *Shaksperian Frauds,* 16.

21. Letter from Samuel Ireland to Mr. Byne, 9 November 1795, found in BL MS 30348, 166v. William-Henry regretted that the play was not published before its representation. See Ireland, *Confessions,* 188.

22. Mr. Barker, quoted in William-Henry Ireland, *Confessions,* 163–64.

23. According to the play's title page, it was presented to Samuel Ireland on 26 April 1795. See the play's title page found in BL MS 30348, 298r.

24. Ireland, *Confessions,* 180.

25. Ibid., 84.

26. According to Samuel Ireland's diary, 12 June 1795, found in BL MS 30346, 90v.

27. Schoenbaum, *Shakespeare's Lives,* 92.

28. Announced by the *Herald,* 12 January 1796, BL MS 30349, 33r.

29. List of contents of trunk found in BL MS 30346, 173r. Presented 14 April 1796, date supplied by BL MS 30346, 173v.

30. Ireland, *Confessions,* 26.

31. Letter from Mr. Hunt to Samuel Ireland, 3 September 1795, found in BL MS 30348, 158r.

32. Letter from John Byng to Samuel Ireland, 1 December 1795, found in BL MS 30348, 176r.

33. Ireland, *Confessions,* 246.

34. Ibid., 178.

35. Ibid., 194.

36. These books were bought from Mr. White, in Fleet St., Mr. Otridge in the Strand, as well as from his father. See Ireland, *Confessions,* 200 and payment for books bought from Samuel Ireland found in BL MS 3047, 10v–11r.

37. Ireland, *Confessions,* 197.

38. Ibid., 200.

39. Ibid., 202–12.

40. Hastings, *"Shakespeare" Ireland's First Folio,* 7.

CHAPTER 5. TALBOT AND WALLIS: TWO CASES OF BLACKMAIL

1. William-Henry Ireland, *Authentic Account,* 14.

2. *Oracle,* 3 October 1795, found in BL MS 30349, 21v.

3. Copy of letter from Talbot to William-Henry Ireland, BL MS 30346, 276r.

4. Letter from Talbot to Samuel Ireland, 16 September 1796, BL MS 30346, 280r.

5. William-Henry Ireland, *Confessions,* 124–25.

6. Ibid., 126.

7. Letter from Talbot to Samuel Ireland, found in BL MS 30346, 137r.

8. William-Henry Ireland, *Authentic Account,* 23.

9. Idem, *Confessions,* 126–27.

10. Ibid., 127.

11. Quoted in William-Henry Ireland, *Confessions,* 128.

12. Ibid., 128–29.

13. Ibid., 130–31.

14. Copy of article, found in BL MS 30349, 107r.

15. Letter from Talbot to Mrs. Freeman, 23 December 1796, found in BL MS 30346, 274r.

16. Letter from Talbot to Mrs. Freeman, 1 July 1796, found in BL MS 30346, 277v–278r.

17. Samuel Ireland's diary, 21 May 1796, found in BL MS 30346, 226r-v.

18. Letter from Talbot to Samuel Ireland, 16 September 1796, found in BL MS 30346, 279r-280v.

19. Copy of a letter from Talbot to Mr. Coles, BL MS 30346, 300r.

20. William-Henry Ireland, *Confessions*, 106–7.

21. Ibid., 183.

22. According to the *True Briton*, 31 December 1795. Article found in BL MS 30349, 32r.

23. William-Henry Ireland, *Confessions*, 222–23.

24. Ibid., 88.

25. Ibid., 89.

26. Ibid., 93. Samuel Ireland's diary records the same events, timing at one hour. See his entry for 30 December 1795, found in BL MS 30346, 171r-172v.

27. William-Henry Ireland, *Confessions*, 93–94.

28. Samuel Ireland's diary, 18 November 1795, found in BL MS 30346, 139v.

29. R.B. Sheridan, *The Letters of R.B. Sheridan*, 1: cf.152.

30. Ibid., 1:cf.167, 166–67.

31. Ibid., 1:213.

32. Ibid., 1: cf.234–35.

33. Ibid., 1: 251.

34. Ibid., 3: cf.321.

35. Ibid., 2: cf.138.

36. Ibid., 2: 138.

37. John Taylor, *Records of My Life*, 256.

38. William-Henry Ireland, *Confessions*, 228.

39. Ibid., 225.

40. Edmond Malone, *Inquiry*, cf.99.

CHAPTER 6. LIES AND MORE LIES: THE TRUTH ABOUT THE IRELAND FAMILY

1. *The Tomahawk*, 31 December 1795, 226, found in BL MS 30349, 34r.

2. *Herald*, 17 January 1796, found in BL MS 30349, 35v.

3. Referred to in John Bower Nicholas, *Literary Illustrations*, 1848, VIII, 8.

4. Edmond Malone, *Inquiry*, 166.

5. Ibid., 239.

6. Ibid., 244 and 219.

7. Ibid., 186.

8. William-Henry Ireland, *Confessions*, 3.

9. Quoted in Farington, *The Diary of Joseph Farington*, 2 January 1796, 2: 464.

10. Schoenbaum, *Shakespeare's Lives*, 135.

11. This was recalled a year before William-Henry died. With some bitterness he must have reflected that his father was right. Manuscript note in Ingleby, *Ireland's Shakespeare Fabrications*, housed in Harvard College Library, TS 680.23.5F, also quoted in Schoenbaum, *Shakespeare's Lives*, 135.

12. Mair, *The Fourth Forger*, 9.

13. Ibid., XV.

14. Document found in BL MS 30346, 183r.

15. Schoenbaum, *Shakespeare's Lives*, 147.

16. Letter from "Mr. H" to Samuel Ireland, 1 February 1795, found in BL MS 30346, 47v–48r.

17. Letter from "Mr.H" to Samuel Ireland, 2 February 1795, found in BL MS 30346, 49r.

18. Letter from Samuel Ireland to "Mr. H.," 7 February 1795, found in BL MS 30346, 61r.

19. Letter from "Mr. H." to Samuel Ireland, 23 February 1795, found in BL MS 30346, 52r-v.

20. Letter from "Mr. H." to Samuel Ireland, 25 July 1795, found in BL MS 30346, 54r-v.

21. Letter from Samuel Ireland to "Mr. H.," 3 March 1796, found in BL MS 30346, 62r-63v.

22. Samuel's diary, 12 June 1795, found in BL MS 30346, 90v. See also Samuel's diary, found in BL MS 30346, 208r-v.

23. Mair, *The Fourth Forger*, 106.

24. Letter from Samuel Ireland to "Mr. H.," found in BL MS 30346, 67r.

25. William-Henry Ireland, *Confessions*, 185.

26. Grebanier, *The Great Shakespeare Forgery*, 177.

27. Mrs. Ireland's account, May 5, 1796, found in BL MS 30346, 204r.

28. Mrs. Ireland's account, BL MS 30346, 205r.

29. William-Henry Ireland, *Vortigern*, 1832, VII–VIII.

30. Letter from Francis Webb to Rev. Dr. Jackson, 30 June 1795, found in BL MS 30346, cf.99r.

31. Letter from Dr. Spence to Samuel Ireland, 2 April 1796, found in BL MS 30348, 255r.

32. Joseph Farington, *The Diary of Joseph Farington*, 4 February 1795, 2:301.

33. Ibid., 2 January 1796, 2:464.

34. *Dictionary of National Biography*, 29:31.

35. Joseph Farington, *The Diary of Joseph Farington*, 23 December 1795, 2:454. I have amended Farington's shorthand.

36. Ibid., 23 December 1796, 2:454.

37. Ibid., 13 January 1796, 2:470. For William-Henry's birth date, see Schoenbaum, *Shakespeare's Lives*, cf.132.

38. Grebanier, *The Great Shakespeare Forgery*, 270.

39. *Dictionary of National Biography*, 29:32.

40. Samuel Ireland, *Picturesque Tour*, 1:130.

41. I have consulted Boyd's "International Genealogical Index for London and Middlesex" as well as Boyd's *Index to Marriages 1538–1837*. But this may indicate incomplete sources rather than any bastardy in the Ireland line. For a detailed study of William-Henry's possible birth and death dates, see my chapter Aftermath: Confessions and Disgrace, n.135.

42. See Herbert Croft, *Love and Madness*, 33, 39, 128.

43. *Dictionary of National Biography*, 38:257.

44. Ibid., first used at XIV and then throughout the book.

45. Idea first mentioned in Grebanier, *The Great Shakespeare Forgery*, 172.

46. Letter from William-Henry Ireland to Samuel Ireland, 3 July 1797, found in BL MS 30346, 307r.

47. Ibid., 307r-308v.

48. Letter from William-Henry Ireland to Samuel Ireland, 13 December 1796, found in BL MS 30346, 302r-v.

49. Letter from William-Henry Ireland to Samuel Ireland, 1 December 1797, found in BL MS 30346, 319v. It should be noted that William-Henry displayed no consistent system when referring to his mother. On 12 April 1797, for instance, he refers to her as his "Aunt" (BL MS 30346, 314r). His sister Jane also refers to her as "my Aunt" (7 June 1796, BL MS 30346, 235r). As for his possible common-law marriage, Boyd's *Index to Marriages 1538–1837 for London and Middlesex* does not list any record of a William-Henry Ireland or Irwin's marriage to his acknowledged first wife, Alice Crudge. Perhaps he followed in his father's footsteps.

50. William-Henry Ireland, *Confessions,* 251.

51. I am indebted to two studies of Chatterton that take similar paradigms: Susan Stewart's *Crimes of Writing,* 140–54; Louise Kaplan, *The Family Romance of the Impostor-Poet Thomas Chatterton,* passim. Stewart, extending a Freudian analysis, links imposture and forgery to day-dreams of masturbation and humiliation. I remain unconvinced. According to Harold Bloom, all literary creativity is based on an Oedipal paradigm of denying the literary father. See Bloom, *Anxiety of Influence,* passim.

52. On Anna-Maria, see Grebanier, *The Great Shakespeare Forgery,* 270.

53. Ibid., 177.

54. Ibid., 53.

55. Anonymous, *A Catalogue of Books,* 4 and 19.

56. Samuel Ireland's diary, 5 July 1796, found in BL MS 30346, 267r.

57. Jones, Barker and Craddock speculated that William-Henry might have also been responsible for a watercolor painting of the Globe Theatre, which was included in Thomas Pennant's *Some Account of London* (1793). See *Fake? The Art of Deception,* 156–57.

If the Ireland family is responsible for the piece, it could not have been William-Henry, as he was artistically incompetent. The suspicion, in such a case, would then fall on Jane. However, I see no reason to include the piece among the Shakspeare Papers. Rather, I think it is a tendency by Jones and company to tidy up history by blaming William-Henry for all the forgeries during this period.

58. See the Anonymous *A Catalogue of Books,* First Day's Sale, 1–4.

59. Mair, *The Fourth Forger,* 3–4.

60. R.B. Sheridan, *The Letters of Richard Brinsley Sheridan,* 1: cf.124.

61. Ibid., 1:124.

62. Ibid., 1:cf.127.

63. Ibid., 1:126–27.

64. Ibid., 1: cf.129.

65. Ibid., 1:cf.130.

66. See *Three Centuries of English and American Plays,* 14.

67. Perhaps Samuel did not escape Dudley's ire. Years later, he joined the attack on the Shakspeare Papers. See my chapter In Defense of the Realm: The Critics Strike Back.

68. See *Catalogue of an Extremely Curious, Highly Interesting and Valuable Library,* Fourth Day's Sale, 92.

69. Mair, *The Fourth Forger,* 5.

70. Farington, *The Diaries of Joseph Farington,* 17 January 1796, 2:472.

CHAPTER 7. NEGOTIATIONS AND THE REWRITING OF *VORTIGERN*

1. Quoted in Grebanier, *The Great Shakespeare Forgery,* 130.
2. William-Henry Ireland, *Confessions,* 33–34.
3. Taylor, *Records of My Life,* 257.
4. Ibid., 257.
5. Rostron, "John Philip Kemble's '*King Lear*' of 1795," 150.
6. Samuel Ireland's diary, 10 May 1795, found in BL MS 30346, 85r. Sheridan said he would come on or about May 24.
7. William-Henry Ireland, *Confessions,* 136.
8. Samuel Ireland's diary, 30 March 1795, found in BL MS 30346, 85r.
9. William-Henry Ireland, Preface to *Vortigern,* 1832, IV.
10. Samuel Ireland's diary, 31 March 1795, found in BL MS 30346,86r-87r. Samuel remained on friendly terms with Harris. He was invited to Harris's house for dinner on 2 January 1796, though it must be pointed out this dinner was later cancelled (BL MS 30348, 213). On 6 March 1796, Harris examined a "packet" sent from Samuel (BL MS 30348, 240r). Though its contents remain unknown, it may well have been *Vortigern* or *Henry II.* It is certain that Harris was invited by Samuel to discuss the future possibilities of publishing *Vortigern* after the play's failure (letter from Mrs. Linley to Samuel, 3 April 1796, BL MS 30348, 257r).
11. William-Henry Ireland, Preface to *Vortigern,* 1832, IV.
12. William-Henry Ireland, *Confessions,* 137.
13. Grebanier, *The Great Shakespeare Forgery,* 157.
14. William-Henry Ireland, *Confessions,* 138.
15. For details of Sheridan's visits, see document found in BL MS 30346, 88r.
16. Quoted in William-Henry Ireland, *Confessions,* 139.
17. Ibid., 139.
18. Ibid., 138–39.
19. Ibid., 136.
20. R. B. Sheridan, *The Letters of Richard Brinsley Sheridan,* 2:17.
21. Letter from Samuel Ireland to R. B. Sheridan, found in BL MS 30348, 6.
22. Copy of Sheridan's proposals, found in BL 30348, 8r.
23. Calculations worked out on document found in BL MS 30348, 14r.
24. R. B. Sheridan, *The Letters of Richard Brinsley Sheridan,* 2:18.
25. Ibid., 2:18.
26. Ibid., 2:18–19.
27. Letter from R. B. Sheridan to Samuel Ireland, 24 July 1795, found in BL MS 30348, 15r.
28. Letter from Samuel Ireland to R. B. Sheridan, 24 July 1795, found in BL MS 30348, 17r.
29. R. B. Sheridan, *The Letters of Richard Brinsley Sheridan,* 2: 20.
30. Ibid., 2: 24.
31. Calculations on document found in BL MS 30348, 19r.
32. Contract found in BL MS 30348, 36v-r.
33. Original draft found in BL MS 30348, 21r-34r.

34. Samuel Ireland, Preface, *Vortigern*, 1799, VI.

35. William-Henry Ireland, *Confessions*, 146–47.

36. Ibid., 146.

37. Ibid., 147.

38. This according to Mrs. Freeman's [Mrs. Ireland's] account, found in BL MS 30346, 210r.

39. *Observer*, 4 October 1795, found in BL MS 30349, 21r.

40. Letter from Samuel Ireland to Francis Webb, 12 October 1795, found in BL MS 30346, 105r-106r.

41. Letter from Jane Linley to R. B. Sheridan, 7 December 1795, found in BL MS 30348, 57r.

42. Letter from Mr. Byng to Samuel, 15 December 1795, found in BL MS 30348, 185v.

43. Letter from Francis Webb to Samuel Ireland, 3 January 1796, found in BL MS 30346, 108r.

44. Jane Ireland's letter to William-Henry, 1803, found in Folger, MS Bd. in PR 4821 I5 A73 1803.

45. Samuel Ireland, Preface, *Vortigern*, 1799, VI.

46. William-Henry Ireland, *Confessions*, 148.

47. The latter hand is discussed in my chapter, Aftermath: Confession and Disgrace.

48. The prologue is by Sir James Bland Burgess; the epilogues are by Robert Merry. These texts are included in my doctoral thesis, which included an edition of *Vortigern*.

49. *Oracle*, copy of article, 18 August 1795, found in BL MS 30349, 19v.

50. Letter from Mr. Powell to Samuel Ireland, 20 February 1796, found in BL MS 30348, 78r.

51. Letter from Mr. Powell to Samuel Ireland, 2 March 1796, found in BL MS 30348, 80r.

52. Letter from Samuel Ireland to Mr. Powell, 2 March 1796, found in BL MS 30348, 81r.

53. Powell's letter to Samuel requesting the copy returned by Larpent, so that it could be altered and sent back for final approval, 3 March 1796, found in BL MS 30348, 82.

54. Letter from Samuel Ireland to Mr. Powell, 5 March 1796, found in BL MS 30348, 83r.

55. Letter from Thomas Caldecott to John Mander, 30 November 1797, quoted in Schoenbaum, *Shakespeare and Others*, 152.

56. Samuel Ireland, Preface, *Vortigern*, 1799, VI.

57. Ibid., VI.

58. Referred to in a letter from Powell to Sheridan, 8 February 1796, found in BL MS 30348, 75v.

59. Kemble quoted in Samuel Ireland, Preface, *Vortigern*, 1799, VI.

60. Samuel Ireland, Preface, *Vortigern*, 1799, VI.

61. Letter from Samuel Ireland to R. B. Sheridan, 24 November 1795, found in BL MS 30348, 40r.

62. For Kemble's lukewarm support see document found in BL MS 30348, 43r.

63. Letter from Kemble to Samuel Ireland, 6 October 1795, found in BL MS 30348, 41r.

64. Letter from Samuel Ireland to R. B. Sheridan, 10 November 1795, found in BL MS 30348, 42r.

65. Letter from Samuel Ireland to R. B. Sheridan, 13 November 1795, found in BL MS 30348, 45r.

66. Letter from Samuel Ireland to Mr. Greenwood, 13 November 1795, found in BL MS 30348, 46r.

67. Samuel Ireland's diary, 18 November 1795, found in BL MS 30346, 139v.

68. Letter from Samuel Ireland to R. B. Sheridan, found in BL MS 30348, 43r-v.

69. Letter from Samuel Ireland to Oliver Beckett, 27 October 1795, found in BL MS 30348, 165r-v.

70. Letter from Kemble to Samuel Ireland, found in BL MS 30348, 47r.

71. Letter from Samuel Ireland to R. B. Sheridan, 17 November 1795, found in BL MS 30348, 48v.

72. Letter from Mr. Greenwood to Samuel Ireland, 17 November 1795, found in BL MS 30348, 50r.

73. Schedule of their meeting in document found in BL MS 30348, 51r.

74. Copy of letter from Sheridan to Greenwood, 18 November 1795, found in BL MS 30348, 53r.

75. Letter from Samuel Ireland to R. B. Sheridan, 7 December 1795, found in BL MS 30348, 58r-v.

76. According to the *Morning Herald,* 12 December 1795, found in BL MS 30349, 23r.

77. Letter from John Byng to Samuel Ireland, BL MS 30348, 185r. Ironically, Sheridan's father, Thomas, had once managed Smock Alley. For further reference, see Sheldon, *Thomas Sheridan of Smock Alley.*

78. *Telegraph,* 15 December 1795, found in BL MS 30349, 27v.

79. Letter from Samuel Ireland to R. B. Sheridan, 19 December 1975, found in BL MS 30348, 59v.

80. According to the *True Briton,* 30 December 1795, found in BL MS 30349, 32r.

81. Copy of article, 15 February 1796, found in BL MS 30349, 37v.

CHAPTER 8. IN DEFENSE OF THE REALM: THE CRITICS STRIKE BACK

1. An accusation reported to Samuel Ireland in a letter from John Byng, found in BL MS 30348, 184r.

2. *Telegraph,* 19 February 1795, found in BL MS 30349, 7r.

3. William-Henry Ireland, *Confessions,* 95.

4. Letter from Mr. Pardoes to Samuel Ireland, 4 April 1795, found in BL MS 30348, 259r.

5. Letter from Robert Relhan to Samuel Ireland, 15 November 1795, found in BL MS 30348, 194v.

6. The source I consulted was J. A. Venn, A Biographical List of *All Known Graduates, and Holders of Office at the University of Cambridge From Earliest Times to 1900.*

7. Mair, *The Fourth Forger,* 28.

8. Schoenbaum, *Shakespeare's Lives,* 139.

9. *Dictionary of National Biography,* 26:310.

10. Schoenbaum, *Shakespeare's Lives,* 145.

11. *Dictionary of National Biography,* 60:96–97.

12. Letter from Francis Webb to Rev. Dr. Jackson, found in BL MS 30346, 99r.

13. Philalethes, *Shakspeare's Manuscripts*, 25. Webb wrote under the alias of "Philalethes." For identification, see Vorbrodt, *Ireland's Forgeries*, 9.

14. Copy of letter from Francis Webb to Rev. Dr. Jackson, found in BL MS 30346, 98v–99r.

15. William-Henry Ireland, *Confessions*, 286.

16. See Samuel Schoenbaum's introduction to Caldecott's account of the forgeries in his *Shakespeare and Others*, 144–53.

17. Letter from Thomas Caldecott to Samuel Ireland, 13 February 1795, found in BL MS 30348, 108r-v.

18. Signed endorsement found in BL MS 30346, 180r-v.

19. Biographical information on these Believers culled from the *Dictionary of National Biography*, 5:45; 25: 334.

20. Ibid., 43:417.

21. Ibid., 58:86.

22. As recounted by Mrs. Mathews, *Memoirs of Charles Mathews*, 1:59.

23. *Oracle*, 23 April 1795, found in BL MS 30349, 13r.

24. Copy of article, *Oracle*, 16 February 1795, found in BL MS 30349, 6v.

25. *Oracle*, 16 February 1795, found in BL MS 30349, 6v.

26. *Oracle*, 28 February 1795, found in BL MS 30349, 8r.

27. *Oracle* on *King Lear*, 28 February 1795, found in BL MS 30349, 8r.

28. James Boaden, *Memoirs of the Life of John Kemble*, 2:163.

29. Quoted in Schoenbaum, *Shakespeare's Lives*, 152.

30. William-Henry Ireland, *Confessions*, 227.

31. Quoted in Schoenbaum, *Shakespeare's Lives*, 150.

32. *True Briton*, 14 January 1796, found in BL MS 30349, 35r.

33. Notion raised in a letter from Webb to Rev. Dr. Jackson, 30 July 1795, found in BL MS 30346, 98v.

34. Grebanier, *The Great Shakespeare Forgery*, 191.

35. Peter Martin ably covers Malone's career and is splendid on Malone's exposure of Chatterton. See his *Edmond Malone Shakespearean Scholar: a literary biography*, esp. 74–80.

36. *Dictionary of National Biography*, 35:437.

37. Quoted in Grebanier, *The Great Shakespeare Forgery*, 141.

38. Evans, "Shakespeare's Text," 33.

39. Gary Taylor, *Reinventing Shakespeare*, 144. In 1797, one year after *Vortigern* was staged, Malone was similarly accused of "using his interest at Oxford" to block the research of a fellow scholar from using papers he had examined at the Ashmolean. See *An Enquiry into the Conduct of Edmond Malone*, 10. But as this episode occurred after the Ireland forgeries they do not merit inclusion in the main body, as I can hardly charge Malone for crimes he had yet to commit.

40. Schoenbaum, *Shakespeare's Lives*, 130.

41. Grebanier, *The Great Shakespeare Forgery*, 137.

42. Quoted in Grebanier, *The Great Shakespeare Forgery*, 138–39.

43. *Dictionary of National Biography*, 54:145.

44. Anonymous, quoted in Gray, *Theatrical Criticism*, 206.

45. William-Henry Ireland, Preface, *Vortigern*, 1832, VIII.

46. Ganzel, "The Collier Forgeries and the Ireland Controversy," 6.

47. Steevens was not only an able forger but someone who used his scholarship to attack his foes. When editing his 1785 edition of Shakespeare, Steevens, in an attempt to irritate Malone, included materials by Isaac Reed. Stevens's 1793

edition was issued as a direct rebuttal to Malone's 1790 edition. Steevens also used the edition to avenge himself on two members of the clergy by attributing obscene footnotes to them. Confusing Malone by forging an entry would suit Steevens's style perfectly. Ganzel acknowledges that many of Steevens's forgeries may, even as yet, be undetected. He raises this possibility in *Fortune and Men's Eyes*, 94–95.

48. Joseph Farington, 23 December 1795, *The Diary of Joseph Farington*, 2:453–54. I have amended Farington's shorthand.

49. *The Gentleman's Magazine*, March 1795, 210. K. S., according to Arthur Sherbo, may be Edmond Malone. Strabo believes that the three letters to *Gentleman's Magazine* in March, April, and June of that year, are by Malone, writing under the pseudonym K. S. This is unlikely as K. S. says that he has seen the papers published in *Miscellaneous Papers* in person. Malone never inspected the displayed papers in person. While it is possible that Malone might have seen some of the papers through Wallis (see my chapter Talbot and Wallis: Two Cases of Blackmail?), these were not the papers to which K. S. refers.

50. *True Briton*, 13 April 1795, BL MS 30349, 11r.

51. Joseph Farington, *The Diary of Joseph Farington*, 2:457.

52. Ibid., 2: 477.

53. The work, he notes, shows Steevens's "influence" and Boaden's "parasitical regard." See Mair, *The Fourth Forger*, 133 and 136.

54. Quoted in Gray, *Theatrical Criticism*, 205.

55. William-Henry Ireland, *Confessions*, 227.

56. Boaden, *A Letter to George Steevens*. This passage appears in capitals in the original.

57. Ibid., 1.

58. Ibid., 2.

59. Ibid., 2–3.

60. Ibid., 3.

61. Ibid., 4, cf.4–5.

62. Ibid., 37–38.

63. Ibid., 40.

64. Ibid., 45.

65. Ibid., 50.

66. Ibid., 30.

67. Ibid., 18.

68. Ibid., 14.

69. Ibid., 27.

70. Ibid., 21.

71. Ibid., 27.

72. Ibid., 20.

73. Ibid., 26.

74. Ibid., 22. The Shakespeare quotations are from Boaden's article, not the modern, Oxford edition.

75. Ibid., 25.

76. Ibid., 26–27.

77. Ibid., 24.

78. Ibid., 33.

79. Ibid., 33.

80. Ibid., 23.

81. Ibid., 24.

82. Ibid., 33.

83. Ibid., 7.

84. Ibid., 27–28.

85. Ibid., 28–29.

86. Letter to Samuel from Isaac Heard, n.d., found in BL MS 30348, 232r-v.

87. Quoted in William-Henry Ireland, Preface to *Vortigern*, 1832, XI–XII.

88. [Francis Webb] Philalethes, *Shakespere's Manuscripts*, 12.

89. I suspect that Wyatt had some help from Webb. Years earlier, Webb used the very same tactic in attacking Johnson for his reversal on Jacobite principles (*Dictionary of National Biography*, 60: 97).

90. John Wyatt, *A Comparative Review*, 24.

91. William-Henry Ireland, Preface to *Vortigern*, 1832, X.

92. Quoted in Samuel Ireland, *An Investigation of Mr. Malone's Claim*, 3.

93. Samuel's diary, 1 February 1795, found in BL MS 30346, 69v.

94. Samuel's diary, 4 February 1795, found in BL MS 30346, 70r.

95. Mair, *The Fourth Forger*, 141.

96. Wally Chamberlain Oulton, *Vortigern Under Consideration*, 54.

97. *Monthly Mirror*, January 1796, found in BL MS 30349, 42v.

98. *Telegraph*, 17 January 1796, found in BL MS 30349, 35v.

99. James Boaden, *Oracle*, 24 December 1795, found in BL MS 30349, 30r.

100. *Morning Herald*, 21 July 1795, copy of article found in BL MS 30349, 19r.

101. Referred to in Grebanier, *The Great Shakespeare Forger*, 137.

102. *Telegraph*, 14 January 1796, found in BL MS 30349, 34v.

103. *Gentleman's Magazine*, February 1796: 93.

104. Samuel Ireland, *Mr. Ireland's Vindication*, 18.

105. Henry Bate Dudley, *Morning Herald*, 17 February 1795 found in BL MS 30349, 7r.

106. *Morning Herald*, February 1796, found in BL MS 30349, 7v.

107. Dudley, "The Mock Trial of Vortigern and Rowena," 23 March 1795, copy of article, found in BL MS 30349, 8v.

108. *Extracts From Vortigern*, Boaden's appendix to his *A Letter to George Steevens*, 57. Passage originally appears in italics.

109. James Boaden, *Oracle*, 21 October 1795, BL MS 30349, 23r.

110. *Extracts From Vortigern*, Boaden's appendix to his *A Letter to George Steevens*, 60.

111. I suspect it was written by James Henry Pye. See note 28 in my chapter, Prologue to Tragedy.

112. *Precious Relics*, 39–40.

113. Waldron was responsible to the 1805 attempted reconstruction of Massinger's *Parliament of Love*. For identification, see W. W. Greg's introduction, XIX.

114. G. M. Woodword, *Familiar Verses*, 10.

115. Ibid., 11.

Chapter 9. Prologue to Tragedy

1. James Boaden, *Memoirs of the Life of John Kemble*, 2:174.

2. No date given for this review, found in BL MS 30349, 37v.

3. Wally Oulton, *Vortigern Under Consideration*, 57–58.

4. A Confidential Friend of the Departed, *Public and Private Life*, 56.

5. Anonymous letter found in BL MS 30348, 241r.

6. Samuel Ireland, Preface, *Vortigern*, 1799, IV.

7. Letter from Samuel Ireland to Mr. Relhan, 20 March 1796, BL MS 30348, 123r.

8. Letter from Samuel Ireland to the prince's secretary, Mr. Tyrwhitt, 22 March 1796, found in BL MS 30346, 188v. Samuel spells the secretary's name "Tyrwhit." My spelling is derived from the secretary's own signature (BL MS 30346, 190r).

9. Letter from the prince's secretary, Mr. Tyrwhitt to Samuel Ireland, BL MS 30346, 190r.

10. Mair gives the date of 18 November 1795 for Clarence's inspection (*The Fourth Forger*, 128).

11. Mentioned in a letter from Thomas Caldecott to Samuel Ireland, 1 April 1795, found in BL MS 30348, 124r.

12. Arthur Strabo, "The Earliest Critic of the Ireland Forgeries," 499.

13. No date nor title to article. Found in BL MS 30349, 47v.

14. William-Henry Ireland, *Confessions*, 141.

15. Mair, *The Fourth Forger*, 163.

16. See *True Briton*, handwritten copy, 3 March 1796. Found in BL 30349, 56r.

17. No title to article dated 4 April 1796. Found in BL MS 30349, 70r.

18. William-Henry Ireland, *Vortigern*, 1832, V. Ireland believed that Kemble and others had colluded with Malone (VI).

19. Ibid., V.

20. Fitzgerald, *The Kembles*, 1:331.

21. A Confidential Friend of the Departed, *Public and Private Life*, 57.

22. Samuel's diary, 28 December 1795, found in BL MS 30346, 159r.

23. *Dictionary of National Biography*, 47:69–70.

24. Samuel's diary, 27 October 1795, found in BL MS 30346, 159r.

25. Letter from Samuel Ireland to Oliver Beckett, BL MS 30348, 165r.

26. Samuel's diary, 23 January 1796, found in BL MS 30346, 159v.

27. The prologue was delivered 4 February 1796, note from James Henry Pye to Samuel Ireland, BL MS 30346, 164r.

28. Pye may have gotten his revenge by writing *Precious Relics; or the Tragedy of Vortigern Rehearsed*. Pye had submitted a prologue for the play which contained the following quatrain:

> As well the taper's *base unlustrous ray*
> *Might* strive to emulate the orb of day,
> As modern bards, whom venal hopes inspire,
> Can catch one spark of his celestial fire. . . .

Precious Relics; or the Tragedy of Vortigern Rehearsed printed the following lines:

> As well the taper's base unlustrous ray
> Might try to emulate the orb of day,
> As modern bards, whom venal hopes inspire,
> Can catch the blaze of celestial fire. . . . (31)

Since Pye's prologue was not published until 1799, Pye must have either written this *Precious Relics,* or someone must have seen his original prologue, which was in the hands of the Irelands.

29. Letter from Francis Webb to Samuel Ireland, BL MS 30346, 114r.

30. See Francis Webb's prologue in BL MS 30346, 195r. I have modenized the spelling.

31. Samuel still printed it in the 1799 edition of the play. After all, he had paid for it.

32. *Dictionary of National Biography,* 7:306.

33. See Sir James Bland Burgess's prologue in BL MS 30346, 192r.

34. It should be noted that Samuel had little problem with the epilogue, written by Robert Merry and passed by the Lord Chamberlain on 22 March 1796 (BL MS 30348, 87r). Merry was quite happy to join Samuel in his box for the premiere and "triumph over the malice of all enemies . . ." (Letter from Robert Merry to Samuel Ireland, 24 March BL MS 30348, 228). Perhaps Kemble did not interfere because he was assuming, correctly, that the play would be well and truly ruined well before the last curtain.

35. Philip Rostron, "John Philip Kemble's '*King Lear*' of 1795," 152.

36. Article in BL MS 30349, 20v.

37. See untitled article in *The Herald,* 12 January 1796. Found in BL MS 30349, 33r.

38. Letter from Samuel Ireland to John Philip Kemble, 9 January 1796, BL MS 30348, 72r.

39. According to *True Briton,* 14 January 1796, BL MS 30349, 35r. However, according to *The Herald,* 12 January 1796, it was Kemble who read the play to the cast (BL MS 30349, 33r).

40. Letter from Samuel Ireland to Parr, 6 February 1796, BL MS 30346, 175r-v.

41. According to Mrs. Freeman's diary, 5 May 1796, BL MS 30346, 224v.

42. Benson married the sister of Mrs. S. Kemble. See the anonymous *Thespian Dictionary.* The *True Briton,* 4 April 1796, noted that one or two of the actors did not "appear to understand" their lines, and appeared in parts "they were wholly unable to perform . . ." (BL MS 30349, 65v–66r). My account of the evening will make it abundantly clear why I think this is a reference to the only two major casting selections left open to Kemble.

43. John Byng's letter to Samuel Ireland, 21 January 1796, found in BL MS 30348, 186r.

44. Letter from Samuel Ireland to R. B. Sheridan, 8 February 1796, found in BL MS 30348, 75v.

45. Letter from Powell to Samuel Ireland, 9 February 1796, found in BL MS 30348 78r.

46. Letter from Powell to Samuel Ireland, BL MS 30348, 78r. Though to be fair, some of these delays were caused by rewritings to the play by the Irelands.

47. Letter from Samuel Ireland to Powell, 12 March 1796, found in BL MS 30348, 84r.

48. Letter from Powell to Samuel Ireland, 12 March 1796, found in BL MS 30348, 85r.

49. Campbell, *The Life of Mrs. Siddons,* 270.

50. Letter from Samuel Ireland to Powell, 21 March 1796, found in BL MS 30348, 86r.

51. Campbell, *Life of Mrs. Siddons,* 270.

52. Letter from Sarah Siddons to Samuel Ireland, 29 March 1795, found in BL MS 30348, 93r.

53. William-Henry Ireland, *Confessions,* 148.

54. Letter from John Byng to Samuel Ireland, 29 March 1796, found in BL MS 30348, 177r-v.

55. See his preface to *Vortigern*, 1832, VI.

56. See article in BL MS 30349, 35v.

57. See letter from Samuel Ireland to R. B. Sheridan February 1796, found in BL MS 30348, 75r-76r.

58. Copy of article, *Morning Chronicle*, 21 September 1795, BL MS 30349, 21r.

59. Copy of article, *True Briton*, 26 September 1795, found in BL MS 30349, 21v.

60. William-Henry Ireland, Preface, *Vortigern*, 1832, VI.

61. Letter from Richard Valpy to Samuel Ireland, 27 March 1796, found in BL MS 30348, 221r-v.

62. Letter from Francis Webb to Samuel Ireland, 27 March 1796, found in BL MS 30346, 116r.

63. Letter from Samuel Ireland to R. B. Sheridan, 8 February 1796, found in BL MS 30348, 75r.

64. Letter from Powell to Samuel Ireland, 1 April 1796, found in BL MS 30348, 96r.

CHAPTER 10. OPENING NIGHT: THE PLAY'S THE THING. . . .

1. William-Henry Ireland, *Confessions*, 141.

2. Malone, *A Letter to Rev. Richard Farmer*, 3–4.

3. Article published, 4 April 1796, found in BL MS 30349, 67r.

4. Fitzgerald, *The Kembles*, 1:340.

5. Article published 7 April 1796, found in BL MS 30349, 72v.

6. William-Henry Ireland, *Confessions*, 143.

7. This according to the *Morning Post*, 4 April 1796, found in BL MS 30349, 61r.

8. Letter from Samuel Ireland to R. B. Sheridan, 8 February 1796, found in BL MS 30348, 76r.

9. Anonymous letter to Samuel Ireland, 1 April 1796, found in BL MS 30348, 241r.

10. Letter from James Burgess to Samuel Ireland, 4 April 1796, found in BL MS 30348, 173r.

11. William-Henry Ireland, *Confessions*, 144.

12. A Confidential Friend of the Departed, *Public and Private Life*, 56.

13. Hogan, *The London Stage*, Part 5, 1843.

14. Burgess's prologue is found in BL MS 30346, 191r–92r. I have modernized the spelling.

15. This according to the *Morning Post*, 4 April 1796, found in BL MS 30349, 61r.

16. *True Briton*, 4 April 1796, BL MS 30349, 65v.

17. William-Henry Ireland, *Confessions*, 149–50.

18. Ibid., 148.

19. William-Henry Ireland, Preface, *Vortigern*, 1832, VI.

20. *The Star*, 4 April 1796, found in BL MS 30349, 73v.

21. Composite of review in James Boaden's *Memoirs of the Life of John Kemble*, 2: 171 and William-Henry Ireland's Preface to *Vortigern*, 1832, VII.

22. *The Times*, 4 April 1796, found in BL MS 30349, 67r.

23. William-Henry Ireland, *Confessions*, 154.

24. Quoted in Marsh, *The Clubs of London*, 2:108. Referred to in Kemble's account as Humphrey Sturt, but the similarity of names and accounts has led to the conclusion that Humphrey Sturt and Charles Stuart are one and the same.

25. William-Henry Ireland, *Confessions*, 153–54.

26. This according to the *True Briton*, 4 April 1796, BL MS 30349, 65v.

27. William-Henry Ireland, Preface, *Vortigern*, 1832, VII.

28. William-Henry Ireland, *Confessions*, cf.152.

29. *Observer*, 2 April 1796, BL MS 30349, 59v.

30. Boaden, *Life of Mrs. Jordan*, 1:297.

31. A Confidential Friend of the Departed, *Public and Private Life*, 57.

32. All act and scene breaks, lineation and punctuation for the performance text are based upon my edition, prepared as part of my doctoral dissertation. See Kahan, "Reforging Shakespeare."

33. Fitzgerald, *The Kembles*, 1: 340. Fitzgerald attributes this shouting to a well-read audience that recognized the passages *Vortigern* was based upon. But in 1787, Malone had published a study which claimed that Shakespeare had not written *I Henry VI* and had only rewritten *II* and *III*. See his *A Dissertation on the Three Parts of Henry VI. Tending to Shew That Those Plays Were Not Written Originally by Shakspeare*. Shouting out *"Henry VI"* during *Vortigern* was in essence an attempt to link *Vortigern* with a play Malone had already said suffered from spurious attribution.

34. Gibbs, *Sheridan*, 191.

35. Farington, 2 April 1796, *The Dairy of Joseph Farington*, 2:518.

36. Article misdated as 3 April 1796, found in BL MS 30349, 59v.

37. According to his *Confessions*, the line was *"And when this solemn mockery is o'er"* (p.157). But William-Henry is misquoting his own play. Most scholars have followed the forger in this error.

38. William-Henry Ireland, Preface, *Vortigern*, 1832, VI.

39. This according to the *Telegraph*, 4 April 1796, found in BL MS 30349, 65r.

40. See Hogan, *The London Stage*, Part 5, 1843 and the *Telegraph*, 4 April 1796, found in BL MS 30349, 65r.

41. *True Briton*, 4 April 1796, BL MS 30349, 66r.

42. Hogan, *The London Stage*, Part 5, 1843 and the *True Briton*, 4 April 1796, BL MS 30349, 66r.

43. Quoted in William-Henry Ireland, *Confessions*, 159. The same speech is given with slight variation but the same significance in the Preface to *Vortigern*, 1832, V.

44. William-Henry Ireland, Preface, *Vortigern*, 1832, V.

45. For a more detailed account of Kemble's destruction of Colman's play, see Fitzgerald, *The Kembles*, 1:327–38.

46. Details from *The Thespian Dictionary*.

47. Box-office receipt, found in BL MS 30348, 102v–103r.

48. James Boaden, *Memoirs of the Life of John Kemble*, 2:172.

49. Boaden recounts the receipts at £103 and William-Henry's total payment at £90 but these figures are probably erroneous. In *Confessions*, William-Henry claims he forgot exactly how much he made. He says his father was given £300 for signing with Drury Lane but that Sheridan did not pay the amount at once,

deferring the sum into smaller payments. From this amount, William-Henry admits receiving only £60 (*Confessions*, 140). Nonetheless, *Vortigern* had such commercial value that even after this performance rumors persisted that the play had been sold to a banking house in Pall Mall for £3000 (*London Recorder*, 15 May 1796, BL MS 30349, 82v). But this is not borne out by the fact that the family retained possession of the play.

Chapter 11. Aftermath: Confession and Disgrace

1. Quoted in William-Henry Ireland, Preface to *Vortigern*, 1832, XII.

2. Quoted in Farington, *The Diary of Joseph Farington*, 29 December 1795, 2:457. Though if I am correct concerning Wallis's involvement, Malone had access to some of the papers without having to visit the Irelands. The poems he studied, however, were not in *Miscellaneous Papers*, nor do they account for more than a footnote in Malone's study. See Malone's *Inquiry*, cf.99. Therefore, my point is still cogent. Only Samuel's publication gave Malone the access to the papers he required to destroy their validity.

3. Malone, *Inquiry*, 314.

4. Ibid., 27.

5. Ibid., 159.

6. Ibid., 198.

7. Ibid., 28.

8. Ibid., 174.

9. Ibid., 209.

10. Ibid., passim, 69–74.

11. Ibid., 135.

12. Ibid., 148.

13. Ibid., 202.

14. Ibid., 71.

15. Ibid., 75.

16. Ibid., 78.

17. Ibid., 81.

18. Ibid., 127.

19. Ibid., 248.

20. Ibid., 286.

21. Ibid., 250.

22. Ibid., 276.

23. Ibid., 147.

24. Ibid., 155–157.

25. Ibid., 312.

26. Ibid., 309.

27. Ibid., 305.

28. Ibid., 88.

29. Ibid., 144–45.

30. Ibid., 162.

31. Ibid., 230.

32. Ibid., 231.

33. Ibid., 235.

34. Ibid., 291–292.

35. Ibid., 239.

36. Ibid., 105–6.

37. Ibid., 106.

38. Ibid., 111.

39. Ibid., 123.

40. Ibid., 137.

41. Ibid., 228.

42. Ibid., 314.

43. Letter from John Byng to Samuel Ireland, 1 April 1796, found in BL MS 30348, 178r.

44. William-Henry Ireland, *Confessions*, 141.

45. Samuel Ireland, Preface to *Vortigern*, 1799, IV.

46. Samuel Ireland, *An Investigation of Mr. Malone's Claim*, 1.

47. William-Henry Ireland, *Confessions*, 189.

48. Malone, *Inquiry*, 359.

49. Ibid., 361–63.

50. Ibid., 366.

51. William-Henry Ireland, *Confessions*, 240.

52. Original draft, 24 May 1796, found in BL MS 30346, 239r-v. The wording of the document is almost identical to an earlier affidavit written to exonerate Samuel. William-Henry signed this earlier document on 17 January 1796. A transcript of it is found in *Authentic Account*, 36.

53. *Massachusetts Magazine*, 8:5, quoted in Hastings, *Shakespeare Ireland's First Folio*, 1.

54. Handbill, BL MS 30349, 111v–112r.

55. Such "vindications" were not unusual. Following Bryant's support of Rowley, Thomas Tyrwhitt issued a similar reply entitled, *A Vindication of the Appendix to the Poems, Called Rowley's, in Reply to the Answers of the Dean of Exeter, Jacob Bryant, Esquire, and a Third Anonymous Writer; With Some Further Observations Upon Those Poems, and an Examination of the Evidence Which Had Been Produced in Support of Their Authenticity* (1792), in which he defended his position, maintaining it was Chatterton and not Rowley who had written the poems.

56. *The British Critic*, May 1796, 522.

57. Hogan, *The London Stage*, 3:1910.

58. Bate, "Shakespearean Allusion in English Caricature in the Age of Gillray," 202, 204–5.

59. "Nest of Ninnies" from a letter from George Steevens to Bishop Percy, 3 January 1797 in Folger MS C.b. 12; "Foodle" reference quoted in Hastings, *"Shakespeare" Ireland's First Folio*, 6.

60. Thomas Campbell, *The Life of Mrs. Siddons*, 269.

61. Letter from Thomas Caldecott to John Mander, 30 November 1797, quoted in Schoenbaum, *Shakespeare and Others*, 150.

62. Copy of article, *Gazetteer*, 27 December 1796, BL MS 30349, 110r. It should be pointed out that Thomas Caldecott maintained that Samuel was innocent. But he never publicly said so. In any case, he also suspected that William-Henry was only one of the "Authors" of the Shakspeare Papers. See his letter to John Mander, 30 November 1797, in Schoenbaum, *Shakespeare and Others*, 153.

63. C. M. Ingleby, *The Shakspeare Fabrications*, Appendix I: 100–101.

64. But for all these bold assertions and speculations Ingleby offered no proof, instead he merely smeared William-Henry's reputation further by recounting a

tale received secondhand concerning the forger's marital infidelities. See his *The Shakspeare Fabrications,* 102.

65. This according to Mair, *The Fourth Forger,* 210.

66. Ibid., 260.

67. Quoted in William-Henry Ireland, *Confessions,* 254–55.

68. Samuel Ireland's diary, May 1796, found in BL MS 30346, 223r.

69. William-Henry Ireland, *Confessions,* 239.

70. Ibid., 260–61.

71. Samuel's diary, no date, although entry begins May 1796. Found in BL MS 30346, 223r.

72. Samuel's diary, 11 June 1796, found in BL MS 30346, 257r-259r.

73. Grebanier, *The Great Shakespeare Forgery,* 252.

74. Letter from William-Henry Ireland to Samuel Ireland, 14 June 1796, found in BL MS 30346, 241r.

75. Samuel's diary, 9 December 1797, BL MS 30346, 303r.

76. Letter from George Steevens to Bishop Percy, 3 January 1797 in Folger MS C.b. 12.

77. Copy of letter from Samuel Ireland to William-Henry Ireland, 16 June 1796, BL MS 30346, 249v.

78. Mair, *The Fourth Forger,* 11.

79. Letter from Mrs. Freeman to Talbot, 16 June 1796, found in BL MS 30346, 250r.

80. Copy of letter from Mrs. Freeman to Talbot, 16 June 1796, found in BL MS 30346, 228v.

81. Copy of letter from Mrs. Freeman to Talbot, 29 May 1796, found in BL MS 30346, 229r.

82. William Mason, dedicatory poem in Mair, *The Fourth Forger. The Dictionary of National Biography* attributes this poem to George Steevens (54:147).

83. Samuel Ireland's correspondence with his lawyer found in BL, MS 30347, 35r–43r.

84. Quoted in Gray, *Theatrical Criticism,* 205.

85. Quoted in Ferrero, "Samuel Johnson and Arthur Murphy: Curious Intersections and Deliberate Divergence," 19. For a fuller account of Murphy's borrowings from live authors, see the same article.

86. Arthur Murphy's letter to Samuel Ireland, found in BL MS 30348, 287r–295v.

87. See his note accompanying a letter from Charles Marsh to Samuel Ireland on the rewriting of *Henry II,* August 1797, Boston Public Library, MS G 70.10.t.

88. Marsh, *The Clubs of London,* 2:107–10.

89. Samuel does note in his records that he paid £50 "To alter the *Vortigern* for Stage" (BL MS 30347, 11v). Aside from a few words added by Byng, all of which were cut for the stage version, the various manuscripts show no new readings by any hand outside that of the family. It seems strange that he should pay his own family and since the next entry is dated 1798, it is possible that this is a reference to some kind of payment to alter the stage version of the play for print. Murphy might have been paid a consultancy fee or for changes to a MS version copied out by Jane.

My personal theory is that this entry, like the others written on 11v, seem to be jottings from Samuel's head, rather than an accurate account of his finances. For instance, under his entry for 11 November 1798, he has the following entry "To attendance and trouble- 100 pounds." Another entry reads "To loss on Shakspeare Public-£53.18.11." Although this is a precise amount, one wonders how Samuel knew how much he has lost? Perhaps these are simply recollections and speculations.

As far as Samuel remembers, he spent £50 on the play, perhaps in paper, errands and hours lost in otherwise gainful employment. He lost roughly the same amount showing these papers to the public, perhaps for the same reasons, and doubles this amount to £100 for the emotional turmoil it had caused his life. Perhaps these numbers served as more than just personal notes. He was thinking of suing some pamphleteers for defamation of character.

90. Copy of article, *Gazetteer*, 5 January 1797, found in BL MS 30349, 109v.

91. Haraszti, *The Shakespeare Forgeries of William Henry Ireland*, 22.

92. Bodde, *Shakespeare and the Ireland Forgery*, 26.

93. Dr. Samuel Parr, *Bibliotheca Parriana*, 522.

94. George Steevens, quoted in Hastings, *Shakespeare Ireland's First Folio*, 8.

95. James Boaden, *Memoirs of the Life of John Kemble*, 2:169.

96. Charles Marsh, *The Clubs of London*, 2: 109–10.

97. Letter from Jane Ireland to Samuel Ireland, 7 June 1796, found in BL MS 30346, 235v–236r.

98. Samuel's diary, found in BL 30346, 206r.

99. Copy of letter from Mrs. Freeman to Talbot, 29 May 1796, found in BL MS 30346, 229r.

100. For example, see document attached to BL MS 30346, 142r.

101. Jaggard, *Shaksperian Frauds*, 7. There is a discrepancy between this account and his *Confessions* wherein he stated that after the failure of the play he was more easy in mind than he had been for a great length of time (159). Most likely the account in *Confessions* is yet another lie.

102. Mrs. Freeman's diary, 19 April 1796, found in BL MS 30346, 224v.

103. Samuel Ireland's diary, 16 May 1796, found in BL MS 30346, 225v.

104. Samuel's diary, found in BL MS 30346, 249r.

105. Copy of letter from Mrs. Freeman to Talbot, 29 May 1796, found in BL MS 30346, 229r.

106. For wedding plans and arrangements, see Samuel Ireland's diary, found in BL MS 30346 206v–207v.

107. Note referring to marriage found in BL MS 30347, 25. For Ms. Crudge's social background see, Mair, *The Fourth Forger*, 208.

108. William-Henry, Preface to *Vortigern*, 1832, II.

109. Hastings, *Shakespeare Ireland's First Folio*, cf.1.

110. Grebanier, *The Great Shakspeare Forgery*, 258–60.

111. A street known for its subculture of hack writers.

112. June 9, 1796, *Public Advisor*, found in BL MS 30349, 104v.

113. Anonymous, "Shakespearean Hunt," No. 11, found in BL MS 30349, 152v.

114. Poster found in the Folger S.B. 157.

115. William-Henry Ireland, Preface to *Vortigern*, 1832, I.

116. Ibid., VIII.

117. Quoted in Haraszti, *The Shakespeare Forgeries of William Henry Ireland*, 8.

118. Letter from Thomas Caldecott to John Mander, 30 November 1797, quoted in Schoenbaum, *Shakespeare and Others*, 153.

119. William-Henry Ireland, Preface to *Vortigern*, 1832, VII.

120. Ibid., XI.

121. Whitehead, *This Solemn Mockery,* 34.
122. William-Henry Ireland, Preface to *Vortigern,* 1832, XIII.
123. Ibid., VIII.
124. Hastings, *Shakespeare Ireland's First Folio,* 2.
125. Ibid., 2–3.
126. Ibid., 8.
127. Charles Hamilton, *In Search of Shakespeare,* 236.
128. William-Henry Ireland, Preface, *Vortigern,* 1832, XIII.
129. For more details on these printed texts and their derivative manuscripts, see my chapter, 'The Counterfeit Presentment: The Texts for *Vortigern,*' in my thesis, "Reforging Shakespeare: A Re Assessment of the Ireland Forgeries Together With The Play *Vortigern.*"
130. List compiled from the *National Union Catalog Pre-1956 Imprints.*
131. Quoted in Schoenbaum, *Shakespeare's Lives,* 155–56.
132. Papers discussed found in BL MS 45850, 42r–44r.
133. Two letter written to himself are found in BL MS 30347, 26r–27v.
134. List compiled from the *National Union Catalog Pre-1956 Imprints.*
135. There is a possibility that the entry in the parish register is not for the forger William-Henry Ireland. There are no wills to confirm his identity under the names Ireland, Irwin, Freeman, or Coppinger. I have consulted the "Archdeaconry Court of Surrey: Index to the Original Wills 1752–1858" and "Index to Surrey Wills: Commissary Original Wills: 1752–1858."

Even if it is our forger, we cannot be sure of his age. The family Bible states that he was born at one o'clock in the afternoon of Wednesday 2 August 1775 (Schoenbaum, *Shakespeare's Lives,* 190). *The Dictionary of National Biography* states that he was born William Henry Irwin in Church of St. Clement Danes in the Strand 1777. However the parish register for St. Clement Danes has no such entry. I have also checked under the names Ireland, Freeman and Coppinger. This same dictionary also states that the forger died at Sussex Place, St. George's-in-the-Fields, 17 April 1835 (*Dictionary of National Biography* 10: 469, 472). This date is very close to the burial date of the William-Henry Ireland in St. George-the-Martyr. Almost certainly, this is where our forger was buried. However, if the birth date is correct, then the parish register erroneously lists his age as 61.

If William-Henry did die at age 61, then he was born in 1774–75, not 1777. I have checked the parish register for 1772–78, without success. Boyd's "Index of London and Middlesex Burials in Parish Register Transcripts-Males, 1538–1853" lists a William Ireland buried at Aldermanbury in 1837. St. Mary's Adlermanbury's parish records list the date as 19 March 1838. But this date is at variance with the *Dictionary of National Biography,* and his age at death (55), would only make this William Ireland 11 years old when the first forgery appeared.

In this rare instance, I believe we can trust an Ireland document at face value, though as stated in my chapter, Lies and More Lies: The Truth About the Ireland Family, there is evidence to suggest William-Henry had problems accepting details concerning his parentage.

136. Shakespeare's birthday is accepted as 23 April 1564, though the exact date itself is only a surmise (Bradbrook, *Shakespeare: The Poet in His World,* 9). Shakespeare died 23 April 1616 (236).

Chapter 12. The Legacy of *Vortigern*

1. James Boaden, *The Memoirs of the Life of John Kemble,* 2: 167. Indeed, it wasn't just Kemble and Malone who attacked William-Henry. For a time after

his confession, he says he was "threatened with a government prosecution . . ." (William-Henry's marginalia in his copy of Boaden's *A Letter to George Steevens,* quoted in *Catalogue of an Extremely Curious, Highly Interesting and Valuable Library, Fourth Day's Sale,* 89). However, I have been unable to substantiate this statement. Normally, I'd accept it but since William-Henry has lied so often, this statement does not merit inclusion to the main body of the book without corroborative proof.

2. Boaden, *The Life of Mrs. Jordan,* 1:294.

3. Quoted in Grebanier, *The Great Shakespeare Forgery,* 157.

4. Jane Austen, *Mansfield Park,* 262.

5. Margreta DeGrazia, *Shakespeare Verbatim,* 10.

6. Quoted in Christopher Norris, "Post-structuralist Shakespeare: text and ideology," 48–49.

7. Jonathan Bate, "Faking It: Shakespeare in the 1790s," 3.

8. Ibid., 7–8.

9. Numbers calculated from *Index to the London Stage.*

10. *The London Stage,* Part 5: 1361.

11. Letter from Thomas Caldecott to Samuel Ireland, 21 February 1796, found in BL MS 30348, 122r.

12. Copy of article, BL MS 30349, 20r.

13. Copy of article found in BL MS 30349, 41v.

14. Quoted in Bate, "Faking It: Shakespeare in the 1790s," 2.

15. Letter from J.B. Burgess to Samuel Ireland, 4 April 1976, BL MS 30348, 173r.

16. Letter from Dr. Spence to Samuel Ireland, 2 April 1796, BL MS 30348, 255r.

17. Quoted in Pearson, *Bernard Shaw, His Life and Personality,* 218.

18. Not a direct quotation, but a paraphrase by a reporter of the *Sun,* 30 March 1796, BL MS 30349, 56v.

19. Charles Marowitz, "Reconstructing Shakespeare or Harlotry in Bardolatry," *Shakespeare Survey,* 40 (1988): 10.

20. Telephone interview, 21 July 1991.

21. Letter from Robert Relhan to Samuel Ireland, 15 November 1795, found in BL MS 30348, 194v.

22. These new devices are discussed in Kenneth W. Rendall, *Forging History: The Detection of Fake Letters and Documents,* 155–60.

23. Grafton, *Forgers and Critics,* 65.

24. Celeste Mitchell, "Fake or Break," *Daily Express.* Saturday November 28, 1992:23.

25. "Lesbian Witches Plot to Bring Back Hitler," *The Best of the Sunday Sport,* 2:50.

26. "Publish and Be Shammed," *Punch,* 10–16 April 1991:30–33.

27. The exhibition was 7–10 June, 1990.

28. Clara Bunting, "Blood on the Canvas," *The Guardian,* July 26:21.

29. Louise Hidalgo, ""Fakes the genuine art of the recession," *The Times,* 17 August 1992: 1.

30. "Antiques swindler took in experts," *Hampstead and Highgate Express,* 4 September 1992:1, 88.

31. "Writing Competition," *The Independent Magazine,* 12 November 1992:60.

32. Honeycombe, "Jack the day tripper? A clever bit of fakery." *The Weekly Telegraph,* No. 120. 26 October 1993: 20.

33. "Are paintings fake or Genuine?" *The Gazette,* Montreal, Canada, 3 March 1996:F3.

34. "100 Van Goghs might be fakes," *The Gazettte,* Montreal, Saturday, 5 July 1997, B8.

35. "Unknown Mozart aria up for sale," *The Globe and Mail,* 20 June 1996:A13; Sian Griffiths, "Novel twist to Defoe's spying," *The Times Higher Educational Supplement,* 30 October 1992:8; "[Three hundred] 300 Coleridge poems found," *South China Morning Post,* 13 February 1995: 12; on Whitman see, "Poet's lost leaves come to light," *South China Morning Post,* 19 February 1995: 10; "Trove of T.S. Eliot's letters," *The Montreal Gazette,* 2 November 1991:E14; "Satre notes find," *South China Morning Post,* 14 February 1995: 18.

36. For a list of other 1990s fakes and quackeries see Simon Hoggart and Michael Hutchinson, "A Sceptic's Guide," *Observer Magazine,* 20 September 1992:14–22.

37. *TLS* (June 8–14, 1990), 619, quoted in Richard Abrams, "Breaching the Canon. Elegy by *W.S.:* The State of the Argument," 54.

38. See Gary Taylor, "A new Shakespeare poem?" *Times Literary Supplement,* 20 December 1985, 1447–48; David Holbrook, "Certainly not by Shakespeare—but is it a literary fake?" *Contemporary Review,* Vol.258 (1991): 25–32.

39. Shakespeare, *Shakespeare's Edmund Ironside: The Lost Play,* edited by Eric Sams; *The Birth of Merlin, or The Childe hathe Found is Father,* edited by R. J. Stewart, forward by Harold F. Brooks, additional chapters by Denise Coffey and Roy Hudd. In terms of bibliographic citation, I list *The Birth of Merlin* as a Shakespeare collaboration with great scepticism.

40. In terms of bibliographic citation, I list *Shakespeare With John Fletcher: Cardinio or The Second Maid's Tragedy* as a Shakespeare collaboration.

POSTSCRIPT

1. For example, when covering the BBC's documentary, *Vortigern* was highlighted in the television section's "Pick of the Day" by *The Sunday Telegraph,* 16 October 1994 and the same day *The Observer* listed it, along with the 1958 classic, *The Blob,* as their choice for television viewing.

2. See, for example, Jeremy Kingston's error-filled review, "Ham Wrote Shakespeare, Not Bacon" in *The Times.* Monday, 27 October 1997: 19. Kingston is mistaken in many of his historical points: Sheridan did not pay £250 to secure the play and Mrs. Siddons was cast as Edmunda not, as Kingston reports, Rowena. See also Robert Hanks's review, "Compare and Contrast" in *The Independent,* 27 October 1997: Reviews, 4. Hanks also thinks *Vortigern* is a bad play, though he admits in what is apparently a convoluted afterthought "that badness is an important element of Shakespeare's greatest."

Works Cited

Abrams, Richard. "Breaching the Canon. Elegy by *W.S.:* The State of the Argument" *The Shakespeare Newsletter.* Fall 1995. XLV:3. 51-2, 52, 54.

Allen, Brian. "Hayman and Rococo." 2 Vols. Dissertation. Courtauld Institute of Art-University, 1984.

"Antiques swindler took in experts." *Hampstead and Highgate Express.* Friday, September 4, 1992: 1, 88.

"Archdeaconry Court of Surrey. Index to Original Wills: 1752–1858. Unpublished index." Greater London Record Office.

"Are paintings fake or genuine?" *The Gazette,* Montreal, Canada, Sunday, 3 March 1996:F3.

Austen, Jane. *Mansfield Park.* 2d ed. London: Signet Classic, Penguin Books, 1979.

Bate, Jonathan. "Faking It: Shakespeare and the 1790's." Unpublished essay. 1991.

———. "Shakespearean Allusion in English Caricature in the Age of Gillray." *Journal of the Warburg and Courtauld Institutes.* 49 (1986): 196–210.

Benthall, Gilbert. "The Life of John Hamilton Mortimer A.R.A." Unpublished manuscript. London: National Art Library, Victoria and Albert Museum Library, Special Collection LL 2261–1961 86.W.50–53.

Bloom, Harold. *The Anxiety of Influence: A Theory of Poetry.* 1973. London, New York: Oxford University Press, 1979.

Boaden, James. *A Letter to George Steevens, Esq. Containing a Critical Examination of the Papers of Shakspeare; Published by Mr. Samuel Ireland. To Which are Added, Extracts From Vortigern.* London, 1796.

———. *The Life of Mrs. Jordan; Including Original Private Correspondence, and Numerous Anecdotes of Her Contemporaries.* 2 Vols. London 1831.

———. *Memoirs of the Life of John Philip Kemble, Esq. Including a History of the Stage, From the Time of Garrick to the Present Period.* Vol 2. London, 1825.

———. *Memoirs of Mrs. Siddons. Interspersed With Anecdotes of Authors and Actors.* 2 vols. London, 1827.

Bodde, Derek. *Shakspere and the Ireland Forgeries. Harvard Honors Thesis in English.* Number 2. Cambridge, Massachusetts: Harvard University Press, 1930.

Bookbinders' Pension Society, 1832. [Poster.] Washington: Folger Library, S.B. 157.

Boase, T. "Illustrations of Shakespeare's Plays in the Seventeenth and Eighteenth Centuries." *The Journal of the Warburg and Courtauld Institutes* 10 (1947): 83–108.

Boyd, Percival. "Index of London and Middlesex Burials in Parish Register Transcripts-Males, 1538–1853." Microfiche copy of Church of Latter-Day-Saints Index, unpublished. Guidhall Library, London.

———. *Index to Marriages 1538–1837 for London and Middlesex.* Salt Lake City: Church of Jesus Christ of Latter-Day-Saints, 1988.

———. *International Genealogical Index.* 3d ed. Salt Lake City: Church of Jesus Christ of Latter-Day-Saints, 1988.

Bradbrook, Muriel Clara. *Shakespeare: The Poet in His World.* London: Methuen and Co., 1978.

British Critic, The. May 1796.

Brown, Sally. "'The marvellous boy': Chatterton manuscripts in the British Museum." *Why Fakes Matter: Essays on Problems of Authenticity,* ed. Mark Jones. London: British Museum, 1990: 83–92.

Buffoni, Clayton. Telephone interview. 21 July 1991.

Bunting, Madelaine. "Blood on the Canvas." *The Guardian.* London, 26 July 1991: 21.

Campbell, Thomas. *Life of Mrs. Siddons.* 1839. New York: Benjamin Blom Inc., 1972.

Catalogue of the Books, Paintings, Miniatures, Drawings, Prints, and Various Curiosities, A. Property of the Late Samuel Ireland, Esq. of Norfolk Street, Strand; Author of the Tour to Holland; Views of the Rivers Thames, Avon, Wye, Medway, Inns of Courts, &c. London, 1801.

Catalogue of an Extremely Curious, Highly Interesting and Valuable Library, Comprising Very Numerous, Rare, and Important Books, Many of Which Are of Early Date, The Works of the Best Modern Authors, Fine Books of Prints, Illuminated Missals and Borae (Including One Used By Mary Queen of Scots in Her Last Moments) Shakesperiana Including the Rare Folio Editions of 1623 (First) and 1632 (the Second), Also Numerous Other Editions By All the Celebrated Commentators; Lucrece, 1624; Early Editions of the Separate Plays; Very Many Historical and Critical Works and Other Books Illustrative of Shakespeare and Dramatic Literature Generally; W.H. Ireland's Own Collections, Relative to the Shakespeare Forgeries, Including the "Confessions" in his own handwriting; Numerous Old English Plays, From the Age of Shakspeare to That of Dryden; etc, etc. London, May 14–17, 1866.

Chalmers, George. *An Appendix to the Supplemental Apology for the Believers in the Supposititious Shakspeare-Papers: Being the Documents for the Opinion That Hugh Mc Auley Boyd Wrote Junius' Letters.* London, 1800.

———. *A Supplemental Apology for the Believers in the Shakspeare-Papers: Being a Reply to Mr. Malone's Answer, Which was Early Announced, But Never Published: With a Dedication to George Steevens, F.R.S.S.A. and a Postscript to T.F. Mathias, F.R.S.S.A. the Author of the Pursuit of Literature.* London, 1799.

Chambers Biographical Dictionary. Edited by Magnus Magnusson. 5th ed. Edinburgh: W&R Chamber Ltd, 1990.

"Choices," Television Section. *The Observer.* 16 October 1994.

[Clarke, Graham]. *W.S. Shakespeare Gent. His Actual Nottebooke Together With Numerouse Illustrations and Annotations By the Very Same Handde. Discovered and Authentickated by Graham Clarke.* Kent: Ebenezer Press, 1992.

Colman, George and David Garrick. *The Clandestine Marriage. A Comedy. As it is Acted at the Theatre-Royal in Drury-Lane,* in *Eighteenth Century Plays.* Edited by John Hampden. Everyman's Library No. 818. 1928. London: Dent; New York: Dutton, 1964.

Confidential Friend of the Departed, A. *Public and Private Life of That Celebrated Actress, Miss Bland, Otherwise Mrs. Ford, or, Mrs. Jordan; Late Mistress of H.R.H. the D. of Clarence; Now King William IV., Founder of the Fitzclarence Family: Delineating The Vicissitudes attendant on her Early Life; The Splendour of her Noon-tide Blaze, as Mistress of the Royal Duke; and her untimely Dissolution at St. Cloud, near Paris,-resulting from a Broken Heart. Accompanied by Numberous Remarks and Anecdotes of Illustrious and Fashionable Characters.* London, n.d.

Croft, Herbert. *Love and Madness.* London, 1880.

Cumberland, Richard. *The Brothers. A Comedy, Adapted for Theatrical Representation, as Performed at Theatres-Royal, Drury-Lane and Covent Garden. Regulated From the Prompt-Books, By Permission of the Managers.* Bell's British Theatre. No. 30. London, 1792.

————. *The West Indian. A Comedy, Adapted for Theatrical Representation, as Performed at Theatres-Royal, Drury-Lane and Covent Garden. Regulated From the Prompt-Books, By Permission of the Managers.* Bell's British Theatre. No. 18. London, 1792.

DeGrazia, Magreta. *Shakespeare Verbatim: The Reproduction of Authenticity and the 1790 Apparatus.* Oxford: Clarendon Press, 1991.

Dictionary of National Biography. Edited by Sidney Lee. London, 1885–1900.

Dobrée, Bonamy, *Restoration Tragedy 1660–1720.* Oxford; Clarendon Press, [1929].

Dobson, Michael. *The Making of the National Poet: Shakespeare, Adaptation and Authorship, 1660–1769.* Oxford: Clarendon Press, 1992.

Edwards, Edward. *Anecdotes of Painters Who Have Resided or Been Born in England; With Critical Remarks on Their Productions; Intended as a Continuation to the Anecdotes of Painting by the Late Horace Earl Orford.* London, 1808.

[Edwards, Thomas] By the Other GENTLEMAN of Lincoln's Inn. *The Canons of Criticism, and Glossary, Being a Supplement to Mr. Warburton's Edition of Shakespear. Collated From the Notes in That Celebrated Work, And Proper to Be Bound Up With It.* 3rd edition. London, 1750.

An Enquiry into the Conduct of Edmond Malone, Esq. Concerning the Manuscript Papers of John Aubrey, F.R.S. in the Ashmolean Museum, Oxford. London, 1797.

Evans, G. Blakemore. Shakespeare's Text. *The Riverside Shakespeare.* Boston: Houghton Mifflin Company, 1974: 27–46.

Farington, Joseph. *The Diary of Joseph Farington.* Vol.2. January 1795-August 1796. Edited by Kenneth Garlick and Angus Macintyre. New Haven and London: Yale University Press, 1978.

Ferrero, Bonnie. "Samuel Johnson and Arthur Murphy: Curious Intersections and Deliberate Divergence." *English Language Notes.* 28.3 (March 1991): 18–24.

Field, Andrew. *The Lost Chronicle of Edward de Vere: Lord Great Chamberlain, Seventeenth Earl of Oxford, Poet and Playwright William Shakespeare.* London: Viking-Penguin, 1990.

Fielding, Henry. *Jonathan Wild.* Edited by David Nokes. London: Penguin English Library, 1982.

———. *The Tragedy of Tragedies, or Tom Thumb the Great. As it is Acted at the Theatre in the Hay-Market. With Annotations of H. Scriblerus Secundus,* in *Eighteenth Century Plays.* Edited by John Hampden. Everyman's Library No.818. 1928. London: Dent; New York: Dutton, 1964.

Fitzgerald, Percy. *The Kembles: An Account of the Kemble Family, Including the Lives of Mrs. Siddons, and Her Brother John Philip Kemble.* 2 Vols. London, n.d.

Foster, Donald W. *Elegy By W.S.: A Study in Attribution.* Delaware: University of Delaware Press, 1989.

Franklin, Dr. *The Earl of Warwick. A Tragedy, Adapted for Theatrical Representation, as Performed at Theatres-Royal, Drury-Lane and Covent Garden. Regulated From the Prompt-Books, By Permission of the Managers,* in *Bell's British Theatre.* Translated by Franklin from De la Harpe. No. 15. London, 1791.

Freehafer, John. "*Cardenio,* By Shakespeare and Fletcher." *P.M.L.A.* 84 (1969): 501–513.

From a Jack to a King. Handbill. London, 1992.

Ganzel, Dewey. "The Collier Forgeries and the Ireland Controversy." *Shakespeare Newsletter.* 35.181 (1984): 6.

———. *Fortune and Men's Eyes.* Oxford, New York: Oxford University Press, 1982.

Gibbs, Lewis. *Sheridan: His Life And His Theatre.* New Yoek: Morrow & Sons; London: Dent and Sons Ltd, 1948.

Grafton, Antony. *Forgers and Critics: Creativity and Duplicity in Western Scholarship.* Princeton, N.J.: Princeton University Press, 1990.

Gray, Charles Harold. *Theatrical Criticism in London to 1795.* New York: Columbia University Press, 1931.

Grebanier, Bernard. *The Great Shakespeare Forgery: A New Look at the Career of William Henry Ireland.* London: Heinmann, 1966.

Greg, W.W. Introduction. *Parliament of Love.* The Malone Society Reprints. London, 1928. I–XIX.

Griffiths, Sian. "Novel twist to Defoe's spying." *Times Higher Education Supplement.* October 30(1992):8.

Halliwell[-Phillips] scrap-books in the Folger Shakespeare Library. Vol. XX. MS W.B. Hamilton, Charles. *In Search of Shakespeare: A Study of the Poet's Handwriting.* San Diego, New York, London: Harcourt Brace Jovanovitch, 1985.

Hamilton, Charles. *In Search of Shakespeare.* San Diego: Harcourt Brace Jovanovitch, 1985.

Hamilton, William. *Vortigern and Rowena* in David Hume, *Illustrated History of England.* London, 1806.

Hamilton, Paul. *Historicism*. London and New York: Routledge, 1996.

Hanks, Robert. "Compare and Contrast." *The Independent,* 27 October 1997: Reviews, 4.

Haraszeti, Zoltán. *The Shakespeare Forgeries of William-Henry Ireland: The Story of a Famous Literary Fraud.* Boston: Trustees of the Public Library, 1934.

Hastings, William T. *"Shakespeare" Ireland's First Folio.* Reprinted from 1:4 *The Colophon, New Graphic Series,* for the Friends of the Library of Brown University. Windham: Hawthorn House, n.d.

Hathaway, Anne [a pen name]. Letter. *Gentleman's Magazine.* February 1796: 93.

Havard, William. *Charles I. A Tragedy, Adapted for Theatrical Representation, as Performed at the Theatres-Royal, Drury-Lane and Covent-Garden. Regulated From the Prompt-Books, By Permission of the Managers,* in *Bell's British Theatre.* No. 21. London, 1793.

Hayman, Francis. *Vortigern and Rowena* in Tobias Smollett. *A Complete History of England From the Descent of Julius Ceasar, to the Treaty of Aix La Chapelle, 1748. Containing One Thousand Eight Hundred and Three Years.* 2d edition. Vol. 1 of 4. London, 1758.

Haywood, Ian. "Chatterton's Plans for the Publication of the Forgery." *The Review of English Studies: A Quarterly Journal of English Literature and English Language.* Edited by R. E. Alton. 36.141 (February 1985): 58–68.

―――. *The Making of History: A Study of the Literary Forgeries of James Macpherson and Thomas Chatterton in Relation to Eighteenth-Century Ideas of History and Fiction.* London and Toronto: Associated Presses, 1986.

―――. *Faking It: Art and the Politics of Forgery.* Brighton: The Harvester Press Limited, 1987.

Hebbron, Eric. *Master-Faker.* London: Pan-Macmillan, 1991.

Hidalgo, Louise. "Fakes are the genuine art of the recession." *The Times.* Monday, 17 August 1992: 1.

Hill, Aaron. *Alzira. A Tragedy, Adapted for Theatrical Representation, as Performed at Theatres-Royal, Drury-Lane and Covent Garden. Regulated From the Prompt-Books, By Permission of the Managers* in *Bell's British Theatre.* No. 5. London, 1792.

Hogan, C.B. *Shakespeare in the Theatre 1701–1800: A Record of Performances in London 1751–1800.* Oxford: Clarendon Press, 1957.

Hoggart, Simon and Michael Hutchinson. "A Sceptic's Guide to the Wonderful World of the Paranormal." *Observer Magazine.* 20 September 1992: 14–22.

Holbrook, David. "Certainly not by Shakespeare—but is it a literary fake?" *Contemporary Review,* 258 (1991): 25–32.

Holinshed. *Holinshed's Chronicles of England, Scotland and Ireland.* Vol. 1. London, 1807.

Home, John. *Douglas: A Tragedy. As it is Acted at the Theatre-Royal in Covent-Garden.* London, 1757.

Home, Henry [Lord Kames]. *Elements of Criticism.* 5th edition. 2 vols. London, 1774.

Honeycombe, Gordon. "Jack the day tripper? A clever bit of fakery." *The Weekly Telegraph.* No. 120. 26 October 1993.

Hope, Jonathan. *The Authorship of Shakespeare's Plays: A Socio-linguistic Study.* Cambridge; New York; Melbourne: Cambridge University Press, 1994.

Index to The London Stage, 1660–1800. Compiled with introduction by Ben Ross Schneider, Jr., forward by George Winchester Stone, Jr. Carbondale: Southern Illinois University Press, 1979.

"Index to Surrey Wills: Commissary Original Wills: 1752–1858." Unpublished index. London: Greater London Record Office.

Ingleby, C. Mansfield. *The Shakspeare Fabrications, or, the MS. Notes of the Perkins Folio Shown to be of Recent Origin. With an Appendix on the Authorship of the Ireland Forgeries.* London, 1859.

Ireland, Jane. Letter to William-Henry Ireland. Washington: Folger Library, MS Bd.in PR 4821 I5 A73 1803.

Ireland, Samuel. *An Investigation of Mr. Malone's Claim to the Character of Scholar, or Critic, Being an Examination of His Inquiry into the Authenticity. [sic] of the Shakspeare Manuscripts, &c..* London, [1797].

————. *Miscellaneous Papers and Legal Instruments Under the Hand and Seal of William Shakspeare: Including the Tragedy of King Lear, and a Small Fragment of Hamlet, From the Original MSS. in the Possession of Samuel Ireland, of Norfolk Street.* London, 1796.

————. *Mr. Ireland's Vindication of his Conduct, Respecting the Publication of the Supposed Shakspeare MSS. Being a Preface or Introduction to a Reply to the Critical Labors of Mr. Malone, in His "Enquiry into the Authenticity of Certain Papers, &c., &c."* London, 1796.

————. *Picturesque Tour Through Holland, Brabant, and a Part France; Made in the Autumn of 1789. Illustrated with Copper Plates in Aqua Tinta From Drawings Made on the Spot.* 2 vols. London, 1789.

Ireland, William-Henry. *An Authentic Account of the Shaksperian Manuscripts, &c.* London, 1796.

————. *The Confessions of William-Henry Ireland. Containing the Particulars of His Fabrication of the Shakspeare Manuscripts; Together With Anecdotes and Opinions (Hitherto Unpublished) of Many Distinguished Persons in the Literary, Political, and Theatrical World.* London, 1805.

————. The Holmes-Shakspeare Correspondence. Washington: Folger Library MS D.b.44.

————. Ireland's Advertisements, ETC. Additional MS 30349. London: British Library Manuscript Department.

————. Ireland's Forgeries. Narratives and Papers. Vol. 1. Additional MS 30346. London: British Library Manuscripts Department.

————. Ireland's Forgeries. Narrative and Papers. Vol. 2. Additional MS 30347. London: British Library Manuscripts Department.

————. Ireland's Forgeries. Correspondence on the Production of *Vortigern* [includes play *The Divill and Rychard*, 298r-322r.] Additional MS 30348. London: British Library Manuscripts Department.

————. Letters Relative to his [William-Henry Ireland's] Forgeries. BL MS 4850.

————. Miscellaneous papers. Folger Shakespeare Library. MS W.B. 496.

————. Manuscript material from Folger Shakespeare Library. Including *Vortigern* MS 3, MS 4, and MS 6. Stratford-Upon-Avon: Shakespeare Institute microfilm, S796.

————. Manuscript material from Folger Shakespeare Library. Including *Vortigern* MS 1, MS 2, MS 7. Stratford-Upon-Avon: Shakespeare Institute, microfilm S796.

————. *Vortigern, an Historical Tragedy in Five Acts Represented at the Theatre-Royal, Drury-Lane. And Henry the Second, an Historical Drama Supposed to be Written by the Author of Vortigern Together With an Account of the Shaksperian Manuscripts, &c.* Introduction by Samuel Ireland. 1799. Preface by Arthur Freeman. *Eighteenth Century Shakespeare.* London: Frank Cass and Co. Ltd., 1971.

————. *Vortigern; An Historical Play; With An Original Preface. Represented at the Theatre Royal, Drury Lane, on Saturday, April 2, 1796, As a Supposed Newly-Discovered Drama of Shakspeare.* London, 1832.

————. Manuscript material from the Larpent Collection. Huntington California MS CA 1110. *Vortigern* MS 5. Stratford-Upon-avon: Shakespeare Institute microfilm S794.

"Irresistible Rise of William Shakespeare, The" BBC television special. 23 October 1994.

Jaggard, William. *Shaksperian Frauds: The Story of Some Famous Literary and Political Forgeries: With Portraits of Lewis Theobald, George Steevens, Samuel Ireland, S.W. H. Ireland, John Payne Collier, and the Ireland Forgeries Caricatures by James Gillray.* Stratford-upon-Avon: Shakespeare Press, n.d.

Johnson, Charles. *The Country Lasses; or, The Custom of the Manor. A Comedy, Adapted for Theatrical Representation, as Performed at Theatre-Royal, in Covent Garden. Regulated From the Prompt-Books, By Permission of the Managers.* Bell's British Theatre. No. 1. London, 1791.

Johnson, Samuel. "Prologue" [speech on the reopening of Theatre Royal Drury Lane, 1747], in *Eighteenth Century Plays.* Ed. John Hampden. Everyman's Library No.818. 1928. London: Dent; New York: Dutton, 1964. XXVII.

————. *Rasselas and Other Tales,* in *The Yale Edition of the Works of Samuel Johnson.* Edited by Gwin J. Kolb. Vol. 16. New Haven and London: Yale University Press, 1990.

Jones, Henry. *The Earl of Essex. A Tragedy, Adapted for Theatrical Representation, as Performed at Theatre-Royal, in Covent Garden. Regulated From the Prompt-Books, By Permission of the Managers,* in *Bell's British Theatre.* No. 8. London, 1791.

Jones, Mark, and Paul Craddock, Nicholas Barker. *Fake? The Art of Deception.* London: The Trustees of the British Museum, 1990.

Jonson, Ben. *The New Inn,* in *Ben Jonson's Plays.* Vol. 2. Introduction by Felix E. Schelling. Everyman's Library 490 Poetry and Drama. 1910. London: J.M. Dent and Sons Ltd, 1957.

Jordan, John. Letter from John Jordan to Edmond Malone, March 19, 1790. Folger Shakespeare Library, MS W.B. 17.

Kahan, Jeffrey. "Reforging Shakespeare: A Re Assessment of the Ireland Forgeries Together With the Play *Vortigern.*" Dissertation. Stratford-upon-Avon: Shakespeare Institute, 1993.

Kaplan, Louise J. *The Family Romance of the Imposture-Poet Thomas Chatterton.* New York: Atheneum, 1988.

Kauffman, Angelica. *Vortigern and Rowena.* Photo from Witt Library, London.

Kelly, Linda. *The Marvellous Boy: The Life and Myth of Thomas Chatterton.* London: Weidenfeld and Nicolson, 1971.

Kenrick, W. *Falstaff's Wedding. A Comedy Written in Imitation of Shakspere. Adapted for Theatrical Representation, as Performed at the Theatre-Royal, Covent Garden. Regulated From the Prompt-Books, By Permission of the Managers,* in *Bell's British Theatre.* No. 31. London, 1795.

Kingston, Jeremy. "Ham Wrote Shakespeare, Not Bacon." *The Times,* Monday 27 October 1997: 19.

"K.S." Letter. *Gentleman's Magazine.* (March 1795): 209–10.

"Lesbian Witches Plot to Bring Back Hitler." *The Best of the Sunday Sport.* Vol. 2. Great Britain: Sphere Books Ltd., 1989.

Linley, William. *Last Whitsunday They Brought Me. Miss Leake's Favorite Song in Vortigern.* London, 1796.

Lipking, Laurence. *The Ordering of the Arts in Eighteenth-Century England.* Princeton: Princeton University, 1970.

———. *She Sung Whilst From Her Eye Ran Down. Miss Jordan's Favorite Song in Vortigern.* London, 1796.

The London Stage, 1660–1800: a Calender of Plays, Entertainments and Afterpieces, Together With Casts, Box-Receipts and Contemporary Comment. Compiled From the Playbills, Newspapers and Theatrical Diaries of the Period. Part 1, 1600–1700. Edited by W. Van Lennep, critical introduction by E. L. Avery and A. H. Scouten; Part 2, 1700–1729, edited with critical introduction by E. L. Avery, 2 vols.; Part 3, 1729–1747, edited with critical introduction by A. H. Scouten, 2 vols.; Part 4, 1747–1776, edited with critical introduction by G. W. Stone Jr., 3 vols.; Part 5, 1776–1800, edited with critical introduction by C. B. Hogan. Carbondale: Southern Illinois University Press, 1965–68.

Mair, John. *The Fourth Forger: William Ireland and the Shakespeare Papers.* London: Cobden-Sanderson, 1938.

Malone, Edmond. *Cursory Observations on the Poems Attributed to Thomas Rowley, A Priest of the Fifteenth Century: With Some Remarks On Commentaries on Those Poems, by the Rev. Dr. Jeremiah Milles, Dean of Exeter, and Jacob Bryant, Esq; and a Salutary Proposal Addressed to the Friends of Those Gentlemen.* 1782. 2d edition. London, 1792.

———. *A Dissertation on the Three Parts of Henry VI. Tending to Shew That Those Plays Were Not Written Originally by Shakspeare.* London, 1787.

———. *An Inquiry into the Authenticity of Certain Miscellaneous Papers and Legal Instruments, Published Dec. 24, MDCCXCV. and Attributed to Shakspeare, Queen Elizabeth, and Henry, Earl of Southampton: Illustrated by Fac-Similes of the Genuine Hand-Writing of that Nobleman, and of Her Majesty; A New Fac-Simile of the Hand-writing of Shakspeare, Never Before Exhibited; and Other Authentick Documents: In a Letter Addressed to the Right Hon. James, Earl of Charlemount.* London, 1796.

———. *A Letter to the Rev. Richard Farmer, D.D.: Master of Emanuel College, Cambridge; Relative to the Edition of Shakspeare, Published in MDCCXC. And Some Late Criticisms on that Work.* 2d edition. London, 1792.

Marder, Louis. *His Exits and His Entrances: The Story of Shakespeare's Reputation.* London: J. Murray, 1963.

Marowitz, Charles. "Reconstructing Shakespeare, or Harlotry in Bardolatry." *Shakespeare Survey: An Annual Survey of Shakespearian Study and Produc-*

tion. Edited by Stanley Wells. Cambridge: Cambridge University Press. 40 (1988 for 1987): 1–10.

Marsh, Charles. *The Clubs of London.* 2 vols. London, 1828.

———. Letter from Marsh to Samuel, August 1797. Boston: Boston Public Library, MS G 70.10.t.

Martin, Peter. *Edmond Malone Shakespearean Scholar: A literary biography.* Cambridge: Cambridge University Press, 1995.

Mathews, Mrs. *Memoirs of Charles Mathews, Comedian.* 2d edition. 4 vols. London, 1839.

McKillop, Alan Dugald. *The Early Masters of English Fiction.* 1956. Connecticut: Greenwood Press, 1979.

Meyerstein, E.H.W. *A Life of Thomas Chatterton.* London: Ingpen and Grant, 1930.

Mitchell, Celeste. "Fake or break." *Daily Express.* Saturday, 28 November 1992:23.

Morris, Sylvia. letter. 12 December 1992.

Mortimer, John Hamilton. *The Meeting of Vortigern and Rowena.* Photo from Witt Library, London.

The National Union Catalog Pre-1956 Imprints: A Cumulative Author List Representing Library of Congress Printed Cards and Titles Reported By Other American Libraries. Compiled and Edited With the Cooperation of the Library of Congress and the National Union Catalog Subcommittee of the Resources Committee of the Resources and Technical Services Division, American Library Association. Vol. 271. London: Mansell, 1973.

Murphy, Arthur. *All in the Wrong. A Comedy, Adapted for Theatrical Representation, as Performed at Theatres-Royal, Drury-Lane and Covent Garden. Regulated From the Prompt-Books, By Permission of the Managers.* Bell's British Theatre. No. 7. London, 1792.

Nicholas, John Bower. *Literary Illustrations.* No. 8. London, 1848.

Nicoll, Allardyce. *A History of English Drama 1660–1900. Early Eighteenth Century Drama.* 3rd edition. 6 Vols. Cambridge: Cambridge University Press, 1952.

Norris, Christopher. "Post-structuralist Shakespeare: text and ideology." *Alternative Shakespeares.* Editor John Drakakis. 1985. London, New York: Routledge, 1986: 47–66.

Ober, William B. *Boswell's Clap and Other Essays: Medical Analyses of Literary Men's Afflictions.* 1979. London: Allison and Busby, 1988.

"Olla Podrida." *The Tomahawk.* 31 December 1795: 226.

"100 Van Goghs might be fakes," *The Gazettte,* Montreal, Saturday, 5 July 1997, B8.

[Oulton, Wally Chamberlain]. *Vortigern Under Consideration; With General Remarks on Mr. James Boaden's Letter to George Steevens, Esq. Relative to the Manuscripts, Drawings, Seals, &c. Ascribed to Shakespeare, and in the Possession of Samuel Ireland, Esq.* London, 1796.

Oxford English Dictionary, The. 2d edition. Prepared by J. A. Simpson and E. S. C. Weiner. Oxford: Clarendon Press, 1989.

Parish Registers, Register Transcripts for St. Clement's Danes. Manuscript on microfilm, London: Westminster City Archives.

Parish Registers, Register Transcripts for St. George-the-Martyr. Manuscript on microfilm. London: Greater London Record Office.

Parish Registers, Register Transcripts for St. Mary's Adermanbury. Manuscript on microfilm. London: Guildhall Library.

Parr, Samuel. *Bibliotheca Parriana. A Catalogue of the Library of the Late Reverend and Learned Samuel Parr, LL.D. Curate of Hatton, Prebendary of St. Paul's, &c.. &c.* London, 1827.

Passages Selected By Distinguished Personages, on the Great Literary Trial of Vortigern and Rowena: A Tragi-Comedy. 3 vols. London, [1795].

Payn, James. *The Talk of the Town.* 2 vols. London, 1885.

Pearson, Hesketh. *Bernard Shaw: His Life and Personality.* 1942. London: Methuen and Co. Ltd, 1951.

Percy, Thomas. *Bishop Percy's Folio Manuscript: Ballads and Romances.* Edited by W. Hales and Fredrick J. Furvivall. Vol. 1. London, 1867.

——. *The Percy Letters: The Correspondence of Thomas Percy and Edmond Malone.* General editors David Nichol Smith and Cleanth Brooks. Edited by Arthur Tillotson. Louisiana: Louisiana State University Press, 1944.

——. *Reliques of Ancient English Poetry: Consisting of Old Heroic Ballads, Songs, and Other Pieces of Our Earlier Poets, (Chiefly of the Lyric Kind.) Together With Some Few of Later Date.* Vol. 1. London, 1765.

"Pick of the Day," Television Section. *The Sunday Telegraph,* 16 October 1994.

Piozzi, Hesther Lynch. *Anecdotes of the Late Samuel Johnson, L.L.D. During the Last Twenty Years of His Life.* Dublin, 1886.

"Poet's lost leaves come to light," *South China Morning Post,* 19 February 1995: 10.

Precious Relics; or the Tragedy of Vortigern Rehearsed. A Dramatic Piece. In Two Acts Written in Imitation of the Critic. As Performed at the Theatre-Royal, Drury-Lane. London, 1796.

Prospero's Books. Directed by Greenaway. With John Gielgud. Elseview Vendex, film 4 International, Canal Plus, NHK VPRO Television, an Allartis-Cinea Camera One-Pentena Co-Production, 1991.

"Published and Be Shammed." *Punch.* 10–16 April 1991: 30–33.

Rendall, Kenneth W. *Forging History: The Detection of Fake Letters and Documents.* Norman and London: University of Oklahoma Press, 1994.

Reynolds, Sir Joshua. *Discourses.* Edited with Introduction and notes by Pat Rogers. London: Penguin Classics, 1992.

Rostron, David. "John Philip Kemble's '*King Lear*' of 1795." *Essays on the Eighteenth-Century English Stage. The Proceeding of a Symposium Sponsored by the Manchester University Department of Drama.* Edited by Kenneth Richards and Peter Thomson. London: Methuen, 1972: 149–70.

Rowe, Nicholas. *The Royal Convert. A Tragedy, Adapted for Theatrical Representation, as Performed at Theatre-Royal, Covent Garden. Regulated From the Prompt-Books, By Permission of the Managers.* Bell's British Theatre. No. 27. London, 1794.

——. *The Tragedy of Jane Shore. Written in Imitation of Shakespear's Style,* in *Eighteenth Century Plays.* Ed. John Hampden. Everyman's Library No. 818. 1928. London: Dent; New York: Dutton, 1964.

"Satre notes find." *South China Morning Post.* 14 February 1995: 18.

Schoenbaum, Samuel. *Shakespeare and Others*. Washington: Folger Books, The Folger Shakespeare Library; London: Scolar Press, 1985.

———. *Shakespeare's Lives*. New Edition. Oxford and New York: Oxford University Press, 1991; rpt. 1993.

Scouten, Arthur. *Great Writers of the English Language: Restoration and Eighteenth-Century Drama*, General Editor James Vinson, assoc. ed. D. L. Kirkpatrick. London and Basingstoke: Macmillan Press, 1980, 1–13.

Shakespeare, William. *The Complete Works*. General Editors Stanley Wells, Gary Taylor. Oxford: Clarendon Press, 1988.

———. *The Double Falshood; or, The Distrest Lovers. A Play, As it is Acted at the Theatre-Royal in Drury-Lane. Written Originally by W. Shakespeare; And Now Revised and Adapted to the Stage by Mr. Theobald, the Author of Shakespeare Restor'd*. London, 1728.

———. *Double Falsehood*. Edited by Walter Graham. Western Reserve Studies. Cleveland, Ohio: Western Reserve University, 1920.

———. *Shakespeare's Edmund Ironside: The Lost Play*. Edited by Eric Sams. Aldershot, Hants: Wildwood House, 1985.

Shakespeare, William and John Fletcher. *Shakespeare With John Fletcher: Cardinio or The Second Maid's Tragedy*. New York: Marlowe and Company, 1994.

Shakespeare, William and William Rowley. *The Birth of Merlin, or The Childe hathe Found is Father*. Edited by R. J. Stewart; Forward by Harold F. Brooks, additional chapters by Denise Coffey and Roy Hudd. Longmead, Shaftsbury, Dorset: Element Books Ltd., 1989.

Sheldon, Esther K. *Thomas Sheridan of Smock-Alley: Recording His Life as Actor and Theater Manager in Both Dublin and London; and Including A Smock-Alley Calender For the Years of His Management*. Princeton: Princeton University Press, 1967.

Sherbo, Arthur. "The Earliest (?) Critic of the Ireland Shakespeare Forgeries." *Notes and Queries*. 35.4 (December 1988): 498–500.

Sheridan, Richard Brinsley. *The Dramatic Works of Richard Brinsley Sheridan*. Vol. 1. Edited by Cecil Price. Oxford: Clarendon Press, 1973.

———. *The Letters of Richard Brinsley Sheridan*. 3 vols. Edited by Cecil Price. Oxford: Clarendon Press, 1966.

Shirley, William. *Edward the Black Prince; or, The Battle of Poitiers. An Historical Tragedy, Adapted for Theatrical Representation, as Performed at Theatre-Royal, Drury-Lane. Regulated From the Prompt-Books, By Permission of the Managers*, in *Bell's British Theatre*. No. 4. London, 1791.

Stafford, Fiona J. *The Sublime Savage: A Study of James Macpherson and the Poems of Ossian*. Edinburgh: Edinburgh University Press, 1988.

Steevens, George. Letter from George Steevens to Bishop Percy, 3 January 1797 in Folger MS C.b. 12.

Stewart, Susan. *Crimes of Writing: Problems in the Containment of Representation*. New York; London: Oxford University Press, 1991.

Stothard, Thomas. *Vortigern and Rowena* in David Hume. *The History of England From the Invasion of Julius Ceasar to the Revolution in 1668. To Which is Prefixed, A Short Account of His Life*. Vol. 1 of 3. Parson's Pocket Edition. London, 1793.

Sunderland, John. *John Hamilton Mortimer His Life and Works. The Walpole Society.* Vol. 52. London: The Walpole Society, 1988.

Taylor, Donald S. *Thomas Chatterton's Art: Experiments in Imagined History.* Princeton: Princeton University Press, 1978.

Taylor, Gary. "A new Shakespeare poem?" *Times Literary Supplement,* 20 December 1985: 1447–48.

———. *Reinventing Shakespeare: A Cultural History From the Restoration to the Present.* London: Oxford University Press, 1989.

Taylor, John. *Records of My Life. Personal Reminiscences by O'Keefe, Kelly and Taylor.* Edited by Richard Henry Stoddard. New York: Scribner, Armstrong, and Company, 1875.

The Thespian Dictionary of Dramatic Biography of the Present Age. Second Edition. London, 1805.

"[Three hundred] 300 Coleridge poems find." *South China Morning Post.* 13 February 1995: 12.

Three Centuries of English and American Plays: A Checklist England: 1500–1800; United States:1714–1830. Edited by William Berquist. New York: Readex Microprint Corporation, 1963.

Tietze, Hans. *Genuine and False.* London: Max Parrish and Co., Ltd., 1948.

"Trove of T. S. Eliot's letters found in a gardener's attic." *Montreal Gazette.* 2 November 1991: E14.

True Briton. 3 March 1796.

Tyrwhitt, Thomas. *A Vindication of the Appendix to the Poems, Called Rowley's, In Reply to the Answers of the Dean of Exeter, Jacob Bryant, Esquire, and a Third Anonymous Writer; With Some Further Observations Upon Those Poems, and an Examination of the Evidence Which Has Been Produced in Support of Their Authenticity.* 1782. London, 1792.

"Unknown Mozart aria up for sale," *The Globe and Mail,* June 20, 1996: A13.

Venn, J. A. *A Biographical List of All Known Graduates and Holders of Office at the University From Earliest Times to 1990.* Part 5. Vol. 5. Cambridge: University of Cambridge, 1940.

Vickers, Brian. Introduction. *Shakespeare: The Critical Heritage.* Vol. 2 of 6: 1693–1733. London and Boston: Routledge & Kegan Paul, 1974. 1–21.

Vorbrort, Oberlehrer. *Ireland's Forgeries. Beilage zum Jahresbericht der Realschule in Meissen.* Meissen, 1884–85.

[Waldron, Francis.] *Free Reflections on Miscellaneous Papers and Legal Instruments, Under the Hand and Seal of William Shakspeare, in the Possession of Samuel Ireland, of Norfolk Street. To Which Are Added, Extracts from an Unpublished MS. Play, Called The Virgin Queen. Written By, or in Imitation of, Shakspeare.* London, 1796.

Wallis, Henry. *Chatterton.* Housed in Tate Gallery, London.

Warton, Thomas. *An Enquiry into the Authenticity of the Poems Attributed to Thomas Rowley. In Which the Arguments of the Dean of Exeter, and Mr. Bryant, are Examined.* London, 1792.

[Webb, Francis] Philalethes. *Shakspeare's Manuscripts, in the Possession of Mr. Ireland, Examined, Respecting The Internal and External Evidences of Their Authenticity.* London, 1796.

Westall, Richard. *Helen at the Scalean Gate.* Photo from Witt Library, London. Picture also found in Rapin de Thoyras. *The History of England. Written in French Done into English, With Additional Notes Marked With an *, by N. Tindal, M.A. Rector of Great Waltham in Essex.* Vol. 1 of 15. London, 1725.

———. *Lady Jane Grey Pleading for Her Children.* Photo from Witt Library, London.

William Shakespeare's Romeo and Juliet. Dir. Baz Luhrmann. Hollywood: 20th Century Fox, 1996.

Whitehead, John. *This Solemn Mockery: The Art of Literary Forgery.* London: Arlington Books, 1973.

[Woodward, G.M.]. *Familiar Verses, From the Ghost of Willy Shakspeare to Samuel Ireland. To which is Added, Prince Robert: An Auncient Ballad.* London, 1796.

Wyatt, John [By a Friend to Consistency]. *A Comparative Review of the Opinions of Mr. James Boaden, (Editor of the Oracle) In February, March, and April, 1795; and of James Boaden, Esq. (Author of Fountainville Forest, and of a Letter to George Steevens, Esq.) In February 1796, Relative to the Shakspeare MSS.* London, 1796.

"Writing Competition." *The Independent Magazine.* 21 November 1992:60.

Young, Edward. *The Revenge. As it was Acted in Drury-Lane. By His Majesty's Servants.* London, 1721.

Index

Ayckbourn, Alan, 223
Addison, Joseph, 22, 23, 30

Barry, James, 76
Barrymore, William, 174, 186
Bate, Jonathan, 223
Beaumont, Francis, and John Fletcher, 73
Beckett, Oliver, 143
Beckett, Samuel, 220
Bensley, Robert, 174, 182
Benson, Robert, 174, 182, 183, 187, 244 n. 42
Bertrum, Charles Julius, 35
Bickerstaff, Isaac, 225 n. 17
Bindley, James, 148
Blackhouse, Edmund, 219
Blakey, Nicholas, 79–80
Bloom, Harold, 23, 236 n. 51
Boaden, James, 34, 148–49, 153–58, 159, 160, 163, 164, 166, 183, 188, 189, 200, 204–5, 213, 247–48 n. 49, 251–52 n. 1
Bodde, Derek, 10
Bononcini, Giovanni, 30
Booth, Barton, 26
Boswell, Alexander, 82
Boswell, James, 19, 25, 41, 82–83, 145, 146, 148, 152, 159, 216, 227 n. 73, 232 n. 1
Branagh, Kenneth, 223
Buffoni, Clayton, 218
Burgess, Anthony, 34
Burgess, Sir James Bland, 173
Burke, Edmund, 39, 66, 82, 151, 214, 215
Byng, John, 44, 92, 148, 160, 174
Byng, Mrs. John, 133

Caldecott, Thomas, 139, 147, 160, 196, 204, 215, 232–33 n. 17, 248 n. 62
Campbell, Thomas, 194

Carlton, Bob, 217
Caufield, Thomas, 174, 182
Cave, Nick, 218
Chalmers, George, 193–94
Chatterton, Thomas, 10, 12, 35, 36, 44, 46, 50, 55, 109, 121, 151, 155, 159, 199, 203, 204, 214, 236 n. 51, 240 n. 35
Chaucer, Geoffrey, 44–47, 50
Cibber, Colley, 28
Clarence, duke of (future William IV), 19, 43, 132, 142, 168, 180
Clark, Graham, 220
Coleridge, Samuel, 221
Coles, Mr., 101
Collier, John Payne, 196, 219
Colman the Elder, George, 29, 187, 225 n. 17, 246 n. 45
Colman the Younger, George, 225 n. 17
Congreve, William, 154
Cowper, William, 66
Croft, Herbert, 10, 47, 117, 148
Crudge, Alice, 11, 202–3, 211, 236 n. 49
Cumberland, Richard, 26, 27
Cunningham, Peter, 219

Daniel, Samuel, 73
Dawson, Charles, 219
Defoe, Daniel, 34, 117, 221, 227 n. 70
DeGrazia, Maria, 9, 11, 39
Dekker, Thomas, 73
De la Harpe, Jean François, 32
Dent, Dr., 200
Derrida, Jacques, 214–15
Dickens, Charles, 122
Dignum, Charles, 174, 183
Dobson, Michael, 11, 22, 34
Dodd, William, 117
Dryden, John, 23, 24, 73, 131
Dudley, Henry Bate, 122, 162–63, 236 n. 67

Eden, Sir Fredrick, 56, 146
Einburg, Elizabeth, 76
Eliot, T. S., 221

Fairchild, John, 220
Farington, Joseph, 50, 114, 168–69
Farmer, Richard, 37, 192
Field, Andrew, 220
Fielding, Henry, 30, 33, 34
Fitzgerald, Percy, 246 n. 33
Foote, Samuel, 27–28
Ford, John, 37, 73
Foster, Donald W., 222
Franklin, Dr. Thomas, 32
Furnivall, Fredrick James, 227 n. 71

Gallini, Andrea, 104
Ganzel, Dewey, 153, 241 n. 47
Garrick, David, 26, 66, 101, 104; and
  George Colman, 29
Gay, John, 225 n. 17
Gibbon, Edward, 25
Gildon, Charles, 23
Gillray, James, 194
Goldsmith, Oliver, 82
Grafton, Antony, 11, 219
Granville, George, 23
Grebanier, Bernard, 10–11, 117, 152
Greene, Robert, 73
Greenaway, Peter, 217
Greenwood, Mr., 141, 142, 143, 144
Griffiths, Francis, and Elsie Wright,
  220

Hackman, James, 118
Hamilton, Charles, 211
Hamilton, Paul, 11
Hamilton, William, 76, 80, 81
Hanks, Robert 253 n. 2
Haraszti, Zoltán, 10
Harding, Silvester, 194
Harmston, Joe, 223
Harris, Thomas, 125, 132, 202, 237 n.
  10
Havard, William, 31
Hayman, Francis, 76, 79, 81
Haywood, Pippa, 223, 224
Heard, Sir Isaac, 148
Hebborn, Eric, 221
Hewlett, John, 146, 148
Hill, Aaron, 23, 25–26

Hitler, Adolf, 220
Hogarth, William, 122
Holinshed, Raphael, 73, 189
Home, John, 33, 96
Hory, Elmyr de, 220
Hoskins, John, 146
Hubbard, Lord John, 29
Hume, David, 81
Humphrey, Mr., 160

Ingleby, C. M., 196, 249 n. 64
Ireland, Anna-Maria, 109, 119, 134, 135
Ireland, Jane, 109, 119, 133, 135, 249–
  50 n. 89
Ireland, Samuel, 9, 10, 41, 44, 47, 54,
  62, 67, 44–45, 51, 71, 73, 75, 86, 87,
  88, 92, 96, 97, 98, 100, 101, 107, 108–
  12, 127–32, 139, 141–44, 154, 157,
  160, 161, 162, 164, 165, 166, 167, 172,
  173, 174, 175, 176, 177, 178, 179,
  180, 184–85, 187, 188, 191, 192,
  193, 197–200, 202, 214, 215, 218–19,
  224, 237 n. 10, 244 nn. 31 and 34,
  247 n. 2, 247–48 n. 49, 248 n. 62, 249–
  50 n. 89; background, 113–23; forgeries, 121; playwrighting abilities, 121–
  23, 236 n. 67; trip to Stratford, 51–53
Ireland, Samuel, Jr., 119
Ireland, Mrs. (maiden name: Anna Maria deBurgh; married name: Mrs.
  Coppinger; also known as Mrs. Freeman), 10, 99, 123, 135, 138, 143,
  198–99
Ireland, William-Henry, 9–10, 11, 12,
  19, 20, 33, 34, 40, 41, 44, 54, 55, 67,
  71, 82, 96–99, 102–3, 105, 123, 124,
  126, 145, 146, 147, 149, 153, 154, 157,
  159, 176, 191, 192–93, 196–99, 232–
  33 n. 17, 235 nn. 11 and 41, 236 n. 49,
  248 n. 62, 250 n. 101, 251 n. 135, 251–
  52 n. 1; marriage, 202–3, 211, 249 n.
  64; novels, 211–12; personae: Mr. H.,
  54–56, 66, 97, 100–101, 111–13, 121,
  138, 154–55, 177, 196, 197, 201–2;
  Saraphina, 138, 211; pre-Shakspeare
  Papers forgeries, 47–51, 236 n. 57;
  post-Shakspeare Papers forgeries,
  138, 205–11; relation to other forgers,
  35–36, 44–47; relationship with Samuel, 46–47, 51, 53–54, 108–21, 123,
  196–98; trip to Stratford 51–53.
  Shakspeare Papers forgeries: Deed

of Gift, 88–91, 119, 149, 155, 161, 189; Deed of Trust, 189; *Miscellaneous Papers*, 86–87, 164, 166; Profession of Faith, 19, 41, 57, 58–62, 149, 189, 200; promised forgeries, 91–94; Shakspeare and Cowley, 66, 189; Shakspeare and the Fraiser Deed, 56, 146; Shakspeare and Queen Elizabeth, 19, 41, 67–68, 70, 87, 189; Shakspeare and Hathaway, 19, 41, 67–68, 70, 87, 155, 189; Shakspeare and Heminges, 57–58, 102, 103, 189; Shakspeare and Leicester, 19, 86, 155, 189; Shakspeare's Library, 19, 41, 84; Shakespeare and Lowin, 189; Shakspeare and his printer, 19, 63–65, 134, 135; Shakspeare and Southampton, 19, 41, 155, 160, 189; paintings and portraits, 43, 66, 84, 146. Plays: *The Devile and Rychard*, 87; *Hamlet*, 19, 41, 84, 150, 155, 160; *Henry II*, 91, 166, 199; *King Lear*, 19, 41, 70, 71, 87, 91, 145, 150, 155–57, 160, 190, 211, 237 n. 10; *Vortigern*, 20, 33, 41, 62, 68, 71, 87, 123, 141, 145, 163, 166, 188, 191, 199, 200, 213, 214, 215–16, 237 n. 10; plotline and Shakespearean parallels, 17–19; premiere, 167, 178–87, 246 n. 33, 246 n. 37; rehearsals, 173–76; revival, 223–24; rewriting, 132, 134–41, 203, 204, 205; sources, 62–63, 72–81; subsequent influence, 217–22

Jaggard, William, 10
Jeffrey, George, 26
Johnson, Charles, 27
Johnson, Samuel, 27, 33, 34, 35, 66, 82, 93, 152, 216, 225 n. 47
Jones, Edward, 35
Jones, Henry, 32
Jones, Mark, and Paul Craddock, Nicholas Barker, 236 n. 57
Jonson, Ben, 28, 37, 73, 119
Jordan, Dorothea, 132, 168, 180, 181, 182, 186, 200
Jordan, John, 38, 51–53, 92, 196

Kames, Lord Henry Home, 39
Kauffman, Angelica, 81
Kemble, John Philip, 43, 133, 139, 140, 141–42, 144, 165, 169–70, 172, 173–77, 183–87, 191, 193, 200, 216–17, 244 n. 42, 246 n. 24, 251–52 n. 1
Kenrick, William, 32, 71
Killigrew, Thomas, 73
King, Thomas (actor), 174, 182
King, Thomas, 121
Kingston, Jeremy, 253 n. 2
Knapton, Robert, and James Dodsley, 79

Larpent, John (Lord Chamberlain), 138–39, 216, 244 n. 34
Lauder, William, 12, 199
Leake, Elizabeth, 135, 172, 177, 182
Lee, Dr., 208
Linley, Jane, 133
Linley, Thomas, 130, 131, 133
Linley, William, 133
Lipking, Lawrence, 34
Luhrmann, Baz, 218

Macpherson, James, 10, 12, 35, 83, 117, 148, 199
Macklin, Charles, 37
Mair, John, 10–11, 110, 168, 202
Malone, Edmond, 9, 36, 37, 38, 39, 40, 41, 48, 66, 82, 102, 106, 109, 116, 133, 146, 153, 158, 159, 160, 168, 169, 177, 178–79, 184, 186, 194, 214, 215, 213, 218–19, 222, 228 n. 90, 240 n. 39, 241 nn. 47 and 49, 246 n. 33, 247 n. 2, 251–52 n. 1; background, 150–52; literary attack on Shakspeare Papers, 188–93
Mander, John, 232 n. 17, 248 n. 62
Marder, Louis, 228 n. 90
Marlowe, Christopher, 37, 73
Marsh, Charles, 135, 200
Martin, Peter, 19, 230 n. 61
Mason, William, 162
Massinger, Philip, 37, 71
Mathews, Charles, 148
Meegereen, Han van, 220
Middleton, Thomas, 17, 153
Miller, James, 29
Morgan, M'Namara, 32
Morris, Sylvia, 229 n. 27
Morrison, Jim, 221
Mortimer, Jane (maiden name: Hurrell), 75
Mortimer, John Hamilton, 74–76, 81
Mozart, Wolfgang, 221

Murphy, Arthur, 199–200, 249 n. 85, 249–50 n. 89

Nixon, John, 194

Otway, Thomas, 73
Oulton, Wally Chamberlain, 160

Palmer, Mr., 174
Pardoes, Mr., 145
Parr, Samuel, 66–67, 145, 146, 148, 152, 160, 193, 194, 200–201
Payn, James, 204
Peele, George, 37
Percy, Thomas, 35, 148, 150, 152, 197, 227 n. 71
Phillimore, John, 174, 182
Pinkerton, John, 148
Pope, Alexander, 39
Powell, Mr., 138, 175
Powell, Mrs., 174, 176, 177, 182
Presley, Elvis, 221
Psalmanzer, George, 34
Purcell, Henry, 23
Pye, James Henry (poet laureate), 43, 169, 172, 243–44 n. 28

Rapin de Thoyras, 76, 81, 231 n. 23
Ray, Martha, 117
Reed, Isaac, 152, 241 n. 47
Relhan, Robert, 146, 219
Rembrandt, van Rijn, 220
Reynolds, Joshua, 66
Ritson, Joseph, 149–50, 152
Rowe, Nicholas, 23, 24, 26, 30, 31, 39, 79
Rowley, William, 73

Sartre, Jean-Paul, 221
Schoenbaum, Samuel, 10, 41, 228 n. 5, 229 nn. 15 and 34, 232–33 n. 17
Scott, Sir Walter, 172
Scouten, Arthur, 30, 226 n. 45
Shadwell, Thomas, 131
Shakespeare, John, 38, 52, 251 n. 136
Shakespeare, William, 73, 126, 186; adaptations of, 22–25; apocrypha, 23, 36–38, 73, 215, 221–22; imitations of, 30–33. Influence on: audiences, 28–30; drama, 11–12, 20–21, 34, 214–17; playwrights, 25–28, 138; Samuel Ire-

land and family, 44–45, 51; subsequent generations, 213–14, 217–18
Shaw, Bernard, 216
Sheridan, Richard Brinsley, 28, 104, 121, 125, 126, 127–31, 132–33, 139, 140, 141–44, 186–87, 225 n. 17, 247–48 n. 49
Shirley, James, 37
Shirley, William, 31, 33
Siddons, Sarah, 169, 171, 175–76, 182, 253 n. 2
Simmons, James, 223, 224
Singleton, Henry, 76
Smith, Adam, 146
Smollett, Tobias, 76, 81, 231 n. 22
Southey, Robert, 172
Spence, Dr., M. D., 114
Steele, Richard, 30
Steevens, George, 37–38, 60, 109, 114, 116, 150, 152, 154, 158, 159, 168, 192, 194, 197, 198, 199, 205, 241 n. 47
Stewart, Susan, 236 n. 51
Strabo, Arthur, 241 n. 47
Stuart, Charles, 183, 246 n. 24
Stuckeley, William, 35
Summerset, duke of, 148
Sunderland, John, 76

Talbot, Montague, 11, 96–101, 112, 114, 197
Tate, Nahum, 131
Taylor, Gary, 11, 21
Taylor, John, 105, 124
Teitze, Hans, 20
Theobald, Lewis, 23, 36–37, 215, 227 n. 77
Thomson, James, 24
Till, Mr., 208
Troward, R., 104
Twain, Mark (Samuel Clemens), 122
Tyrwhitt, Thomas, 192, 248 n. 55

Valpy, Richard, 148, 176–77
Van Gogh, Vincent, 221
Van Thiel, Peter, 220

Wacker, Otto, 220
Waldron, Francis, 165, 242 n. 113
Wales, prince of (future George IV), 19, 43, 101, 167
Wallis, Albany, 12, 103–7, 110, 119, 127, 147, 192–93, 202, 241 n. 49

Walpole, Horace, 121
Warburton, John, 39
Warton, Joseph, 66, 67, 145, 148, 200, 230 n. 61
Warton, Thomas, 40, 228 n. 98, 230 n. 61
Watt, Ian, 34
Webb, Francis, 114, 132–33, 143, 146–47, 148, 149, 158, 172–73, 242 n. 89
Wells, Stanley, 225 n. 7
West, Richard, 28

Westall, Richard, 76–78, 114
Whitfield, Mr., 180
Whitman, Walt, 221
Williams, Mr. 52–53
Wise, Thomas, 219
Woodward, G. M., 165
Wordsworth, William, 213
Wyatt, John, 148, 158–59, 162, 242 n. 89

Young, Edward, 33

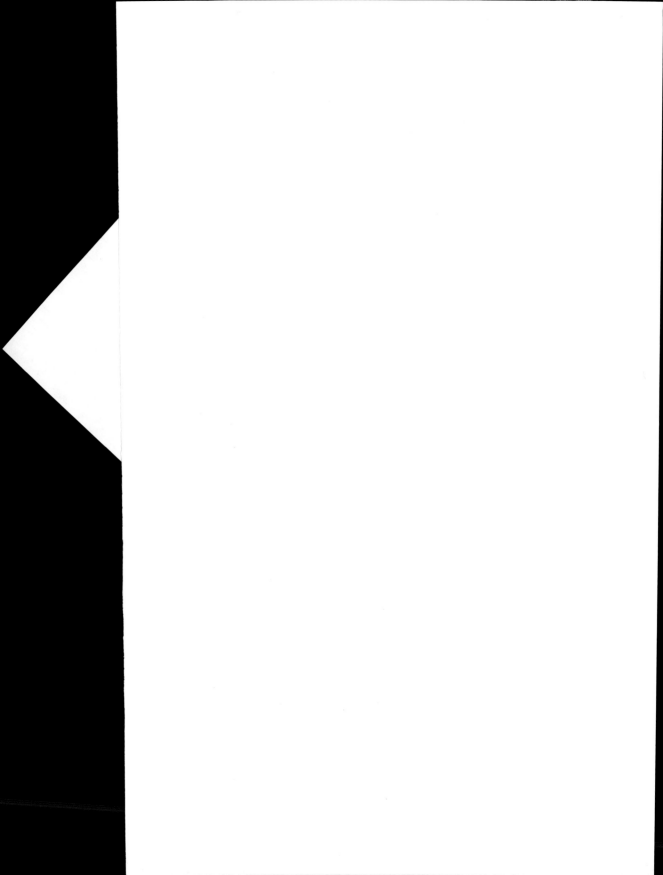

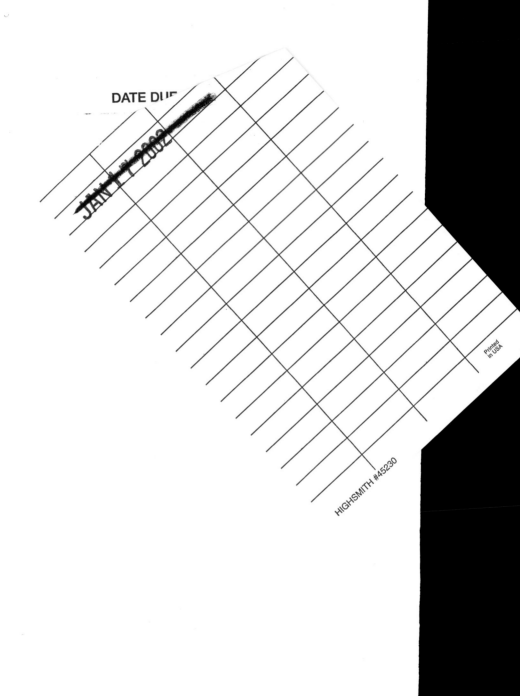

DATE DUE

JAN 1 1 2002

HIGHSMITH #45230

Printed in USA